PRAISE FOR *HITMAN*

"A chilling exploration of Yves 'Apache' Trudeau's legacy, a feared hitman whose lethal skills fuelled Canada's criminal underworld. *Hitman* reveals his brutal career and critically examines the justice system's readiness to strike deals with dangerous offenders. By exposing both the violence of one man and society's struggle to confront organized crime, you are drawn into a dark, often hidden battle unfolding in the shadows of our world."

—Jacques Duchesneau, former Montreal Chief of Police

"A must read. *Hitman* highlights how Yves (Apache) Trudeau's influence extended far beyond his actions; it shaped the very landscape of the biker underworld in Quebec and, by extension, across North America. Julian Sher and Lisa Fitterman remind us of the complexities of criminal life, where ambition, violence, and betrayal intertwine, leaving an indelible mark on the world of organized crime."

—Garry Clement, former RCMP Superintendent, National Director of Proceeds of Crime Program

"A rare and detailed glimpse inside the Montreal gangster era of the 70s and 80s. Supported by painstaking research, this book is a must read for anyone seeking to understand Canadian organized crime."

—Andy Richards, former inspector of the British Columbia Organized Crime Agency

"Gripping from beginning to end. *Hitman* is shocking both for its insight into the brutal biker underworld and for exposing a legal system unable to hold mass murderers to account. A must-read!"

—Kim Bolan, *Vancouver Sun*

"I can't think of a more loathsome representative of Canada's underworld than hitman Yves Trudeau. *Hitman* deftly captures his important, chilling story."

—Peter Edwards, author of *A Gangster's Life: War and Addiction in the New Underworld*

"A smart and fascinating true crime story with some unpredictable twists."

—Sam Wiebe, author of *Ocean Drive* and *The Last Exile*

HITMAN

THE UNTOLD STORY OF CANADA'S DEADLIEST ASSASSIN

JULIAN SHER
AND LISA FITTERMAN

HarperCollins*PublishersLtd*

Hitman

Published by HarperCollins Publishers Ltd

First published in Canada by HarperCollins Publishers Ltd in a hardcover edition: 2025
This HarperCollins Publishers Ltd trade paperback edition: 2026

HarperCollins Publishers Ltd
Bay Adelaide Centre, East Tower
22 Adelaide Street West, 41st Floor
Toronto, Ontario, Canada
M5H 4E3

www.harpercollins.ca

HarperCollins Publishers
Macken House, 39/40 Mayor Street Upper
Dublin 1, D01 C9W8, Ireland
https://www.harpercollins.com

Library and Archives Canada Cataloguing in Publication information is available upon request.

ISBN 978-1-4434-7153-4

Printed and bound in the United States of America
$PrintCode

To our parents, for their support and inspiration.

CONTENTS

CAST OF CHARACTERS

THE HITMAN

Yves (Apache) Trudeau

THE HELLS ANGELS

California

Ralph (Sonny) Barger

Sorel (South) Chapter

Réjean (Zig-Zag) Lessard

Jacques (La Pelle) Pelletier

Robert (Ti-Maigre) Richard

Robert (Snake) Tremblay

Luc (Sam) Michaud

Michel (Sky) Langlois

Gerry (Le Chat) Coulombe (prospect)

Laval (North) Chapter

Jean-Pierre (Le Croisseur) Mathieu

Michel (Willie) Mayrand

Richard (Bert) Mayrand

Laurent (l'Anglais) Viau

Guy-Louis (Chop) Adam

Yvon (Le Père) Bilodeau

Yves (Le Boss) Buteau

Jean-Guy (Brutus) Geoffrion

Michel (Jinx) Genest

Gilles (Le Nez) Lachance

Régis (Lucky) Asselin

Denis (Le Curé) Kennedy

Claude (Coco) Roy (prospect)

THE NOMADS

Maurice (Mom) Boucher

David (Wolf) Carroll

Normand (Biff) Hamel

BIKER ASSOCIATES

Paul April

Michel Blass

Robert Lelièvre

WEST END GANG

Frank (Dunie) Ryan

Allan (The Weasel) Ross

Melvin Mingo

Jimmy Holt

John Slawvey

Eddie Phillips

David Singer

MONTREAL POLICE

John Dalzell

Mario Dumont

André Savard

John Westlake

PROSECUTORS

France Charbonneau

René Domingue

Sonia Paquet

Dave McGee (Florida)

DEFENSE LAWYERS

Daniel Rock

Sidney Leithman

Léo-René Maranda

Jacques Bouchard

Robert LaHaye

Christiane Filteau

JOURNALISTS

Dan Burke

D'Arcy O'Connor

André Cédilot

Paul Cherry

Richard Desmarais

PROLOGUE
DEATH COMES CALLING

Darlene Weichold was worried.

It was 9 p.m. on December 8, 1978, and her older brother had promised to call hours earlier to arrange to take her and her cousin Janet shopping the next day. The fourteen-year-old sat by the phone in the living room of the little house she shared with her mom in southwest Montreal, but it remained silent. When she tried to call him, it rang and rang until she hung up, frustrated.

"What's he doing?" Darlene asked Janet, who'd stopped by to keep her company while her mom had a girls' night out. "Billy's not like this. When he says he's going to do something, he does it."

"Billy is a guy," Janet replied. "They do things like this sometimes."

"Nope," Darlene said, shaking her head. "Not Billy. For me, he has always done what he said he'd do."

Of her three older brothers, Billy, who at twenty-one was seven years older than his little sister, was the one Darlene was closest to. He was a railway worker, like the other men in the family, and a ladies' man who held doors open for women and always seemed to have one on his arm. The drum player in a garage band, he could practice for hours at a time, his three dogs so accustomed to the racket, they could sleep through it without a twitch.

If Darlene had a problem, Billy was the brother she'd go to for help. If she was feeling lonely, he would come to pick her up and take her back to his place in Greenfield Park, just across the Champlain Bridge on Montreal's South Shore—a trim two-story home with a peaked roof and driveway.

It's why, on that cold December evening, Darlene was worried. He'd never do something to hurt her or make her feel she didn't count, at least not intentionally. Even though she tried to keep calm in front of Janet, deep down she knew something was wrong. But what?

Her mom was out at the horse races, then planned to continue the get-together at one of her friends' homes. There was no way for Darlene to reach her until later, when she was in a house with a phone, to ask that she come home with the car so they could go check on Billy. To pass the time, the girls turned on the TV and began to switch channels, idly looking for something to watch. Click. *Donny and Marie*. Click. *The Rockford Files*. Click. *The Love Boat*. Darlene couldn't concentrate.

Where is he?

Just after 11 p.m., she turned the TV dial to CFCF, CTV's Montreal affiliate station, and came to a sudden stop. On the screen was the report of a shooting on Verchères Street. That was where Billy lived! There were flashing red lights, sirens, and cops—cops everywhere. The journalist was at the scene, holding a microphone in gloved hands as he reported on multiple bullets being fired in front of a house. It appeared the unidentified victim, who'd been struck in the back, died instantly.

Billy was probably stuck in the mayhem, unable to reach her, Darlene thought. Unnerved, unsuspecting, and hopeful, she went to sleep. But not for long. She would soon waken to news that would upend her life for good.

It would be more than six years before Darlene would find out who had killed her brother, what seemed like an eternity, during which she tried to harden herself against the whispers that Billy had been a biker and that's why he was dead, that the family itself was no good. Finally, in 1985, she learned the truth, not from the police, but from the radio and newspaper articles screaming headlines about a killer with the nickname "Apache."

His real name was Yves Trudeau. He had been a founder of the first Hells Angels chapter in Quebec, and then became a relentless hitman for the outlaw bikers. For fifteen years, he had carried out his kills in the shadows, unknown and undetected by police. Only a shocking turn of events in 1985 would catapult him onto the front pages and all over the TV news.

Darlene, like most people, was horrified to learn that Trudeau, by his own admission, had stabbed, shot, bombed, strangled, beaten, and otherwise helped murder at least forty-three people over the last decade and a half. That puts him far ahead of more infamous Canadian serial killers from the 1980s and 1990s, such as Clifford Olson, who confessed to murdering eleven children and teenagers; Paul Bernardo, who was convicted of killing three girls and admitted to raping at least another ten; and Robert Pickton, who was found guilty of murdering six women and boasted of slaughtering many more.

Unlike those men, who killed for sex, lust, or pleasure, for Trudeau, the bloodshed was all business. He was a contract killer hired to do a job, and for the most part, he did it well. So well that the bikers sometimes loaned him out to other organized crime empires to do their dirty work, including the east-end French gangs led by the deadly Dubois brothers and the upstart Irish Mafia in west-end Montreal.

The numbers meant nothing to Darlene, and only one of the names counted. Among the roster of murders Yves Trudeau confessed to was her brother's. Her body went numb as she read that

Billy's death had been a case of mistaken identity. Trudeau had been contracted by the Hells Angels to kill Roxy Dutemple, Billy's landlord, who was a member of a rival biker gang. While staking out the house, Trudeau saw a car pull into the driveway and a man exit from the driver's side to gallantly open the passenger door for the woman who'd been sitting next to him. As she screamed, the killer let loose with a hail of bullets into the man's back and head.

Darlene's brother never had a chance.

"Why?" Darlene whispered. Maybe, in the waning winter light, Billy and Roxy looked alike, both with tall, thin silhouettes. Or maybe Trudeau just didn't care. After all, as he would later tell police, when he discovered his fatal error he laughed hysterically and joked that people who looked like Roxy Dutemple should be killed just in case they were him.

"You destroyed our family," Darlene told the black-and-white photo staring out from the newspaper page. "All that pain and suffering, for a mistake."

It was not the first, or the last, mistake Yves (Apache) Trudeau would make.

He was not a lone wolf. As a serial killer, he survived and thrived because he was part of a global crime empire in which murder and silence dictated the rules, and it needed someone like Trudeau to do its dirty work. Although he was unilingual and reluctant to travel beyond Quebec, his infamy spread across borders. "Necessity is the mother of invention, and that's why she invented Apache Trudeau," says an American federal prosecutor who took on Canadian drug traffickers for whom Trudeau had worked.

This is the story of a killing spree that would span fifteen years and reverberate through society for decades longer. It is an account of the tragic failure of police to stop or catch a serial assassin and then, worse still, the controversial sweetheart deal the confessed killer would get from authorities desperate to quell biker violence.

It is the tale of one man's journey down a road that began with adventure and ended with anguish and agony for him and many others. The journey of a man filled with, as one judge put it, "an instinct that is evil."

A journey that would call into question the very underpinnings of our justice system.

PART ONE

“TO KILL WAS A NECESSITY”

1. THE YOUNG POPEYE

Yves Trudeau's first public run-in with police did not involve handcuffs and trouble. Instead, it was all smiles and firm handshakes—and even a trophy or two.

He was one of hundreds of people attending a gathering in a large hall at the Montreal Botanical Gardens on November 22, 1969, posing for photos, laughing, and engaging in animated conversation. Seen from afar, the gathering could have been any convention, complete with multiple speeches and awards given, votes taken, minutes recorded, and a question period.

But the attendees were not classic businessmen from the traditional worlds of, say, banking, real estate, or insurance. They were not dressed in suits and ties, with their feet shod in proper oxfords. No, these were bikers, among the roughest and toughest men in Quebec, and they looked the part in leather and sneakers, their tattoos and club patches displayed in all their oft-gory glory.

A young Trudeau worked the crowd, at once observant and in constant motion. He was slight, thin, and sharp-featured, his hair slicked back in a modified pompadour. Others in the room included members of the many other biker gangs that had expanded throughout the province in the 1960s, burly, bearded, and shaggy-haired men proud to be riding in packs with names like the Devil's Disciples and the Death Riders.

It was the first-ever meeting of the United Motorcyclists of Quebec, a federation that had been founded the previous April to promote the notion that bikers were just regular guys who deserved to be treated with respect, rather than horror or fear. What made the convention even more extraordinary was the heavy presence of uniformed police officers who rode motorcycles, not to keep a wary eye on the bikers but to mingle with them as fellow attendees. Honored guests included Louis Chantigny, Quebec's High Commissioner for Sports, whose government had just handed over a $3,600 grant to the new federation, and, even more startling, none other than the police chief of Montreal, Jean-Paul Gilbert.

It was all part of a bold, if ill-fated, attempt to head off the ugly violence and deadly turf wars that had started to simmer in Quebec as the biker gangs flexed their muscles. The idea was to promote peace and friendly sports competition between clubs instead of skirmishes with chains and, worse still, sharp blades and bullets.

"Motorcycles are just like baseball bats," Chief Gilbert told the appreciative crowd. "There are good things to do with them and not-so-good things." His department didn't want to suppress the bikers' way of life, he continued, but rather, make it more acceptable to the public by emphasizing the sporting nature of motorcycling in general. To that end, he noted that members of the federation would be able to use police buildings for meetings and a large tract of undeveloped land in the northeast end of the city that had been donated by British Petroleum, where they could host races on cross-country terrain.

The photographs in the local papers captured Gilbert, neatly attired in a light-gray business suit, handing out a number of sporting trophies to the bikers. In one, Trudeau poses with two other leather-clad men as he is presented with a trophy that depicts a biker doing a wheelie, bucking the bike in the air on its rear wheel, much like one would do with a horse. In another picture, Trudeau smiles tightly as he shakes the chief's hand. An unadorned pinkie ring glints from the left hand hanging idle at his side.

Looking on at the event with a mixture of satisfaction and hope was John Dalzell, a Montreal beat constable and motorcycle enthusiast who had been appointed the department's first-ever (and only) official liaison to the bikers. One of the main architects of the police peace initiative, he prided himself on being able to move between biker clubhouses and police stations with ease. Indeed, on that day, he was named secretary-general of the short-lived federation.

"Back then, in '68 and most of '69, I'd say eighty percent of members were regular jacks who worked for the city or in construction," Dalzell recalls. "They were guys who had a blast drag-racing, doing wheelies, and getting drunk on beer."

In hindsight, it's hard not to see the tragic naïveté of the Montreal gathering, a foreboding calm before the violent storm. Many of the more aggressive bikers were accustomed to flouting the law and were already beginning to finance their activities through trafficking drugs and killing anyone who got in the way; there was no way they would be content to swap their rough lifestyle for a genteel, fun weekend hobby.

Dalzell would get to know and, in a way, even befriend the soft-spoken biker named Yves Trudeau. Almost two decades later, Trudeau would be exposed as a serial assassin, while Dalzell would go on to become the Montreal police department's director of communications. Both would witness the terrible violence and death toll that plagued Montreal in the 1980s and 1990s.

But looking back on those hopeful moments in 1969, Dalzell points out that the police could never have predicted what would become of the bikers and the young man with the goatee and slicked-back pompadour. "You can't regret or think, *What if we knew then what we know today?* What's the use in that?"

Yves Trudeau was born on February 4, 1946. Little is known about his early years. The man whose criminal exploits would make him infamous never talked much about his childhood, and court transcripts and, later, parole board hearings disclosed little about his upbringing. There was never a hint of any of the stereotypical explanations for what turns someone into a relentless killer—no mention of a broken family, a deprived childhood, or an early life of drugs and criminality.

The young Trudeau came of age in a conservative Quebec of the 1950s, still dominated by the church and traditional family values. He described his father as strict and controlling, obsessed with all things military, according to media accounts. But he remained close to his mother, talking about her until a month before his death. "I want to show my mother that I am good," he would say.

Whether it was to escape the constraints of family and society or just plain boredom, as Trudeau grew into a lean and wiry young man, he sought excitement in two things: bombs and bikes. He fell in love with blowing things up, a pastime he pursued and perfected when as a teenager he landed a job at Canadian Industries Limited, or C-I-L, a manufacturer known for its paint and fertilizers—and explosives for use by police, military, and industry. "C-I-L has served industry with explosives for 140 years," the company boasts to this day on its website. "The tradition continues with specialty explosives for every need." C-I-L made everything from detonating cords to blasting machines. What the young Trudeau learned in the brief time he worked at the company plant in McMasterville, just south of Montreal, would serve him well in the years to come.

If explosives were work for Trudeau, riding bikes was fun. And why not join the biggest and baddest biker gang at the time: the Popeyes Motorcycle Club. Trudeau was just twenty-two, a quiet, diminutive outsider when, in 1968, he became a member of the boisterous Quebec gang that would eventually transform into the Hells Angels' first chapter in Canada. They took their name from the cartoon sailor man with bulging biceps who always fought to the "finich 'cause I eats my spinach" and bragged that he never left his foes standing. The patch on their gray leather jackets showed a pipe-smoking Popeye on a red motorcycle nicknamed "Le Cruiser." After forming in east-end Montreal in the early 1960s, the club quickly became the largest of the many motorcycle gangs that had sprung up across the province, boasting several hundred members, with chapters in cities including Drummondville, Quebec City, Sherbrooke, and Trois-Rivières.

For the young bomb aficionado, the club became family.

Trudeau's background fit the profile of those who joined the motorcycle gangs at the time: blue collar or unemployed, with a limited education and fewer prospects. They were rebels without a cause, society's outcasts, who knew how to absorb hits and not back down, with little respect for conventional authority.

"These are people who are attracted to this family because theirs has been less than satisfactory," says Dr. Louis Morissette, a criminal psychiatrist for many years at Montreal's respected Philippe-Pinel Institute, who interviewed and studied several bikers. "It's really a search for belonging which we all have: 'Hey, they're giving me a sense of value.'"

For a young man seeking adventure and excitement, mixed in, perhaps, with a bit of crime, Yves Trudeau could not have chosen a better city than Montreal.

By the late 1960s, Montreal was beginning to lose ground to Toronto as Canada's biggest city and as the country's business and financial capital. But it never lost its spot as the country's crime capital, if not one of the premier crime cities in North America. It was a dubious honor that the city had held going back several decades as various ethnic groups and families rose to the top of the crime world.

In the 1920s, Montreal became the continent's preferred party town and bootlegging center when the United States enacted Prohibition, banning the sale of alcohol. Canada left the decision on booze to local governments, and while many cities in Canada followed the US example, Montreal remained ferociously wet and wild. It became the only large city in North America not under the booze ban.

Famous American jazz musicians such as Duke Ellington and Count Basie came to the city. Indeed, so many Americans flocked across the border that the popular composer Irving Berlin wrote and recorded a hit song called "Hello Montreal" that heralded how easy it was to "make whoop-whoop whoopie night and day" in the city.

Joining the revelers were the booze-runners and gangsters. Chicago crime lord Al Capone was known to hang out at the Montreal Pool Room, and prominent Montreal families made their fortunes shipping alcohol across the border. Prostitutes were readily available in Montreal's famous Red-Light District, and the drug trade flourished even during the lean Depression years of the 1930s.

The 1940s saw the emergence of Jewish criminals like Harry Ship, called "the King of the Montreal Gamblers," who ran innumerable bookmaking houses along Saint Catherine Street and the popular Chez Parée nightclub, where big-time celebrities like Frank Sinatra and Dean Martin would perform.

Police corruption was endemic, and a crusading lawyer named Jean Drapeau vowed to clean up the city when he was elected mayor in 1954. The results were mixed. Brothels and bookmaking establishments were shut down, but organized crime was already moving into drugs as the main money-maker. Montreal became a major transit route for heroin manufactured in France and destined for New York and the lucrative American market—what became known as "the

French Connection." The 1950s saw the emergence of the Italian Mafia as the top crime group in the city, starting with the Calabrian mob, notably the Cotronis, and then their Sicilian rivals, the Cuntreras and the Rizzutos—family names that would become notorious.

Fittingly for a city so steeped in crime and underworld mayhem, the 1950s also saw the birth of a uniquely Quebec phenomenon: the crime tabloid. *Allo Police* debuted in 1953 and would continue its gory, gratuitous, and graphic coverage for the next fifty years. Eventually, it was joined by the more picture-friendly *Photo Police*—not that *Allo Police* ever shied away from displaying stomach-churning murder scenes. The tabloid often favored the lurid and the sensational, occasionally even dabbling in pornography to boost sales. *Allo Police* had a knack for turning both the bad guys and the good guys (sometimes it was hard to tell which was which) into heroes, or at least likable rogues. At the same time, its journalists and photographers had exceptional contacts with cops and criminals, which often put the paper at crime scenes way ahead of conventional newspapers and allowed them to cover the events in much more detail. Over the years, *Allo Police* did an impressive job of painting a frightening picture of the Montreal underworld in which Yves Trudeau would emerge and flourish.

By the time Trudeau burst onto the crime stage at the tail end of the raucous and rebellious sixties, all the elements were there—drugs, corruption, and a tabloid press—to make Montreal the perfect venue for a new crop of criminals to come roaring in: the bikers.

Quebec was coming out of what is known as the Great Darkness, turning its back on the Catholic Church and the father-knows-best fiefdom of long-time Quebec premier Maurice Duplessis. They had run the province in tandem for decades, enforcing traditional church mores, favoring business over unions, and persecuting those who did not fall into line. But with the Quiet Revolution, the province was convulsed by political change and the breakdown of age-old social boundaries.

The biker world offered restless young men like Trudeau the perfect blend of rebellion and regimentation. Externally, they projected a devil-may-care disrespect for law and order, but internally they tried to maintain an almost paramilitary structure dictated from the top down, with a simple code of behavior Trudeau would later describe as "no rape, no burn, no shoot." In other words, a biker could not steal another biker's girlfriend or wife, cheat another biker in a drug deal, or use drugs that had to be injected. And what happened in the clubs stayed in the clubs, whether it was an internal dispute or a fight with another gang that resulted in injuries or worse. With their long hair, leather jackets, jeans, and chains, with club names and logos that evoked images of flaming death, destruction, and physical strength, the bikers found their power in a group, one for all and all for one. And woe betide those who didn't fall in line.

The Popeyes' headquarters were in La Fontaine Park, in the Plateau neighborhood in east-end Montreal. Once, the park had been home to a British army garrison, which used the land to train on. The biker club, considered the best-organized in the province, used it as its home base for typical gangster activities: drugs, prostitution, extortion, and theft.

About a year after joining the gray-jacketed Popeyes as a "striker," or prospective member, Yves Trudeau was already moving up the ranks, earning his patch and befriending Yvon (Gorille) Bilodeau, one of the club's founders. Despite his "gorilla" nickname, Bilodeau was not as beefy or menacing as most bikers, with neat hair, a well-trimmed beard, warm eyes, and an easy smile. He was shy, said one police officer who knew him, and was not fond of appearing in public. So Trudeau got the job of speaking for the club at that special biker gathering with police at Montreal's Botanical Gardens.

Although there would later be claims that Trudeau earned the nickname "Apache" because he scalped the ear of one of his victims, it appears he was called that from the start, long before he made his first kill. Perhaps it was due to his long, straight dark hair, dark eyes, and complexion, but really, there was often no specific reason for the nicknames the bikers conferred on each other, save to give a sense of secret fellowship and confuse others not part of their fraternity. Trudeau cherished that fellowship—at least until many years later, when it turned dark and menacing.

Ironically, one of the people the young Popeye would become friendly with was a cop who had taken a very different path into the biker world.

Many young boys growing up in the 1950s dreamed of becoming a cop. Not John Dalzell. He was Anglo-Irish to his core, and the Montreal police were almost exclusively a French-speaking force. Raised in the working-class neighborhood of Rosemont, in the east end of the city, Dalzell learned early about tensions between French and English, about territory, fighting, and having to sneak onto an ice rink at a francophone college up the street because it was so much better maintained than the pitted one in a nearby park where English speakers were supposed to play.

"If the French kids caught us, we'd fight," Dalzell recalls. "The relationship was, shall we say, very contentious."

But Dalzell did have one francophone friend whose family lived on the same street as his. At the time, that was practically unheard of; most streets in Rosemont were occupied by either English or French residents.

In the spring of 1965, Dalzell noticed his friend had cut his hair short. It turned out that he had just joined the Montreal police. "It's quite interesting," he said. "You should join too, John. They're looking for English guys big time."

Dalzell demurred at first. His French was "brutal," mostly swear words and street joual. But he soon applied, and the self-described "rug rat" from Rosemont began his career as a patrol cop out of Station 10, on the west side of downtown. It was a more English part of the city, and many of his colleagues and bosses were Anglos too—a little sea of them in an overwhelmingly French police department.

If Dalzell joining the Montreal police force was out of the ordinary, his journey into the world of the bikers was even more unusual. It began on a cold night in December 1966, when he was still living in his parents' basement. He got home around midnight, tired from a late shift as a beat cop. Rather than take his beloved Triumph motorcycle down a set of cement steps to the basement, as he usually did, he decided to leave it out, chained to the metal picket fence that surrounded the home. He could practically smell the snow on the frigid air—his signal that it was time to put the bike away for the season.

I'll clean it in the morning before putting it away, he told himself as he got ready for bed.

The next thing Dalzell knew, it was two in the morning and his father was shaking him awake.

"John, someone is stealing your bike," the older man said.

"What? No!"

Dalzell jumped up. In his pajamas, he ran to the front door in time to see a white truck taking off with his bike in the back. Wait, was that a hand waving at him in the van's rearview mirror? Or giving him the finger? He stood there, berating himself. What was he thinking, leaving a motorcycle outside like that, protected by just a chain and lock that could be broken by anyone with strong pliers? The Triumph was his pride, joy, and only mode of transport other than public transit, and there was no way, on his salary, that he could afford to buy another one, new or used.

So, on his own time, using his cop skills but not his badge, he started a quest to find his bike, frequenting "chop shops"—stores where stolen vehicles and bikes are dismantled and their parts sold or used for repairs and upgrades. One shop in particular, on Ontario Street in Montreal's working-class east end, was a repository for parts such as engines, brake rods, and fenders, and the owner didn't think twice about the tall guy he'd never seen before who asked questions in French with a heavy English accent. It was winter, after all, when bikers couldn't ride, so they spent their time looking for merchandise to improve their bikes in time for spring or, if they were feeling flush, a new motorcycle.

"The owner let me go down to the basement to check out things on my own while he worked upstairs," Dalzell says. "It was dark and dusty, and I would surreptitiously take down serial numbers on the parts, lots of them. Then, back at work, I'd ask the detectives working in stolen vehicles to check the numbers and their provenance."

Soon, the detectives invited the beat cop down to police headquarters. There, in a meeting room on the second floor, Dalzell saw a massive blackboard mounted to the wall with a dizzying chart composed of columns of numbers and lines that connected them. In effect, it was the 1960s version of a computer spreadsheet. It proved that many of the parts Dalzell had found in the basement of the chop shop belonged to motorcycles that had been reported stolen.

"Well, who's investigating this?" he asked, his gaze riveted on the chart.

"Nobody," came the answer. "We don't know anything about motorcycles. We just put the numbers up on the board."

The response drove home for Dalzell the fact that motorcycle theft presented a prime opportunity for crooks looking to make quick and easy cash. If the people who were supposed to investigate these kinds of crimes didn't know what to do, then there was no hope for anyone else in law enforcement. Biker gangs were still too new a phenomenon, no matter that they were, as he describes it, "springing up like flowers all over the place."

That summer, Dalzell was assigned to walk the beat at Expo 67, Montreal's popular world's fair. He continued to search for his own stolen bike, or its parts, in what free time he had left. The assignment was a change from his regular beat on the west side of downtown, but as he dealt with the hordes of tourists, pickpockets, and grifters drawn to the Expo, the biker gangs were undergoing a change of their own: ramping up the production and sale of narcotics such as cocaine after discovering that the illicit proceeds could finance their activities and help them expand.

By then, Trudeau had risen through the ranks of the Popeyes to become one of the club's leaders, and the Popeyes began to entrench their wealth and power through the drug trade and other illegal activities. In response, rival clubs such as the Ontario-based Satan's Choice and the Devil's Disciples, based in Dalzell's old neighborhood of Rosemont, decided to muscle in on Popeye turf. The ensuing battle, which would cement Quebec's place as one of the most dangerous places in North America for organized crime to do business, foreshadowed the two deadly biker wars to come: the first between the Hells Angels and the Outlaws from 1977 to 1984, in which Trudeau would play a key killer role, and the second and even bloodier battle between the Hells Angels and the Rock Machine from 1994 to 2002.

But those events were still years away.

With biker tensions simmering as the 1960s came to an end, Dalzell was called into a meeting with the chief of police. Jean-Paul Gilbert was a graduate of the Université de Montréal who had progressive, innovative views on law enforcement. He believed it was not a time to be ham-fisted, or to storm into clubhouses with billy clubs and guns blazing, arresting everyone on the spot. Rather, after hearing about the beat cop from Station 10 who was moonlighting undercover in chop shops, he called Dalzell in with a proposition: become the official liaison between the department and the bikers.

Dalzell balked. Blow his cover with the bikers? What would happen when he revealed his true identity?

But Gilbert persisted. To that point, authorities had concentrated their efforts on thwarting bank robbers and combatting established criminal organizations like the Italian Mafia, the emerging Irish gangsters in the west end, and the French-Canadian gang known as "le clan Dubois," a deadly east-end group who engaged in everything from extortion to drug trafficking and murder. But when it came to bikers, a much newer phenomenon, the police were at a loss, and Dalzell, who had loved motorcycles since he was a kid, was in a position to help.

Gilbert believed the twenty-two-year-old constable could show bikers that someone they considered a friend, or at least not a threat, could actually work for the enemy—and could help them. He would be the go-between between them and the force. He could help stop random searches and seizures, when cops didn't even bother to show a search warrant before cavalierly tossing motorcycles onto the back of a police truck with the excuse that the serial numbers looked suspicious. At the same time, he could keep tabs on the bikers because he was allowed into their clubhouses, drank beers with them on Friday nights, and rode with them on weekends.

"We have to find a way," Gilbert said.

Dalzell decided to go for it. After three years of walking the beat, he needed a new challenge, and he figured he had one thing the bikers would respect and appreciate: a Harley-Davidson he had purchased (with the help of the police department) to replace his stolen Triumph. "That was the ultimate class for the bikers," he recalls, since back then most of them had Triumphs or other smaller models. "But I had a Harley, and holy shit, that was the holy grail for bikers. So I reintroduced myself to them as a cop."

Not surprisingly, it did not go over well. The bikers' initial response to Dalzell's revelation that, when he wasn't wearing leather, he was sporting police blue, was along the lines of "You fucking kidding me?" Still, using his charm and the street creds he had earned over the years, Dalzell managed to convince José Martindale, the head of the Devil's Disciples, and Yvon Bilodeau, one of the leaders of the Popeyes, that he could help mediate—not necessarily between their groups, but between them and the local police.

If the police saw the bikers as bums, the motorcyclists saw the cops as bullies who were constantly hounding them and seizing their property without showing proper warrants. Dalzell figured he could fix that and please both sides.

For the next two years, he lived a double life as a constable and a biker. The first year was the best. He'd drop into a clubhouse without a second thought, hoist a beer, and socialize. He even escorted scores of bikers to training sessions with rookie cops. The idea was that the bikers would role-play as the heavies—they played their parts with gusto—and pretend to be hanging out en masse in front of a restaurant, taking up the sidewalk and the road and intimidating everyone they met. "Some rookies reacted by just beating the crap out of the bikers from the get-go. Others were more circumspect and managed to talk the bikers into leaving," Dalzell recalls.

Back then, to him, most of the bikers weren't the fearsome figures they would become when serious drugs came on the scene. Rather, they were like adolescent boys who'd all had bikes equipped with two gears and banana seats, grown up to own a machine that was bigger and fiercer, with a motor and the ability to stoke fear in others. Once they acquired motorcycles and signed up, they became somebodies.

To most of Dalzell's fellow officers, though, the bikers were a mysterious, strange outfit. "It drove police crazy when they were listening in on wiretaps, because they would hear names like Apache, Gorilla, Sky, and Chesterfield, and it was like listening to a secret code that made no sense," Dalzell remembers. "They would come to me and ask, 'Who are these people?'"

When Dalzell first met Trudeau in the summer of 1968, the biker was still a prospect, with a vest that had a modified club crest lower down on his chest. At the time, the future killer didn't have a motorcycle—maybe it had been seized by police or was in for repairs—and was a bit of a sad sack, hanging back, the ultimate outsider in a clubhouse full of them.

On a few occasions, after drinking with the guys in a South Shore bar, Trudeau asked Dalzell for a ride back to his home in McMasterville, on the nearby Richelieu River. The two couldn't talk much on the way because of the noise from the cop's Harley, but Dalzell can't recall anyone ever sitting down and having a good laugh or a deep conversation with the biker.

"You know what I remember most about Apache in those days?" Dalzell asks. "There was an abandoned airport tarmac in Les Cèdres, just northeast of Montreal, where we'd ride sometimes, and he was really good at doing wheelies. He'd raise his bike up on its rear wheel like it was a horse, and he could go for a long time without crashing."

It wasn't all fun and games. While Dalzell was keeping an eye on the bikers, there was an occasional outbreak of violence. During a melee in June 1968 between the Devil's Disciples and the Popeyes near the Jacques Cartier Bridge on the South Shore, a Disciple named Jean-Yves (Fidel) Piquette was fatally stabbed—a death Trudeau would later say happened because the young biker got "cocky." But it wasn't until the winter of 1969, after the convention at the Montreal Botanical Gardens, that the young cop sensed he was no longer welcome.

"Dope changed everything," he says.

Drugs—first marijuana, then heroin and finally cocaine—changed the biker landscape dramatically in three ways. It turned the clubs from party-making machines into profit-making ones, sparking deadly turf wars over trafficking territory. It made some bikers, who often came from working-class if not downright poor backgrounds, suddenly and fabulously wealthy. And it turned others, like Trudeau and some of his buddies, into coke-addicted "sniffers."

For Dalzell, it turned his one-time chums into dangerous criminals. "I quickly got to know when they didn't want a cop present," he recalls. "I saw that transformation. Maybe it's a skill I've got, able to anticipate when to be there and when to leave, and at one point, I wouldn't even drop into a clubhouse unless I knew who was there."

Dalzell and Trudeau, the happy-go-lucky young man doing wheelies, would not see each other again for fifteen years. Each would steadily climb the ranks in their respective worlds. When they finally did reunite, it would be under circumstances neither could have imagined.

As Dalzell's time was running out with the bikers, Trudeau's was only ramping up, complete with a British-made motorcycle, a taste for drugs, and a willingness to do anything to make money.

Even murder.

Especially murder.

2.
THE FIRST KILL

The house in Saint-Luc-de-Vincennes was in ruins when provincial police, cadaver dogs, and an excavation truck descended upon it in October 1986. Wood planks were broken and rotting, and the roof had caved in. Where there had once been windows, only black holes remained, silent witnesses to what hitman Yves Trudeau would claim was his first murder, more than sixteen years earlier.

Jean-Marie Viel was about twenty years old, a small-time hood and skinny biker wannabe whose disappearance in September 1970 was not remarked upon, not in a newspaper story or on a radio or TV program. He was just gone, leaving little behind save for an out-of-focus photo that would surface years later of him sitting casually on a motorcycle in front of a wire fence, eyes gazing down beneath dark brows, unsmiling, his right hand on the handlebar and his left on his lap, fingers poised as if he was smoking a cigarette. He was all angles and shadows, with dark-brown hair parted on the right and curled over his ears, a jean jacket, and lace-ups rather than solid, clunky biker boots on his feet.

Around the time Viel disappeared, tensions were ratcheting up in Quebec's increasingly violent biker world. The year before, in an effort to stop the turf battles, the Montreal police department had spurred the creation of the United Motorcyclists of Quebec, complete with the ceremony at the Botanical Gardens attended by Trudeau, who got to shake hands with the police chief. But the spectacle of police brass mingling with the bikers did little to stem the violence. And Yves Trudeau would have his hands all over it.

As Trudeau would later tell it, his first kill was an accident. It was biker justice, part of a dangerous trend as biker violence slowly, inexorably began to creep up across Quebec.

In April 1969, the Popeyes' clubhouse was damaged by fire. Then there were gunfights, stabbings, and the occasional murder. In July 1970, a police search of the clubhouse following one of those gunfights turned up three machine guns and a machete.

By then, Trudeau, once the quiet guy on the sidelines who rode on the back of John Dalzell's motorcycle, the biker who loved to do wheelies, was front and center as one of the leaders of the Popeyes. For him, showing any kind of weakness personally or as a Popeye was anathema. Power was paramount: power that fed his ego and the club's coffers, power that came from wearing the Popeyes patch on the gang's singular gray jacket. Power that made people walk a wide circle around him on the street, strutting, dangerous, and, as it turned out, deadly.

As Trudeau would later tell it, the killing of Viel started out as a simple plan for retribution: the younger man had stolen a Popeyes' motorcycle, and Trudeau was determined to wreak vengeance, but he claimed he had intended to beat up the hapless bike thief, not murder him. Despite the time that had passed, his memory of the theft was still as clear as if it had happened the day before. A code had been breached, and payment must be exacted—and in biker terms, that meant violence. Besides, a stolen motorcycle was bad news for the gang's reputation.

Just as he would do for so many of his later assassinations, Trudeau hunted down his target, stalking him like prey. He found Viel in the small city of Trois-Rivières, about 150 kilometers northeast of Montreal. There was a hail of bullets and lots of blood. And then Trudeau was burying the body in the dirt behind the house in nearby Saint-Luc-de-Vincennes that sixteen years later would be abandoned and decrepit.

At the time, the Popeyes were a presence in the region, with two clubhouses, one of which burned down in August 1970. Although police opened an investigation, it went nowhere because the biker code of silence was strong.

It is not known how Trudeau reacted to his first kill. Did he have a sleepless night because he did not mean to murder Viel? Or, on the contrary, did he simply join his fellow gang members for some drinking and drugs to celebrate the retrieval of the motorcycle? Perhaps the young biker realized that if he played his cards right, murder could cement his reputation as a tough biker not to be messed with, heightening his place within the clubhouse.

Louis Morissette, the criminal psychiatrist, believes that first kill set Trudeau on his path as a career assassin. "That was a big driving force. Once he had done that and the guy was dead, he would have thought, *Oh, that wasn't so hard. They keep asking me to kill, and it works.*"

"That's how it works: he had found that was his way in," Dr. Morissette continues. "He was accepted, and after that, there were opportunities that kept coming. To do what he did and to last as long as he did, for sure he had the ability, the intelligence, and the competence."

Death would become Trudeau's calling card in an underworld where contract killings were par for the course—a violent settling of accounts. The man who would be known as both the Mad Bumper and the Mad Bomber would become a hitman because he was good at it. And because he had to, to survive.

It would be almost two years before Trudeau took another life. After that, the murders would become more regular, more brutal—and seemingly unstoppable.

In between his first two assassinations, Yves Trudeau found time for a more common criminal activity: robbing banks. By 1971, according to his later testimony, he had become a president of a Popeyes chapter. Soon after, though, he was busted for an armed bank robbery in Saint-Hyacinthe, about sixty kilometers east of Montreal. He had to quit his position as a Popeye president while doing a short stint in prison, but that only seemed to bolster his stature.

The Popeyes were considered the most vicious of Quebec's biker gangs. Their reputation, and the mystique around Yves Trudeau, began to grow, so much so that a new pattern emerged that would mark Trudeau's career as an assassin for years to come: he was so good, other gangs would contract him to do their bidding.

Trudeau's first partnership was with the Dubois brothers, several Montreal-born siblings who grew up in the working-class west-end neighborhood of Saint-Henri and claimed they were teased at school because of their hand-me-down clothes and molasses sandwiches for lunch—that was all their parents could afford. They were tight-knit, fierce, and cruel, these brothers, having gained a reputation for toughness and a criminal bent when they were only teens. They ran an outfit that the Quebec Commission of Inquiry into Organized Crime once called the most important criminal organization in the province, one that frightened even the Mafia and other biker gangs.

It didn't take long, though, for the Dubois gang to turn to Trudeau and the Popeyes for help: they became the Dubois brothers' muscle, enforcing punishment for unpaid debts and other transgressions. Police believe that several of Trudeau's next murders, after the killing of Viel, were exactly that: retribution carried out on behalf of the Dubois gang.

On March 25, 1972, Trudeau and another gunman lay in wait for Michel Berthiaume, twenty-four, and Robert Cadieux, thirty-one, to leave a cabaret on Saint Denis Street in east-end Montreal. It was a clear night, dry and chilly. Finally, at 2:30 a.m., their quarry, both of whom had police records, walked out together—right into a hail of bullets. Berthiaume, a burglar, was hit in the head and chest, and died on the spot. Cadieux, with bullets lodged in his neck, throat, and stomach, somehow staggered across the street before collapsing behind a parked car. As the sound of police sirens got closer, the gunmen took off. Cadieux, a fraud artist, was rushed to Notre-Dame Hospital, where he died of his injuries five days later. Police speculated the assassinations were due to a dispute over unpaid loans that had been granted at a usurious rate.

Ten months later, Trudeau struck again. At eight in the morning on January 23, 1973, a resident of Saint-Basile-le-Grand stumbled across the bloodied, half-frozen skinny body of Joseph-Jacques Saint-Laurent, thirty-two. The victim lay with his limbs at impossible angles at the edge of a remote, undeveloped tract of land that bordered the Chemin des Quarante, beaten black, blue, and red, with a bullet from a .12-gauge gun lodged in his head. A forensic pathologist estimated that Saint-Laurent, who had been released from Bordeaux Prison only three weeks earlier, after serving time on fraud charges, had been killed two days before. Homicide investigators from the Sûreté du Québec (SQ), the provincial police, believed it was "a settling of accounts." Trudeau would later say he had three accomplices for the killing, all the better to keep kicking and punching Saint-Laurent senseless before the final bullet finished him off.

Less than a month later, Trudeau notched up his fifth kill.

It was Valentine's Day, 1973. Muhammad Ali was fighting British boxing champion Joe Bugner in Las Vegas for the world heavyweight championship—twelve slow rounds, with no knockout. Meanwhile, Trudeau and two accomplices waited outside a brasserie called Joey, on Saint Hubert Street. They were stalking two men, Robert Côté and Pierre Bélisle, both twenty-two, who were inside, drinking and watching the fight. Both were members of the Outlaws biker gang, the Popeyes' enemies in a turf battle. When they walked out of the brasserie into the crowded street on a frigid night, Trudeau and his accomplices followed quietly, waiting for an opportunity to kill when there weren't any witnesses. About fifteen minutes later, at the corner of Saint Hubert and Castelnau, the assassins let loose in the dark with a hail of bullets. Bélisle wasn't hit, but Côté was struck several times and died five days later in the hospital.

It was the official start of a war between Trudeau's Popeyes and their biker rivals—the Outlaws, the Devil's Disciples, and Satan's Choice, three gangs who at the time dominated the manufacturing and smuggling of chemical drugs into Quebec. The lucrative drug trade began to take off in the 1970s and would explode even more in the 1980s, and the Popeyes decided they wanted in on the action, by any means necessary. The war would heighten the gang's reputation for violence and give Trudeau the opportunity to hone his métier on the way to becoming what the tabloids would later call "the 'Best' Killer in Canada."

In 1977, the war would also draw the fearsome California-based Hells Angels to Canada and set Yves Trudeau on his path to criminal glory—or infamy, depending on where you stood on the battle lines.

The first stop in the expansion tour of the most famous outlaw biker gang in the world was Montreal, where anything was available for a price and where a port provided easy entry to the rest of the continent.

3. HITMAN FOR THE HELLS

Before the Hells Angels swept into Trudeau's life, he was a dabbler—a killer, to be sure, who worked irregularly for the Dubois brothers as an enforcer, but it was as if he had something to prove. He was the outsider, smaller and quieter than his boisterous biker buddies, so he had to be more fearsome in other ways. He needed to show he was stronger and more decisive. "Look at me!" he seemed to be saying as he did wheelies on his bike. When it came to murders such as Viel's, he wanted to show he was tough and unforgiving. Anything other bikers could do, he could and would do better, including murder.

The Hells Angels would tap into that need, turning Trudeau from a casual killer into a hitman who would garner infamy as the most prolific assassin Canada has ever seen. He would become part of an inner circle determined to make the world's most powerful motorcycle gang predominant in Quebec and to ensure that its power was absolute.

When the Hells Angels came to town, war was inevitable, and Yves Trudeau would be at the center of it.

Trudeau, like all his fellow bikers, would have long been in awe of the legendary Hells Angels. For three decades they had roared through the back roads and cities of America on their Harleys, sporting their black leather jackets with the fearsome Death's Head logo: a gruesome skeleton face with what looks like a devil's horn, a red bike helmet, and long golden wings with the appearance of flames.

Their gang's name came from American bomber pilots who were stationed in England during the Second World War. Some of them, upon returning home afterward, joined various groups of loosely organized bikers that had sprung up in southern California. In 1947, things got nasty when a large army of bikers took over the small California town of Hollister, later made famous in the popular Marlon Brando movie *The Wild One*, in which a character is asked what he is rebelling against. "Whadda ya got?" comes the reply.

In 1948, a small gang of bikers in San Bernardino formally called themselves the Hells Angels and set up the club's first chapter. But it was only in 1957 that the HA slowly and steadily began its meteoric rise as the world's leading outlaw biker gang, thanks to the shrewd and determined leadership of a tenth-grade dropout named Ralph (Sonny) Barger. He formed an HA chapter in Oakland, and by 1958, the Angels had relocated their headquarters there. Until his death in 2022, Barger would remain the inspirational leader of what became a remarkably successful global crime empire.

"He's not a big guy, not a physically threatening guy," recalls Jay Dobyns, a former undercover cop for the United States Bureau of Alcohol, Tobacco, Firearms and Explosives who infiltrated the Angels and met Barger several times. "But he's got this charismatic leadership personality that allowed him to build this club."

Barger realized if his Angels were going to dominate the increasingly competitive and violent biker world, he would have to mix an almost military-type discipline with the free-wheeling outlaw spirit that was at the heart of being a biker. So, over time, he and the HA developed a series of strict rules to bring order to a rowdy army.

At least six members—all riding the mandatory Harleys—were required to form an official HA chapter, which had to be sponsored by an already existing franchise. For all their talk of being rebels, inside each chapter there was a clearly defined hierarchy, with an all-powerful president assisted by a sergeant at arms. There were rigid recruitment protocols, obliging aspiring members to prove themselves as "prospects" in "puppet clubs" that helped the HA carry out its dirty work. There were even policies about drugs: "No using dope during a meeting" and "no drug burns," which meant, simply, don't rip off your fellow bikers. These were rules that would later come back to haunt Trudeau and the other members of his misbehaving chapter.

In 1966, Barger took the unusual step of incorporating the Hells Angels as an officially registered business—a bold and brash move for a proud gang of self-styled "outlaws"—and he later trademarked the name Hells Angels and the winged Death's Head insignia. (Many years later, that move became useful on several occasions when the Angels, listing themselves in court documents as a "non-profit mutual benefit corporation," sued mega-companies such as Disney and Saks Fifth Avenue for trademark infringement.) Barger realized that being serious bikers meant being serious about business. And more and more, that business meant drugs.

The Hells Angels' timing was perfect, for the 1960s gave them the two things they needed to expand across America and onto the world stage: the counterculture movement that made them into anti-establishment heroes for many and, more importantly, the explosion of recreational drugs: marijuana, heroin, acid, and, most popular of all, cocaine.

As Barger put it in an interview with the *Washington Post*: "In the '60s, we got a lot of publicity. It was all fun and games. In the '70s, we all became gangsters." Later, in his autobiography, the Angels leader was even more blunt: "The seventies were a gangster era for us. I sold drugs and got into a lot of shit."

That "gangster era" coincided with a deliberate and well-organized battle plan, along with their rivals in the other major biker gangs, to expand beyond America's borders. Up until the middle of the 1960s, the Hells Angels had been exclusively Californian. The second-largest gang, the Bandidos, was based in Texas. A third group, called the Outlaws, was founded in Illinois. For all of them, the power and profits of global expansion were too alluring to resist. By the late sixties, the Angels claimed a membership of about five hundred, most of them still in the southern United States but with chapters in the northeastern states and slowly moving abroad, first in Switzerland, then England and West Germany. Eventually, they would boast over 2,500 members in more than twenty-five countries, becoming as familiar and popular an American icon worldwide as Disney or McDonald's. On a global scale, the Bandidos were close behind, with an estimated 2,000 members in twenty-two countries. The Outlaws, for their part, would move into France, Australia, and Norway.

When the Outlaws executed three Hells Angels in Florida in 1974, in retaliation for an early beating of one of their bikers by the HA, war was officially declared between the two gangs, a battle that would last for years and claim hundreds of lives. That rivalry, and its body count, would spill over into Canada in unimaginably brutal ways when both gangs moved north of the border.

Up until then, Yves Trudeau and his Popeye pals had been battling it out in a small-time turf war with Satan's Choice, the country's largest gang, with chapters not just in Montreal but throughout Southern Ontario. Now they were ready to join the big leagues.

Canada would eventually become the largest center for the HA's power outside the United States, accounting for about one in five of every Hells Angel in the world and remaining the only country where the Angels had a complete monopoly of the biker underworld, unchallenged by any significant rivals. That dominance, which would come slowly and bloodily, began on December 5, 1977. On that date, almost thirty years after their birth in California, the HA "patched over," or absorbed, about thirty-five members of the Popeyes in Quebec, thus making Yves Trudeau one of the founding members of the Hells Angels in Canada. Others who joined included Michel (Sky) Langlois, a Popeyes cofounder, who would become the HA's second national vice president.

The Hells Angels chapter was located in Laval, just north of Montreal, so it was often called the "North" chapter. Trudeau would later boast that he served as the chapter's sergeant at arms, in effect the second in command.

From that first foothold in Quebec, the Angels spread across the country—slowly at first, to be sure, but relentlessly. By 1984, they had one more chapter in the province, in Sherbrooke. Then they expanded across Canada, starting with one clubhouse in Halifax and four in British Columbia.

Their hated rivals, the Outlaws, moved in to take over Satan's Choice—and the war was on.

Within a year of joining the Hells Angels' army, Yves Trudeau got his first murder mission: eliminate one of the leaders of the rival Outlaws gang, Roland (Roxy) Dutemple.

By this time, Trudeau had already racked up five kills. This would be number six, a murder that would turn out to be a tragic mistake.

On December 8, 1978, Trudeau thought he had his man when he saw a tall, thin figure get out of a car in the driveway of the house he was renting in Greenfield Park. "Are you Roxy?" he called out in the waning winter light. But he didn't give the man time to answer. Instead, he unloaded multiple shots into the back and head of William Weichold, called "Billy" by his friends and family, killing him on the spot. A railway worker who had been introduced to Dutemple by his brother, Billy was only renting the Outlaw's house.

The next day, Trudeau discovered his error while reading an account of Weichold's death in a local newspaper. He laughed and blurted out that those who merely looked like Dutemple deserved to die too.

What was a joke for Trudeau was a life-altering tragedy for Billy Weichold's little sister, Darlene. She had stayed up late that night, wondering why her brother hadn't called, as he had promised to take her shopping. She caught the TV news at 11 p.m. about a random shooting on Billy's street and went to bed assuming he had been delayed by the commotion.

Then came the pounding on the front door in the middle of the night. *Bang. Bang. Bang-bang-bang.* Darlene, startled out of sleep, looked at her bedside clock. It was 2 a.m. Bewildered and scared, she checked through the peephole to see who it was before opening the door to admit her brother Richard. He was breathing hard and crying. "Is Mommy here?" he asked.

Mommy? When had Richard ever called their mom *Mommy*? Come to think of it, when had she ever seen her tough older brother cry?

"No, she's out at a friend's place, but I'm waiting for Billy to call me," Darlene said. "Do you know why he hasn't called? He was supposed to arrange to take me shopping."

It was as if Richard didn't hear her. "Where's Mommy?" he repeated.

"At her friend's house," Darlene said again.

"Call her. I need to talk to her. *Now.*"

Scared, Darlene got her mom on the phone and told her to get home fast, that Richard was there and crying. Only when her mother, Patricia, walked through the door did the teenager find out why her brother was acting so strange.

"Mommy, there's no more Billy," Richard said. "Billy's been shot dead."

What came after still unspools for Darlene like a film reel, the edges frayed from being played over and over again, images jumbled together so that they make no sense.

The police screeching up to the house in Verdun.

Billy's blood staining the length of the driveway on Verchères Street.

Police sharpshooters standing guard at his funeral in Saint-Bruno, armed to make sure violence didn't break out, and the police van with its back doors wide open to show a supply of guns.

Billy's three dogs racing through the cemetery to his grave, howling because they could sense their master was there, in the ground beside his father.

Her mom's face, mottled and swollen from constant crying, her tears the soundtrack to the tragedy that would destroy their lives through guilt, blame, and recriminations. Somehow, they were all lost that night and couldn't find their way back to each other.

In the immediate aftermath of Billy's death, Darlene felt like she was wading through a landscape of thick gray mud. The planned-for shopping trip was from another, more innocent time. Now she found herself clenching her fists against an onslaught of police questions.

"Did William belong to a biker gang?"

"No!" she answered.

"How do you know that?"

"He was my brother!"

"Did he sell drugs?"

"No! Well, maybe some marijuana sometimes. But *not* for the bikers. For petty cash."

"Then why was he living in a house that belongs to a leader of the Outlaws biker gang? How did William even know Roxy?"

"I don't know," Darlene sobbed. "I don't know. Ask my brother Richard. He introduced them. And my brother was *Billy*, not William. Why did he die?"

It would take years before Darlene—and the police—would get an answer to that question. At the time, the police wrote it off as just another "gangland slaying," one of two catchall phrases that would become frustratingly common for law enforcement over the coming years, the other being a "settling of accounts."

The rough translation? "We have no idea who did it."

Then and for many years afterward, the police knew nothing about the committed serial assassin who was just beginning to make a frightening name for himself, a man who was whispered about in the criminal underworld as the go-to guy if you needed someone eliminated.

After Billy Weichold's murder, Trudeau had three dozen more kills to pull off for the bikers and other gangsters before he would stop.

Trudeau had the nerve to attempt to collect his fee for the Dutemple contract, despite having shot the wrong man. The Hells Angels refused to pay up. But it wasn't fair, Trudeau whined. He had been at the right address, and the car looked right too. As far as he was concerned, he'd done a job that he should be paid for. Still, business was business: to get his money, he'd have to bump off the right guy. Three months later, he did.

Dutemple had been targeted to die because the Hells Angels suspected he had helped get three of their gang members killed in October 1978. A tough Outlaws member with dark-brown hair worn in a comb-over, Dutemple was, at the time, working at the Tourbillon Bar in Pointe-aux-Trembles, in Montreal's far east end, as a doorman and bouncer. That night, two men walked into the seedy bar, whose French name aptly translates as "Whirlwind." They were so well and conservatively dressed, patrons thought they were undercover cops. They ended up sitting at a table near the partying Hells Angels bikers. They calmly finished their drinks before standing up, pulling pistols from their jackets, and spraying the bikers' table with bullets.

Two HA members, Jean Brochu and Georges Mousseau, were killed instantly, while a third biker visiting from Hamilton, Ontario,

Guy Davies, a member of an Angels support club, succumbed to his injuries five days later in the hospital.

Convinced that Dutemple, as the bar's bouncer, had given information to the killers, the Hells Angels decreed that he had to pay the ultimate price. Yet another verdict in biker justice, and Trudeau was tasked with carrying out the sentence. Three months after he had mistakenly slain Billy Weichold, on March 29, 1979, Trudeau tracked down Dutemple at his new job, as a bouncer at the Guyro nudie bar in Longueuil, on Montreal's South Shore. The unsuspecting Dutemple finished his shift around 8:30 p.m. and walked to his car, a 1973 Pontiac Astre coupe—nothing flashy, even forgettable. He opened the door, settled himself in the driver's seat, and put the key in the ignition.

BOOM! A bomb exploded, tearing him to pieces.

It was quick. It was efficient. This modus operandi would become Trudeau's trademark: a painstakingly constructed bomb, each ingredient carefully measured. It would earn him one of his many nicknames: the Mad Bomber.

And this time, Trudeau got paid.

4.
THE NOISY BARBARIANS

The bombing murder of Roxy Dutemple was the first of Yves Trudeau's many contract killings for the Hells Angels. He may have started killing as part of his allegiance to the biker code, helping first the Popeyes and then the Hells Angels punish or eliminate their enemies. He continued, no doubt, because he was so good at it. Murder made him feel menacing and feared, and the power of fear was an important commodity in the dangerous world of the bikers. Then there was the money. Trudeau would later testify he was paid anywhere between $5,000 and $200,000 for each of his many killings. One of his final jobs—the fatal bombing of four men—came with the promise of another $200,000 payday.

Increasingly, Trudeau had a pressing need for that blood money, to fuel his new and growing addiction to cocaine. Like many of his fellow bikers in the undisciplined and unruly Laval chapter of the Hells Angels, he was committing the risky mistake of snorting more cocaine than he was selling. That was bad for business and the bottom line, because the outlaw biker gang was changing its priorities from partying with drugs to profiting from them.

In the beginning, Trudeau managed to keep his addiction under control. He'd always been wiry and edgy; if anything, the cocaine gave him more energy and made him more inventive. As he continued to prove himself such a valuable asset to the gang, the time lag between his kills kept shortening. A month, a week, mere days. He was an assassin who would do anything to get the job done, be it bombing, strangling, stabbing, shooting, or beating—whatever was easiest.

"To kill was a necessity," Yves Trudeau would later tell a court.

Steadily, the body count kept rising. Victim number eight was Robert Labelle, a former president of the Huns, a biker gang in Laval that had been affiliated with the Devil's Disciples, the longtime rivals of the Popeyes. It happened on April 3, 1979, fittingly one day before the Quebec Commission of Inquiry into Organized Crime warned that biker gangs had supplanted criminal organizations like the Mafia as the most fearsome and violent in the province. "Bikers: Hordes of Noisy Barbarians," screamed a headline in *La Presse*.

"They are willing to use violence to get their way, not just amongst themselves but in the public at large," Judge Denys Dionne, the commission's head, declared.

Although the majority of bikers still wore traditional leather vests adorned with lots of badges, their leaders looked different, more refined, Dionne pointed out, with short, styled hair, the latest in respectable fashion, and a penchant for sports cars rather than motorcycles. They *looked* like businessmen, but their ways of conducting business were becoming ever more deadly. "It's a scourge," the judge said.

As if to illustrate Dionne's observations, Trudeau's assassination that same week was swift and brutal. The target, Robert Labelle, was in his Laval bungalow at 10 a.m. when Trudeau and two accomplices came calling. Labelle opened the door, and the Hells Angels fired two bullets, killing their enemy on the spot. That was it, a job done. As with most police investigations into such murders around this time, this one went nowhere. Detectives speculated that the death was a settling of accounts, and Labelle just another casualty of the violent war between biker gangs.

No arrests were made. Trudeau's name never even came up as a suspect. He was, as always, an unknown, a deadly ghost.

Eliminating a rival biker like Labelle was business. Sometimes, however, the murders Trudeau helped carry out were simply for petty revenge. Forty-three days later, on May 16, 1979, Trudeau struck again. Richard Joncas was found slumped over the steering wheel of his Dodge Econoline van on a service road behind the Promenades St-Bruno mall, on Montreal's South Shore. The van's lights were on. He had been ambushed and shot. Again, police would attribute the murder to the proverbial "settling of accounts." Joncas, it would later emerge, had been part of a recent rampage at a place called the Terrasses de Chevalier in Laval, damaging some vehicles belonging to the Hells Angels in the process.

Another deadly notch in Trudeau's belt, but for the police, it was just another anonymous biker murder. They had no idea they had a serial assassin on their hands.

The tenth murder occurred six weeks later, on July 3. Once again, it was a small-time altercation that, once Trudeau was involved, had deadly consequences. Serge Boileau, a twenty-four-year-old public service employee, was playing billiards at the Brasserie des Pivoines on Rachel Street in Montreal's east end. Despite its flowery reference to peonies, the brasserie was an establishment frequented by bikers. It was Boileau's misfortune that he had words with two of the bikers, including Trudeau, around 9 p.m. The three went outside to chat some more, then Boileau went back in as if that was it, end of argument—until one of the bikers returned and shot him in the head.

Once again, a familiar pattern emerged. The police were mystified. No one in the bar admitted to witnessing anything, and the police weren't able to get a description of the killer. It was never clear if it was Trudeau or his companion. Like all the other biker-related killings, the death was attributed to a gang squabble, perhaps a drug deal gone wrong. But the curious thing was that the victim, Serge Boileau, did not seem to have any gang connections. Police had never heard of him before. There was not even a mention of him in files on other suspected criminals. That night, he may simply have been unlucky: in the wrong place at the wrong time, cussing off violent killers with no idea whom he was talking to.

He would not be the last innocent victim of Yves Trudeau's wrath.

And so it went. Barely one week after killing Boileau, an ordinary bar patron, Trudeau was back in business knocking off troublesome gangsters. On July 10, 1979, Trudeau and two accomplices drove fifty kilometers to the home of Jean-Charles Vincent, thirty-six, in the village of Saint-Lin, nestled in the picturesque lower Laurentians north of Montreal. They rang the bell, the drug dealer opened the door, and Trudeau and his men promptly mowed him down with six bullets. There was no time for comments or questions. That was it.

In a rare move for a gang-related slaying, two members of the Hells Angels (though not Trudeau) were taken in for questioning. But they were soon let go, and the murder remained unsolved. Only later would police learn from Trudeau the details of the hit; he told them Vincent died because of a speed deal gone bad.

Seven months later, Trudeau again went after a fellow criminal, only this time, he slaughtered innocent family members in his zeal to get the job done. André Desjardins had been a Hells Angel, with "had been" being the operative words. In the strict code of the bikers, you could leave the Hells Angels in "good standing," or you could leave on bad terms, which rarely ended well for the person exiting the club. Desjardins was suspected of having become a police informant, and the penalty for such a transgression was extreme. In February 1980, Trudeau was dispatched to mete out the proper punishment, accompanied by two other bikers named Charles Labrie and Jean-Pierre Mathieu. (Mathieu's nickname was Matt Le Croisseur, which roughly translates to "Matt the Liar" or "Matt the Double-Crosser." Within five years, he and Labrie would find themselves at the other end of biker guns in gangland slayings.)

The three men went looking for Desjardins at the home of his mother, Jeanne, where gang members had often been spotted. It was a second-story dwelling on Drolet Street, not far from Montreal's Mount Royal—a classic city apartment with winding exterior stairs leading up to the front door. Jeanne Desjardins was a short but feisty woman with a guarded smile, always holding a cigarette between the second and third fingers of her left hand. Did she welcome the visiting bikers into her home, not suspecting they were looking for her son? Or did she stand up to them from the get-go, trying unsuccessfully to shut the door in their faces?

Either way, she ended up dead.

Her body was found on February 12, wedged in the foyer between the front door and a set of stairs that led to the upper floor. She had been beaten black and blue, the blows so hard and vicious, her skull was cracked open.

It marked at least the third time, after Billy Weichold and Serge Boileau, that Trudeau had murdered someone with no history of criminal activity. Maybe André Desjardins's mother refused to divulge her son's whereabouts. Maybe she didn't know. But in Trudeau's mind she had to die, and for the same reason the bikers had gone to her home in the first place: she was related to someone slated for death and thus had become a witness.

Next up for Trudeau and his accomplices were Desjardins himself and his wife, Berthe. They were a handsome couple, Berthe with short, dark hair that framed an open face and wide smile, and André, clean-shaven, with wavy brown hair and a knowing grin. Trudeau tracked them down, and like Desjardins's mother, they were both beaten to death. Their bodies were dumped unceremoniously in the St. Lawrence River. André's body surfaced six months later, on August 4, bloated and unrecognizable. Berthe's would not turn up for another five years—and then only accidentally, when police were investigating what would become the most infamous massacre in biker history.

Women often seemed to be collateral damage in Trudeau's revenge. It was a few months before he struck again, this time accompanied by Jean-Pierre Mathieu and Yves Buteau, a former Popeye who had risen to become the national president of the Hells Angels in Canada. Their target this time: Donald McLean, thirty, a former Satan's Choice member turned Outlaw.

Neighbors called McLean a "sweet guy." He was a thickset, bearded man who kept his dark hair trimmed to his shoulders and loved to talk about hockey and baseball with anyone who would listen, but went quiet when anyone dared to ask about his gang affiliation. Two years earlier, he'd escaped a murder attempt when a bomb blew up the Chevy Camaro he was sitting in outside Outlaw headquarters on Bordeaux Street in Montreal's east end. McLean's companion in the car, Gilles Cadorette, the head of the Outlaws, was killed instantly, but McLean escaped with a minor eye injury and a shaken disposition.

This time he would not be so lucky.

At 7 p.m. on May 27, 1980, McLean and his girlfriend, Carmen Piché, twenty-two, descended from their second-floor apartment on 4th Avenue in the southwest Montreal neighborhood of Verdun and went around to the dirt-covered courtyard in back, where the biker's chrome-slick Harley-Davidson was parked.

Piché, a petite woman with long brown hair who worked nights as a cocktail waitress, was quieter and more reserved than her

Outlaw boyfriend. She knew the neighborhood well, and her mother lived just down the street, perhaps one of the reasons the couple had chosen to move into the apartment the year before. As she got on her boyfriend's motorcycle, a bomb placed under the seat went off. The blast was so powerful, it flung what was left of her body twenty feet away. McLean, standing by the bike, was burned and blown to bits too.

Piché's grieving mom spent hours at the morgue identifying her only child from what was left. When she returned home, she had a few choice words for a journalist who was waiting outside. McLean wasn't good enough for her Carmen, who was more educated than he was and worked hard to build a life for them. "But she loved this boy, Donald, something terrible," she added, before going inside and shutting the door.

Two and a half months later, Trudeau racked up his final murder of 1980: Donald Arseneault, victim number seventeen. At about 11:30 p.m. on August 11, the twenty-year-old, who looked like Ringo Starr's older, more self-indulgent brother, complete with a thick mustache, luxuriant brown hair, and a tiny gap between his front teeth, was found shot to death in a stolen car that was abandoned in a lane just off De Courcelles Street in Saint-Henri, near some train tracks. His crime? He had apparently caused problems for the bikers during an earlier stay in the Cowansville prison, in the Eastern Townships.

Trudeau stayed quiet for the next seven months before striking again. And this time, as with Billy Weichold, he killed the wrong person. Murder number eighteen was a twenty-six-year-old trucker named Robert Morin. On March 14, 1981, Morin was whiling away the early hours of the late-winter Saturday afternoon at the Darling Bowling Alley on Ontario Street, on Montreal's east side. Just before

3 p.m., he returned to his parked car, a 1974 Pontiac LeMans, got in, and began to drive south along Darling, en route to his home on Du Havre Street.

All of a sudden, on a quiet stretch of road near railroad tracks, a loud boom rent the air. Trudeau had staked out his target, accompanied by an associate named Paul April, an ambitious east-end drug dealer with ties to the Hells Angels and other gangs. They had planted a remote-controlled bomb under Morin's Pontiac, then waited until the LeMans was moving through a less-populated area—no families strolling on the sidewalk or children playing soccer or street hockey—before triggering the explosive device. Morin was killed instantly. Parked cars were damaged, their windows shattered or blown out, and there was debris everywhere.

Only later did Trudeau discover that, once again, he had murdered the wrong man. His target had actually been a member of the Outlaws known as "Michel G.," about whom little else is known. Robert Morin paid the price of Trudeau's zeal and mistakes.

Less than two months later, on May 9, Donat Lemieux, thirty-seven, and his girlfriend, Lucille (Lucie) Vallières, thirty-two, would become Trudeau's nineteenth and twentieth victims. It is not known why they were shot to death, their bodies bloodied from a hail of bullets and left on the balcony of the apartment they shared in Rosemont. Their deaths went unnoticed and unremarked upon in the mainstream media, as if the very history of their presence had been erased from the world. As if Quebec had become so jaded, the deaths of two more victims were not worth dwelling on. As if they had never existed.

With all these kills, Trudeau's reputation was reaching new heights. To the police, the killer remained ephemeral, unknown, with nary a description or name raised to lead them to a suspect, despite the growing pile of bodies scattered across the province. But in organized crime circles, interest in his talents was growing. They knew who he was. Word was spreading about the man who had gotten away with killing twenty people in a little over a decade. That made Trudeau famous enough that gangs other than the Hells Angels became interested in benefiting from his deadly special services, a turn of fate that would dramatically alter his life and his future with the Angels.

5.

THE IRISH CONNECTION

They came from opposite ends of the city, one French, the other Irish. But they were both working-class Catholics raised in the hard-scrabble streets. They both found that gangs and crime were the easiest route to power and prestige. And they were both willing to use unrestrained violence to get power and hold on to it.

It was a contract for murder that would bring together Frank (Dunie) Ryan, the leader of the West End Gang, and Yves (Apache) Trudeau. It would not end well. Both would be betrayed by people they considered allies, if not friends. One would soon end up dead at the hands of a business partner; the other, in order to avoid certain death at the hand of his supposed biker buddies, would have to make a fateful choice.

Growing up poor and Irish in Montreal meant you had three strikes against you. You were at the bottom of the food chain—and literally at the bottom of the city, crammed between the railway tracks and the St. Lawrence River and the port. You were a minority in a largely French-speaking city. And the wealthier English community looked down on you for being what you were: poor and Irish.

Frank Peter Ryan Jr. saw his father abandon his family when he was three. His mother called him "Junior," which the young boy mispronounced as "Dunie," and it became his nickname for life. By his teens, Dunie had dropped out of school and racked up an impressive juvenile rap sheet for everything from jewelry store robberies to heisting fur coats from the back of delivery trucks. Ryan became part of an informal network of Irish criminals known, at least in the crime tabloids and in the streets, as the West End Gang.

"They grew up poor. All of them. And it was a hardscrabble life," recalls D'Arcy O'Connor, the author of *Montreal's Irish Mafia*. "They were tough, Irish, working-class kids who grew up with similar backgrounds and that made them very tough criminals."

Unlike the French bikers who came out of the city's east end and the traditional Italian Mafia based in the northern part of the city, the West End Gang was a gang in name only. It had no official structure, membership, or rules. "The West End Gang is great because it's actually not a gang, it's a network of people. It's very flexible. You also don't give the police a structure to look at and penetrate," says journalist Dan Burke, who investigated Ryan and his cohorts for years. "Dunie Ryan was a very, very, very sharp criminal operator. Very intelligent guy. He's at the top." Burke and O'Connor were featured in the 2022 documentary about the West End Gang, *Kings of Coke*.

Ryan had the guts and brains to become an accomplished thief at an early age. "He could tell the difference between a good fur and a bad one, between a valuable gem and a worthless one. He's a money launderer as well," Burke recalls. "Dunie would do anything. Dunie loved the game."

Initially, the West End Gang's speciality was holding up banks. In the 1960s, Montreal earned the dubious distinction of being labeled "the bank robbery capital" of North America, and no one did it better than the Irish stickup men. They would sometimes rob the same bank two or three times a week—and get away with it. Dunie Ryan was not as lucky when he went across the border for a holdup. He was busted after robbing a small Massachusetts bank in 1966 and served six years in an American prison. But upon his return to Montreal, he emerged as the dominant figure in the West End Gang. "What made Dunie a good crime boss?" Melvin Mingo, a prolific bank robber and long-time member of the West End Gang, asks rhetorically. "He had a good gang. To me that would be the simplest answer. He just had good people around him that supported him, and people knew who they were."

Ryan and his cronies never looked back. In 1976, they helped to pull off the "crime of the century" by stealing $2.8 million from a Brink's truck. They tried to foster a reputation as "Robin Hoods," honorable thieves who never forgot their roots in Pointe-Saint-Charles, Griffintown, and other poor Irish communities. Everyone knew someone connected to the West End Gang. There were Christmas turkeys handed out to the needy and contributions to the local church. When one of his men got out of jail, Ryan was there with a helping hand and some money. "He'd say, 'Well, I'll see what I can do for you. Here's five hundred bucks; go get yourselves some clothes and whatever the fuck you need.' Dunie was like that. He was generous to a fault," one former gang member told D'Arcy O'Connor.

But in the end, they were ruthless criminals who settled their problems not with generosity but with guns. After pulling off a store heist, one of Ryan's closest pals, John Slawvey, randomly machine-gunned a police officer standing on a sidewalk nearby, even though the cop had not witnessed the holdup. Slawvey was gunned down himself in 1976 by police when they tried to arrest him, in what Ryan saw as a revenge execution. As was the gang's way, Ryan then put out a $50,000 contract on the head of the lead police investigator on the case, André Savard.

"I always put my .44 Magnum under the bed," recalls Savard in the *Kings of Coke* documentary. He earned the nickname "Dirty Harry" because of his no-nonsense approach to going after the gangs. "We are not easy targets, you know. So we are not going to let ourselves get killed without defending ourselves."

By the 1980s, the West End Gang was moving into more serious crimes than robbing banks. "Dunie Ryan realized the big money to be made was in drugs," O'Connor explains. Unlike the global crime organizations based in Montreal, such as the Italian Mafia and the Hells Angels, the local Irish mobsters' clout never extended beyond the city. But they had one distinct advantage over the more established rivals: they controlled the port of Montreal, where the Irish had been working for years and where the West End Gang had a tight control over the union and what moved where in, around, and through the port. That forced the Mafia and the HA to deal with the upstart Irish gang as cocaine exploded onto the North American scene in the 1980s and huge amounts had to be smuggled in containers through the port. Much of it was destined for New York and other major American markets. The demand was insatiable, making Ryan and his cohorts extremely powerful and rich.

"The money had become almost a joke to the guys—that was the legend. They were lighting cigars with hundred-dollar bills," says Burke. The police estimated Ryan was worth at least $50 million. Rumors of his wealth were legend in the criminal underworld; some said he had a briefcase with $500,000 that he always kept close to him, while others believed he had buried millions of dollars in various hideouts because, as befitting a bank robber, he never trusted the institution.

But with that huge wealth from the drug trade came rivalries and jealousies—and murder. "Dunie used to bury all his money. It's millions of dollars, but it's such a big headache," warned fellow bank robber Melvin Mingo. "It's not like you're selling Chanel N°5 or stuff like that. You're involved with drugs, with money laundering, with racketeering, you got an organization that is the worst thing on the face of the earth. Everyone gets challenged.

"Somebody always wants to take over an empire."

For all his charm and generosity to his team, Dunie Ryan was a ruthless enforcer. "Ryan might have been an 'honest thief,' as a lot of people called him. However, if you crossed Dunie, there could be hell to pay," notes O'Connor.

Patrick (Hughie) McGurnaghan would find that out the hard way. A low-level drug dealer associated with the West End Gang, McGurnaghan had an "extensive file on his criminal activities since 1956," according to police, mainly for fraud and bookmaking. He allegedly bought cocaine in huge quantities from Ryan for distribution, but he ended up snorting more than he was selling. By 1981, he had run up a debt of at least $100,000 with Ryan. "Every time Dunie tried to collect, McGurnaghan would blow him off," recalls O'Connor.

So Ryan decided to send an unmistakable message to McGurnaghan—and consequently to anyone else who might think of crossing him. That was not unusual for the leader of the Irish mafia. What *was* remarkable was the messenger Ryan chose to deliver it: the Hells Angel enforcer Yves Trudeau. "It makes sense that Dunie would turn to someone like Trudeau to do his dirty work," says retired Montreal police detective Ken Sweeney,* one of the few anglophones on the force, who spent years tracking the Irish mafia and other gangs. "They're both ruthless and willing to do anything."

As turns-of-events go, it was precedent-setting.

A decade after his first kill, Trudeau was, at this point, still largely unknown to police, even though he was a serial killer knocking off contract murders for the Hells Angels. They knew, of course,

* *A pseudonym to protect the identity of a police officer who made many enemies in the criminal underworld.*

that bodies were piling up in what they presumed were drug disputes; they just never suspected that many of those murders had been carried out by a single person. But if he was below the radar of the authorities, in the criminal underground, Trudeau's reputation had spread well beyond the bikers. He had done contracts for the French-Canadian Dubois gang, and now the Irish saw the value of his skills. His work was so professional and prolific that rival gangs wanted to use him, and the Hells Angels seemed willing to farm out their best assassin.

The HA and the West End Gang were not exactly enemies—they collaborated in the cocaine trafficking business—but they were competitors. Still, business was business, and if Ryan was willing to pay for a bit of Trudeau's time to knock off one of his own, why not?

As was his wont, Trudeau was meticulous and methodical. He staked out McGurnaghan. He learned where he lived, what kind of car he drove, and what his habits were. The Irish drug dealer may have had ties to the West End Gang, with its roots in the poor Irish enclaves on the wrong side of the tracks, but he was living in a family member's apartment complex on a quiet tree-lined street in Westmount, one of Montreal's richest neighborhoods. The car he drove, borrowed from a dealer, was a sleek beige 1977 Mercedes-Benz 280SE sedan.

It would end up being his coffin.

Trudeau knew that McGurnaghan left his car parked overnight in the building's outdoor parking lot, and it was easy to plant a powerful bomb underneath the car's chassis, connected to a remote-controlled radio device. October 27, 1981, dawned damp, chilly, and gray, with a steady drizzle when McGurnaghan got into his car with a passenger, a former bookie named Joseph Frankel. They drove east on York Street, then turned up Victoria Avenue and then right on Sherbrooke Street, one of Montreal's busiest roads. As the car passed a large park near a school, McGurnaghan turned right on Melville. It would be the last move he ever made.

At 12:40 p.m., a tremendous explosion rocked the quiet neighborhood. Windows shattered nearby. The mangled car flew from the road to a field at a corner of the park. Pieces of the destroyed vehicle were scattered as far as twenty-five meters away, a hub cap here, a front grill there.

Not that Trudeau ever cared about killing innocent bystanders, but it was only a miracle that weather and school schedules had kept the park empty. At lunchtime, it was usually packed with students, dog walkers, and nearby residents. "Near the park, there is a school that usually has hundreds of children outside," said one local. But thanks to the rain and a school holiday, no one was there that day.

Frantic witnesses who had watched from their homes rushed out to help. "The man just fell out and his arms and legs were blown off," said one distraught woman.

"I opened the car door, and the guy had no feet," another man recounted to O'Connor. "There was a smoking hole in the bottom of the car. The guy was conscious but bleeding to death and screaming 'Get me out of here.'"

As luck would have it, a doctor was shopping at a nearby antiques store when he heard the blast. "I knew it was a bomb right away," he recalled. He got to the crime scene within twenty-five seconds. After quickly determining that the passenger, Joseph Frankel, was injured but would survive, the doctor turned his attention to a desperate McGurnaghan. The doctor pulled off his belt to use as a tourniquet and told a neighbor to get another belt.

He stayed with the suffering victim in the ambulance as it raced to a nearby emergency room, but it was no use. "He died in my arms when we were about fifty feet from the hospital," the doctor said. "He bled to death."

Frankel got away with multiple cuts and perforated eardrums.

Police knew McGurnaghan was the target, and they knew it was a gang-related hit, but they had no idea who had done it. With more than two months left to go in 1981, it was Montreal's sixty-fifth murder of the year, more than double the rate of the previous year. "It was probably a settling of accounts," one cop at the scene said, trotting out the usual phrase police use when they have no idea what really happened.

"Police Fear Gang War after Westmount Blast," read one headline the next day. A police investigator who kept tabs on the Irish mob was more accurate, if rather blunt. "Things could really go pop," the unnamed cop told the *Montreal Gazette*. "It all depends on who is behind the bombing. If his own people gave the order, then that will be that. It's not a nice way to go, but if you play on the dung heap you usually end up covered in the stuff."

Every person, even a criminal, is a loved one to someone—a husband, a father, a brother, an uncle. McGurnaghan's family diplomatically noted in the obituary printed in the newspaper shortly after his murder that he had died "accidentally." "You were taken from us without a goodbye," said one printed tribute. "We had no chance to say farewell," said another. "No one will ever know the pain we felt that day when the phone rang and we were told that you had been taken away," wrote his sisters. His mother noted that "the shock I received that day no one can ever tell. It broke my heart to lose you, but you did not go alone. For part of me went with you that day."

Dunie Ryan couldn't have cared less about the passing of a former friend like McGurnaghan. "Dunie had made an example of him," O'Connor says. "And the word was out very quickly: you do not fuck with Dunie."

André Savard, the homicide cop who had a price put on his head by Ryan, knew how far the leader of the West End Gang would go to cling to power. An informer inside the gang came to him and made a chilling recorded statement. "Dunie Ryan had ruthless control. Anyone who didn't do what he wanted or how he wanted, that person was killed," the informant said. "As a matter of fact, anyone who worked for Dunie long enough ended up in jail or dead. He was bad news. He is responsible for at least a bare minimum of fifty murders in the city."

Dunie Ryan and his new pal Yves Trudeau were not done yet. The bodies—the hits—continued to pile up.

With a cocaine addiction that needed to be constantly fed, Trudeau kept busy accepting contracts to kill prospects, members of rival gangs, former Popeyes buddies, and even full-patch members of his own Hells Angels. At the beginning of 1982, mere months after the McGurnaghan bombing, Denis Kennedy disappeared. An influential member of Trudeau's own Laval chapter, Kennedy was known as "Le Curé," the French word for "priest." His friend Charles Hachey, a long-haired and lanky biker with a penchant for sunglasses and cowboy hats, was also nowhere to be found. Kennedy had been seen several times in the Hells Angels' Sorel chapter clubhouse before he vanished.

In a time before computers and cellphones, perhaps his buddies assumed Kennedy, a rare English-speaking member of the Quebec Angels, was out west for an extended period, as he had been in the recent past, when the Satan's Angels Motorcycle Club in British Columbia was considering a merger with the HA. Only later did it come out that Trudeau, accompanied by three other bikers, had shot Kennedy to death in Sainte-Marthe-sur-le-Lac, a bucolic beachside town forty kilometers west of Montreal along the shore of the Lake of Two Mountains. Kennedy's body was unceremoniously tossed into the St. Lawrence River, which Trudeau used as a graveyard.

According to some accounts, Dunie Ryan had heard that Kennedy and Hachey were plotting to snatch Ryan's children to gain leverage and oblige the Irish mobster to forget about the money they owed him for drugs. Ryan reportedly contacted Yves (Le Boss) Buteau, at the time the leader of the Canadian Hells Angels. Ryan warned Buteau to deal with the wayward bikers pronto, or he would cut off the Hells Angels' drug supply.

Buteau was just as ruthless as Ryan; he had helped spearhead the Angels' merciless battle against the Outlaws, and he had often dispatched Yves Trudeau as one of his principal assault weapons in that war. Denis Kennedy had also been a reliable foot soldier, involved in several shootouts with the Outlaws, but in the Angels, loyalty only runs so deep. Buteau, always an astute businessman, knew money was more important than friendships. If his drug suppliers in the West End Gang wanted Kennedy gone, so be it. He turned once again to his most reliable killer to solve the problem.

Kennedy's body was never recovered, although police would later conduct an intensive underwater search in the St. Lawrence. On June 26, 1982, the bullet-riddled body of Charles Hachey was found behind a nondescript house in Saint-Sulpice, forty-six kilometers east of Montreal. His body was secured in three plastic bags and chained to a block of cement.

With these murders for the West End Gang, along with the killing of McGurnaghan, Trudeau had crossed another line, never to come back. He was a hitman, plain and simple—no longer just an avenging Angel, but a hired gun. A contract was a contract, no matter whom he was paid to kill or who was paying.

Trudeau kept up the pace in 1983, even working for former enemies. At the start of the year, according to later court testimony, he was hired by two brothers, Guy and Raymond Filion, ex-members of the Devil's Disciples, who ran the drug trade in the east-end Montreal neighborhood of Rosemont and had been the hated rivals of the Popeyes. Their history apparently didn't bother Trudeau in the slightest. The Filions paid Trudeau a mere $5,000 to kill Guy Maltais, a bespectacled fraud artist from Chicoutimi who owed them money. On the evening of January 15, 1983, a passerby found Maltais's body splayed out on the icy ground by his Buick, shot to death.

The Filions should have known better than to deal with an unscrupulous contract killer who was willing to do business with anyone. Nine months after they hired Trudeau to clean up their mess, someone in turn hired him to kill Raymond Filion. He did so coolly and efficiently, gunning him down on the doorstep of his sister's home in Laval. It would not be the last time Trudeau would turn against someone who had hired him or helped him to carry out a killing.

That brought the hitman's body count to thirty-one. The Mad Bumper was on a roll.

Trudeau also expanded the scope of his targets. A contract was a contract, after all, even if it meant killing a man with family ties to Montreal's Mafia. Michel Desormiers, thirty-nine, was more powerfully connected than many of Trudeau's other victims, though hardly more sympathetic. Slim, with a much-groomed mustache, he was the brother-in-law of Montreal Mafia boss Frank Cotroni, a relationship he relied heavily upon to further his illegal businesses. According to André Cédilot of *La Presse*, the Mafia did not trust him because he wasn't a blood member of La Famiglia, while the bikers feared that he knew too much and tended to brag indiscriminately.

Early in 1983, Desormiers was rumored to have been the getaway driver in a quadruple murder on Ampère Avenue in Laval; soon afterward, he was severely beaten by unknown assailants at a nightclub in the Mont-Rolland neighborhood of Sainte-Adèle, a town in the Laurentians about eighty-five kilometers north of Montreal. His sister, Pauline Desormiers—Cotroni's wife at the time—was injured when she tried to intervene to save her brother.

As far as the police were concerned, Desormiers was living on borrowed time. And in the early hours of July 15, 1983, that time ran out. Desormiers was shot three times in the head and twice in the back while on the doorstep of his bungalow, in a bold execution Trudeau had orchestrated with two biker associates. For the police, it was yet another unsolved gangland slaying. For the killer, it was just another contract, an agreement whispered over and shaken on. Money for his cocaine habit. Money that helped keep him alive.

Trudeau seemed to like killing people in their homes, probably because that's where they were easiest to find and at their most defenseless. And he never thought twice of dispatching a girlfriend who happened to be there. A few minutes after midnight on March 20, 1984, Trudeau, accompanied by Paul April, who had helped Trudeau three years earlier with a deadly car bombing, walked into a quiet apartment on Cartier Street in Montreal's trendy Plateau-Mont-Royal neighborhood. A drug dealer named Philippe Galipeau was sitting at the kitchen table with his partner, an exotic dancer named Rachel Francoeur. Galipeau, thirty-seven, was facing a court case over his drug dealing and had angered the wrong people. Trudeau and April shot him in the abdomen and back. They killed Francoeur, twenty-one, with a bullet in her back. The weapon, a 12-gauge shotgun, was found in a nearby laneway. Payment for the killings was $5,000.

For those murders, Yves Trudeau and Paul April were partners in crime. They would soon find themselves at opposite ends of another contract. Before the year was out, Trudeau, April, and the West End Gang leader Dunie Ryan would all be connected in a fateful—and for two of them, fatal—triangle of guns, bombs, and murder.

6.
A CONTRACT FOR REVENGE

Frank (Dunie) Ryan had found Trudeau to be a useful killing machine. But by the end of 1984, the Irish mobster was growing increasingly worried about staying alive himself.

Ryan had become wealthy enough to move far from the poor Irish working-class districts of Montreal and buy a comfortable home in the city's upscale west island. He had a fancy car and an expensive yacht. But he was running scared. "By 1984, Dunie Ryan is looking over his shoulder and wondering how safe his perch might be because he knows that people are jealous of him," writes gang chronicler D'Arcy O'Connor. Journalist Dan Burke, who chronicled Ryan's life, adds: "Dunie is worth between fifty and one hundred million and he did express his concerns about his own safety, and he was worried about his kids being possibly kidnapped."

On November 13, 1984, Ryan was holding court, as he often did, at Nittolo's, a gaudy motel and restaurant on Saint Jacques Street that served as a kind of unofficial headquarters for the leader of the West End Gang. That's where members would congregate and drink, pay tribute to him, and receive his gifts of money or drugs when they needed a helping hand. Ryan felt safe there because he felt he was on his home turf. "That was where he hung out, did business; he wouldn't think twice about something happening to him there," explains Burke.

So Ryan was not worried that November evening when Paul April approached him at the bar. With scraggly dark hair, a droopy mustache, and beady eyes, April was a rare francophone who was close to the West End Gang. While trafficking drugs in Montreal's east end, April had racked up a debt of at least $200,000 with Ryan, his main coke supplier. So Ryan was perhaps hopeful when, that night at Nittolo's, April asked Ryan to accompany him to room 40, at the far end of the motel's parking lot. There are different stories about what April used as a lure: some say it was sex with a young woman; others probably more accurately insist it was the promise of the cash owed. Either way, the two men made their way to the room in the dark. Once inside, Ryan immediately realized he was in mortal danger. He was confronted by one of April's associates, Robert Lelièvre, wielding a shotgun.

Police and gang members later surmised that the pair wanted to strap Ryan to a chair and torture him to give up the locations where he had buried his rumored loot. "Dunie knows he's doomed unless he gets out of there. He's got to fight his way out of there or he's finished," Burke recounts in *Kings of Coke*. "So he picked up the chair and smashed it into the window to make a break for it. He went down swinging."

It was an unfair fight from the start. Lelièvre let loose with his shotgun, riddling Ryan's body. As the West End Gang leader was bleeding out on the floor, a third man, named Eddie Phillips, reportedly put a bullet in his head on the floor with a .45-caliber handgun. "I shot a dead man!" he would later say.

Frank Peter Ryan Jr. was dead at age forty-two. "Dunie wanted to 'Live Fast, Love Hard, Die Young.'" Burke remarks. "If that was his motto in life, then all three wishes came true, unfortunately."

As usual, the police had at best only a vague understanding of what had gone down at Nittolo's. As with McGurnaghan, they knew it was a gang slaying. It was clearly not a robbery. The murder done, April and his cohorts fled without any clues to the buried riches they had hoped to secure. They also left behind $6,350 in cash, which police found in Ryan's wallet, along with a gold chain around his neck and a Rolex watch on his wrist.

Police surmised it was almost certainly an inside job. Ryan had been shot at close range, presumably by people he knew, in a room at a motel where he felt safe and comfortable. A motel on his own turf.

According to a later court filing, police caught an early break when they received an accidental tip about Paul April's possible involvement in the murder. Sidney Leithman, a high-powered criminal lawyer whose clients included Mafia bosses and the Hells Angels—and Dunie Ryan—was close to the West End Gang and corrupt enough to get a steady supply of cocaine from them and others. When he learned that police cars were surrounding his client's favorite motel, he called police and asked if Ryan and the man he identified as Ryan's companion that night, Paul April, had been arrested. April became a suspect in Ryan's murder after Leithman's phone call alerted the police to "April's presence with Ryan," the court document stated.

Unaware that he was already on the police radar, and with more braggadocio than brains, April wasted little time boasting about his coup. At an east-end bar, he was heard proclaiming: "The king is dead. Dunie Ryan is dead and now I'm the king."

It was laughable. April was in no position to lead anything, and his brash action only meant he now had a target on his back.

In the power vacuum that was created after Ryan's murder, his right-hand man, Allan Ross, quickly claimed his spot on the throne. Unlike most members of the West End Gang, who had grown up poor, Ross was born and raised in middle-class Notre-Dame-de-Grâce. At the age of eighteen, he was arrested three times within five months for car theft and breaking and entering. "When I first met Allan Ross, he was charged with shoplifting. He didn't have two cents to rub together," says Jeffrey Boro, a prominent criminal defense lawyer. "Allan Ross kind of was Dunie's gofer boy."

With ruthlessness and cold-blooded determination, Ross rose through the ranks of the West End Gang. "You could stop Allan Ross on the street, and you could see the hate in his eyes for police, you could see it while talking to him. You know, that scar he had on his face and his beady eyes looking at you," recalls John Westlake, a former Montreal police drugs and gang investigator. "He was a violent human being, and if he wanted something, I believe he would have killed you for it. Allan Ross would destroy you if you were not careful."

Short and sharp-featured, with thin lips that seemed fixed in a permanent scowl, Ross earned the less-than-complimentary nickname "The Weasel." The most charitable explanation was that, with his beady eyes and crooked nose, he looked somewhat like a ferret. A more likely reason was his reputation for being a slippery operator. "He tried to get away with everything," explains Jimmy Holt, a former bank robber and member of the West End Gang, in *Kings of Coke*. "Trying to get out of things, trying not to be too involved, and taking the easy way out. They called him a weasel for a reason, you know."

His one-time lawyer Jeffrey Boro agrees. "He would weasel out of tight spaces, and that's how he rose up in the organization, so to speak. That was his moniker for sure. He was a street-smart person. He would weasel out of everything."

Even more ruthless and ambitious than Dunie Ryan had been, Ross took his predecessor's drug empire and expanded so quickly and widely that it even came to the attention of American authorities who were tracking the cocaine trade. "The West End Gang was an extraordinary surprise to us," recalls Dave McGee, who was the lead federal prosecutor in North Florida on the drug file. "They became an organization with global power, an organization that imports tons and tons of cocaine into the United States and into Canada. You've got small-time hoods that rose up and had the initiative to go down and meet personally with Colombian cartel guys—that's ambition. That's gutsy too. Those are dangerous people."

McGee meant that the Colombians were dangerous, but the same could be said of Ross and the West End Gang. Both were ruthless. Both were dangerous to their enemies. And for Ross to solidify his power, he needed to quickly exact revenge on the men who had killed his patron, Dunie Ryan. At Ryan's funeral on November 17, just four days after his murder, Ross set in motion the explosive events that would follow.

About two hundred people gathered to pay tribute to the slain West End Gang leader at St. Augustine of Canterbury Catholic Church, an ornate stone building in Notre-Dame-de-Grâce, not far from where Ryan held court in the bars along the Saint Jacques strip, or from where his gang flooded the streets with cocaine. His family was on hand, of course, as well as dozens of members of Ryan's wider family—the Irish mob, along with an impressive representation from the Hells Angels and the Mafia. Yves Trudeau was among the many bikers to show up. "I went with other members of the Laval chapter out of respect, because he was a friend," he later said.

In his sermon to the unusual crowd, the priest, who knew all too well the unsavory history of many of those in attendance, had a message for the burly and bearded men squeezed into the pews of his church. "The priest had said perhaps the gathering of people should reconsider their lives," Dan Burke recalls. "But the priest told me after that, obviously what he said fell on deaf ears. Which was understandable."

Indeed. For Allan Ross was already planning more deaths. At the church, he was seen talking with three men: Michel Blass, a longtime criminal and murderer, and two Hells Angels from the Laval chapter, Laurent (l'Anglais) Viau and Yves Trudeau. Ross knew that

Trudeau had carried out several assassinations for Ryan. Now he wanted the hitman to turn his talents to avenging Ryan. Ross offered him a juicy contract to eliminate Paul April and anyone else connected to the slaying.

"We knew who had killed Ryan," Trudeau would later testify. "I was offered $200,000, plus other considerations, such as wiping out the drug debts of the North chapter."

Having killed for Ryan, Trudeau was only too happy to avenge his death on behalf of the new leader of the West End Gang. The executions that Trudeau would subsequently carry out to fulfill that contract would be among his last. And the fallout would change his life—and the history of the Hells Angels in Canada—forever.

7.
THE BOMBING

The fans were packed into almost every seat in the Montreal Forum. Just a typical Saturday night in Montreal as the hallowed Canadiens and their fading superstar Guy Lafleur were trying to save a lackluster hockey season.

On November 24, 1984, the team eked out a 6–4 win against the Detroit Red Wings, but Lafleur, at thirty-three no longer the young artist and sharpshooter on ice he once was, had failed to score. No one at the game knew it then, but by the time the weekend was over, the news would leak that Lafleur, the man with flowing blond locks who had helped the Canadiens win four Stanley Cups, had perhaps played his last game for the home team. There was an acrimonious press conference, and Lafleur would hang on for bit, but the bloom was off "The Flower." Montreal hockey fans were devastated.

Despite the rumblings of Lafleur's unhappiness, another event blasted all news of hockey from the front pages that weekend. Yves Trudeau had struck again, with the biggest, loudest, and deadliest killing he would ever pull off.

As he always did with his targets, Yves Trudeau staked out Paul April, his old buddy in crime, to study his routines and habits. It didn't take him long to realize it would be a challenging kill. Probably suspecting they were in the gunsights of some very unhappy people in the West End Gang, April and his cohorts were always armed, the hitman determined. That would make killing them with firearms a bit more challenging. "It was necessary to find a way to approach them without arousing their suspicions," he would later say.

But how? Trudeau quickly settled on one of his favorite weapons in his arsenal: a bomb. He was already known as "the Mad Bomber," after all. Only this time, instead of setting off an explosive under a motorcycle or a car, Trudeau decided to take out an entire apartment to eliminate his prey.

Trudeau had discovered that, for the previous two months, April, along with three other fellow criminals, including Robert Lelièvre, who had helped him kill Dunie Ryan, had rented a small three-and-half-room unit in a large apartment building on de Maisonneuve Boulevard, just west of Montreal's downtown core. The nineteen-story complex took up almost an entire city block, with the Montreal Forum on its east corner and Station 10, the police outpost that, ironically, was in charge of keeping tabs on the West End Gang, on its west side.

On November 18, one day after Ryan's funeral, Trudeau went to an address on Papineau Avenue in the east end, where, he later testified, a courier from Ross delivered a $25,000 advance for the killing, along with thirty-five pounds of C-4 plastic explosives to carry it out. Cyclonite is the primary compound that makes C-4 so deadly; easily malleable, it can be molded into any desired shape and will thus also determine the direction of the resulting explosion, which was exactly what Trudeau wanted.

Trudeau then dropped in to visit Paul April, whom he knew well, given that they had collaborated in a couple of murders. "I noticed he didn't have a TV," he would recount later. "I offered to get him a TV, a video recorder, and a cassette of . . . a documentary on the life of a gang member." The movie, called *Hells Angels Forever*, was billed as "The True Story of an American Phenomenon." The opening words on the screen declared: "What starts off as a squadron of American daredevil bombers in World War II, branded by society as renegades, turns into a revealing ride into the world of honor, violence, and undying passion for motorcycles on the road."

Trudeau knew the movie would appeal to April, who was close to the Angels and, like most hangers-on, probably yearned to be part of the club. "I told him I wanted him to have it so he could see how the HA operates, what they're all about," the hitman explained, in words that had a deadly double meaning.

April, apparently, was not at all suspicious, especially because he had been considering hiring Trudeau himself, for yet another contract killing. He never suspected that his own name was next on Trudeau's list.

To carry out the plan he was devising to eliminate April, Trudeau recruited one of his newest associates, Michel Blass. Just two months earlier, the two men had worked together on a job where they blew up a car to get rid of Sylvain Dagenais, a troublesome drug dealer. More importantly, Trudeau was confident that Blass had the stomach for cold-blooded murder, given his impressive family pedigree when it came to violence and death.

Until Yves Trudeau's history of murder was splashed across the front pages of the newspapers—a revelation that was still a year away—Quebec's most infamous gang killer was without a doubt Michel Blass's older brother Richard. Known as "Le Chat" because he seemed like a cat with nine lives, Richard had survived not one, not two, but three Mafia assassination attempts over three months in 1968. He had also managed to escape twice from prison.

An amateur boxer, Richard Blass got into trouble as a young man when he knifed a fighter who had bested him in the ring. He then graduated to a series of violent feuds with the Italian Mafia, showing no fear when, in 1968, he tried to assassinate mob boss Frank Cotroni. (He succeeded only in slaying two of his bodyguards.) The Mafia first tried to retaliate in August 1968 by sending two hitmen into a bar Blass was drinking at, but he got out unscathed. A few weeks later, the Mafia set fire to a motel Blass was at, killing three people. Again, "Le Chat" emerged unharmed. A couple of months later, Blass remarkably survived another attempted Mafia hit, despite having been shot several times in the head.

In 1969, Blass was arrested for a bank robbery, but escaped from prison twice. He then set out to take revenge on two of his cronies who had testified against him, tracking them to a bar in October 1974 and shooting them to death. Worried that the bar patrons might be able to identify him, Blass returned a few months later, locked ten men and three women inside a locker, and proceeded to slaughter them all. That prompted what, at the time, was one of the largest police manhunts in Quebec history. In January 1975, police tracked Blass to a Laurentian chalet; in a shootout, he ended up with twenty-seven bullets in his body. The cat's nine lives had run out.

Now, eight years later, his brother Michel was standing beside another serial killer, ready to carry out a complicated execution. Though he would never reach the infamy of his older brother, Michel Blass was no slouch in the killing department. He would later confess to police that he had carried out at least a dozen murders.

But his operation with Yves Trudeau at the Maisonneuve apartment building was his tour de force—and his final series of murders.

It was Blass who knocked on the door of apartment 917 several hours after thousands of hockey fans had left the Forum and emptied out the bars. It was shortly after 4 a.m. on Sunday, November 25.

Blass had come to deliver to Paul April the promised presents: a TV, a VCR, and the Hells Angels movie. (Blass would later claim it was his idea, not Trudeau's, to plant the bomb inside the TV—two murderers vying for the glory of the kill.)

On the one hand, it's hard to imagine why April and his roommates weren't suspicious about a delivery at that hour of the morning. On the other hand, considering that they were also up at 4 a.m., perhaps all four criminals were too stoned, tired, or just plain stupid to worry.

"As soon as Blass left, I parked behind the building and I blew up the bomb that was hidden in the TV set," Trudeau later recounted. Recalling his earlier words to April that the HA movie tucked into the VCR would help April see how the gang operates, Trudeau joked about the cruel irony of his plot: "That night, Paul April learned just how powerful the Hells Angels were."

Indeed, soon after April and his cronies gathered around to watch the movie, an explosion equivalent to ten pounds of dynamite took out their apartment, along with much of the surrounding building. The blast was deafening. It shattered the walls in seven of the eight apartments on the ninth floor. It blew out the windows on nine of the floors in the complex. It cut off heat, plumbing, and electricity to every home in the top half of the building. Much of the outside wall of the building was shorn off, the rubble collapsing onto the downtown street, not far from the police station. "I've never seen anything like it," said Montreal police spokesman Charles Poxon. "It was like a Middle East–type bomb you see on television with all that debris everywhere. You think it can't happen here but it did."

Abdenbi Massaoui lived just a few doors down from the targeted apartment with his wife and three children. "The door to our apartment was shattered, the walls came down," he told the *Montreal Gazette*. "I really thought it was the end for us."

There were early reports that the explosion had severed the cables in the elevators, sending them plummeting to the basement, but that turned out to be wrong; the safety controls kicked in, and the circuits to the elevators were cut. But that didn't diminish the terror for Wana Nugent, a tenant who was in one of the elevators. "Suddenly there was a violent explosion," she told the *Gazette*. "The doors of the elevator shot open, and I was thrown out."

As far away as the second floor, tenants felt the impact. "I thought my ears were gone, the detonation was enormous," said Vanya Paskaline. "It looked like half the building blew up."

"We were blown out of bed," said another neighbor, who dashed out of her apartment and heard others clamoring for assistance. "It was awful. It was frightening. They were banging on our walls for help."

Miraculously, no innocent bystanders were killed, although a twenty-four-year-old woman was rushed into surgery and lost an eye after being hit by flying glass. Seven others were treated for lacerations and shock. The more than four hundred tenants were forced to leave their homes until repairs could be done to make the building safe.

Trudeau didn't care about the collateral damage. His handiwork had done its intended job: Paul April and his three companions had been shredded to pieces. Forensics showed they were facing the bomb when it went off; April and two others were blasted "from head to toe" a police report later concluded. The fourth man was hurled thirty meters away from the explosion into an alcove behind an elevator shaft.

All four victims were well known to police. At sixty-three, Robert Lelièvre had survived longer than most criminals. His record dated back to the 1960s, when he was part of a bank robbery gang run by Monica Proietti, better known as "Machine Gun Molly." Proietti held up more than twenty banks until she was killed in a police shootout in 1967. Lelièvre was arrested and labeled a "habitual criminal," but was soon released and continued a predictable if ultimately futile career of crime.

The two other victims were Gilles Paquette, twenty-seven, who had been convicted of arson, and Louis Charles, fifty-four, who had served time for armed robbery. While in prison, Charles was convicted of killing another inmate with a knife, but was acquitted in a second trial.

The building was so badly damaged, police had to use a crane to bring what was left of the men from their destroyed apartment down to the street. Crime scene photos showed disfigured faces, torn limbs, and a hand strewn across a ripped-open torso. The corpses were quickly put into red, green, and black body bags and taken away into the night.

Using pails and shovels to sift through the debris amidst the shattered rooms and crumbling walls, ten homicide officers, three bomb squad experts, and an arson investigator looked for clues about what had caused such devastation. As usual, the police would get most things wrong about what Yves Trudeau had done.

There were hints that the police, for the first time, may have been on a trail that would lead them to Trudeau. "Drug Dealers' War Suspected," screamed the headline in the *Montreal Gazette* the day after the bombing. The article revealed that police suspected the bombing "may have been an act of revenge for the November 13th killing of reputed cocaine dealer Frank Peter Ryan," noting that Paul April "had been wanted for questioning" in Ryan's murder. There was even an intriguing mention that bomb squad investigators had found "fragments of a suspected remote-control device," which suggested that the four men "were victims of a bomb that had been sent or taken into their apartment."

But the newspaper also reported that, first and foremost, police were working on the theory that "the four were making a bomb that went off prematurely." And that, as it turned out, was the erroneous conclusion the police quickly and confidently settled upon. There was evidence that no doubt helped push the police in that direction. April's chest had been blown away, leaving some to wonder if he had been trying to build a bomb that would be strapped around his body. Forensics suggested that the men had been "seated in a circle facing the device." A police report concluded: "Explosion occurred on a table in the centre of the living room of apartment 917. Hypothesis: occupants were making a bomb."

In reality, of course, the four hapless gangsters were watching the Hells Angels movie on the new TV Trudeau had given them, but the authorities didn't know that. Within three days of the blast, the police announced that their investigation was over. "They're off the scene as of today," declared Charles Poxon of the Montreal police department. "There is no evidence that anyone other than the four men killed were involved. The results of the autopsies performed on the victims . . . indicated they were building a bomb."

"Bomb Likely Killed Its Makers: Police," the *Gazette* headline declared.

"The Bomb Exploded in Their Hands," echoed *La Presse*.

Even *Allo Police*, which was usually more reliable—at least when it came to gang violence—labeled the bombing a "work accident," speculating that April and his men had been planning "an important hold up elsewhere" and were planning to use a bomb as a diversion.

The Maisonneuve bombing brought Yves Trudeau's kill list up to forty. And yet the authorities still remained ignorant that they had a serial gang killer on their hands. Aside from the apparent fragments of a remote-controlled device found at the crime scene, there were other clues, if the police had been at all inclined to notice them.

André Savard, the homicide cop who was targeted by the West End Gang for his investigations, had been talking to a confidential source close to the Irish Mafia. "The Mad Bomber was a freelance hitman," the snitch told Savard in a tape-recorded interview, referring to Trudeau. "I can positively identify him as the man that blew up the building on de Maisonneuve. I will put the Mad Bomber on the spot." But the information went nowhere; the police were stuck on their own theory of a bomb-making accident.

Years later, in a letter to author D'Arcy O'Connor, Allan Ross all but confessed to ordering the hit. "Dunie was my best friend and like a brother to me," he declared. "And there was [sic] only two things that could happen when Dunie got killed. I was going to get killed or the people responsible for Dunie's death were going to get killed. Hey, I won. Paul was in a tavern bragging that he had killed the King. Paul was looking to see which way the wind was blowing and 13 days later he saw which way it was blowing—it was blowing him to hell. Ha, ha, ha."

Ross wasn't finished having the last laugh—or getting retribution. With Paul April and Robert Lelièvre eliminated thanks to Trudeau, Ross went after Eddie Phillips, the third man in the motel room with Ryan on that fatal night. Phillips was shot five times in the back outside a bar by a West End Gang member named David Singer. Then, to keep Singer quiet about what he had done, Ross had Singer murdered in Florida, where he had fled to hide until things died down.

That Florida connection would eventually contribute to The Weasel's undoing and arrest—strangely not in Canada, where he had operated untouched for years, but in the United States, where the authorities had their eye on the emerging drug kingpin from Montreal.

Two days after the bombing, a confident Trudeau went to see Allan Ross to collect his bounty. That's when things got complicated. Ross, ever "The Weasel," told a disappointed Trudeau that the balance of $175,000 was not available. Instead, he suggested the contract killer collect his fee from his fellow bikers, since the Hells Angels owed the West End Gang—who still had a firm grip on smuggling through the port—a lot of money for cocaine.

There would be slightly different accounts of the exact sums. In later testimony, Trudeau would say Ross told him to collect $195,000 from the Sorel and Halifax chapters. Other testimony put it at $75,000 from Sorel and $110,000 from Halifax.

The exact figures don't matter. It was a lot of money, and the Angels were unlikely to be pleased. Yves Trudeau, fresh off another big kill and high as ever on cocaine, would have to go cap in hand to his fellow bikers, asking for money. That would trigger a chain of events that led to even more deaths than had occurred in the Maisonneuve bombing—and pushed Trudeau into the most dangerous position he had ever been in.

8.
THE MASSACRE

Eager to collect his money, Yves Trudeau set off to Nova Scotia to meet with David (Wolf) Carroll, the leader of the new Hells Angel chapter in Halifax, who would go on to become one of the most powerful figures in the outlaw biker world.

The two men could not have been more different, even if they both wore the same HA patch. Trudeau was dedicated to earning money to pay for his cocaine habit. He had little respect for the gang's decorum or rules: he would kill anyone, even a fellow Angel, if the money was good. Carroll, on the other hand, was deeply committed to Hells Angels traditions.

Good-looking, with curly hair, a neatly trimmed beard, and a disarming smile, Carroll had been born and raised in Dartmouth, Nova Scotia. In December 1984, barely a week after Trudeau set off the bomb in the apartment building on de Maisonneuve Boulevard in Montreal, Carroll's local gang, the Thirteenth Tribe, patched over to the Angels. He would rise rapidly to the top of the HA hierarchy, soon moving to Quebec to join the francophone leaders of the Angels there in running their expanding drug empire, even though for a long time he spoke only English.

At the same time, Carroll kept a firm grip on his Halifax fiefdom, transforming what had been a ragtag local bike gang into a powerful crime syndicate based in a bunker in Fairview, a residential neighborhood in the city's west end, complete with a bright red-and-white neon Hells Angels sign in front and a splashy Death's Head mural on the side.

Unlike Trudeau, Carroll was a firm believer in biker discipline and hierarchy. "Everybody bowed down to him," says Tom O'Neill, a former RCMP investigator who took on the HA. O'Neill described what would happen whenever Carroll came back from Quebec to check on his Halifax boys: "It was like the general is coming down; they've got to snap to attention and salute the flag: 'Wolf's in town, everybody's got to go to the clubhouse. Get your bikes out, get your colors out, Wolf is here!'"

As wedded as he was to the old biker traditions, Carroll quickly embraced the new ethos of drugs and money. His Halifax crew dominated the Nova Scotia drug market, while in Montreal, he ran a prostitution agency and extortion rackets in the downtown nightclub scene. In the Laurentian tourist town of Saint-Sauveur, sixty kilometers north of Montreal, he partnered up with a member of a Mafia clan to run a popular bar.

Although he would never rival Trudeau when it came to killing, Carroll did not shy away from violence. He owned a Cobray machine gun and was behind a bomb blast in Quebec City that cost the victim a leg. And in a move that might have made Trudeau proud, Carroll began experimenting with new ways to set off car bombs, using pagers and car alarms.

So when Trudeau showed up in Halifax and explained that Allan Ross had told him to collect his fee for the Maisonneuve bombing from the Hells Angels chapters who owed him drug money, Carroll, however reluctantly, was able to help. In two installments, according to Trudeau's later account, he gave the hitman $98,000. Most of that money was for Trudeau, but some was supposed to be shared with his Laval chapter. Soon enough, though, Carroll learned that most of the money went straight up Trudeau's nose in the form of cocaine. And that is when things got ugly.

Outlaw bikers were by definition unruly, hard-partying, garrulous boys. They liked to have their fun. But even by the no-holds-barred standard of the Hells Angels, the Laval (or North) chapter was increasingly erratic and uncontrollable. Most of its members continued to be violent, undisciplined, and irresponsible men who partied as if they were still Popeyes, with allegiances only to themselves rather than the Hells Angels as a whole. They thought nothing of siphoning off profits and snorting cocaine they were supposed to be selling. And they spared no thought for the ramifications when they kept the profits from selling $300,000 worth of speed to the West End Gang instead of sharing it with the other chapters, as they were supposed to do.

The North chapter president, Laurent (l'Anglais) Viau, a small man with unkempt long hair, a thick beard, and eyes he hid behind sunglasses, had no desire to enforce discipline. Trudeau, one of the chapter's founders, was focused on making and misappropriating money to feed his cocaine addiction. In stark contrast, the bikers at the Sorel clubhouse (often referred to as the "South" chapter), led by Réjean Lessard, were becoming *more* businesslike and organized in their approach to crime. Increasingly, they were allied with groups such as the Mafia and the West End Gang, both of whom had a laser-like focus on profits above all else. For the new breed of Angels, cocaine and other drugs were a business, not a pastime, and woe betide anyone who crossed them.

Lessard, nicknamed "Zig-Zag," allegedly because his angled beard resembled that of the cartoon character imprinted on packages of Zig-Zag rolling papers, was not a typical biker. He preferred to drive a sports car over a motorcycle and often wore white button-down shirts to hide his tattoos, thus making him look more professional. He had been born into a comfortable middle-class family in Quebec's Eastern Townships, but as an adolescent, he rejected the values his parents had tried to instill in him, growing up to become a tough guy, a hard guy, a violent man who was an original member of a biker gang called the Marauders. Soon, the Marauders patched over to the Popeyes and then, in 1977, to the Hells Angels. For the next four years, Lessard—at the time a member of the raucous North chapter—was as hard-partying as anyone else in the clubhouse, and he became friends with one of the other serious cocaine addicts in the chapter, Yves Trudeau.

Things changed in 1983, when Lessard began to suffer epileptic seizures, a condition that was not helped by his extreme lifestyle and the drugs he was putting into his body. All of a sudden, he summoned the discipline to go straight, quitting cocaine and becoming a vegetarian. From this new, clean vantage point, and with all the passion of a former addict who has rejected his former pastimes, he came to hate what the guys in the North chapter had become—"les sniffeurs," as he called them. In a momentous decision that would change his life, and Trudeau's, Lessard quit the Laval chapter and joined the more serious Sorel club. There, he quickly rose through the ranks to become the chapter leader, forging ever-closer ties with the other crime groups that ran the province. Like his new allies, he understood that in unity lay power and riches. Significantly, he also connected with David Carroll, the ambitious biker leader from Nova Scotia.

In early 1985, Lessard met with an enraged Carroll at the Sorel bunker. The Halifax chapter, although wealthy by most standards, was still establishing itself and was certainly a lot poorer than Trudeau's club in Laval. And yet Carroll had managed to gather the not insignificant sum of $98,000 to pay Trudeau, money that Allan

Ross said the bikers owed him. So he was not pleased when he discovered that much of the money was being used to support the cold-blooded killer's drug habit.

To add insult to injury, Lessard informed Carroll that the Laval chapter was not sharing the estimated $150,000 it was earning each week from a lab it had created to make and market speed, opting instead to enrich only themselves. The two leaders agreed that something had to be done before the out-of-control Laval boys ruined things for all of them. Something drastic. A punishment carried out in the extreme terms that bikers would understand. "In joining the Hells Angels, I signed up for criminality," Lessard would later say. "In that milieu, it was the club above all else. I saw the ship sinking because of the risk of internal dissension. We needed to take action."

So, because they did not play by the rules, the North chapter was officially, and quietly, declared to be in "bad standing." In biker language, that was a death sentence.

There would be a culling.

Plans came together quickly. Along with Carroll from Halifax and Lessard from Sorel, Georges (Bo-Boy) Beaulieu, the head of the Hells Angels' Sherbrooke chapter, agreed that the Laval chapter had to be eliminated. The three powerful chapters from eastern Canada were united in taking an unprecedented action: the mass slaughter of their own.

Lessard called on his aide-de-camp, the bearded, barrel-bodied Robert (Ti-Maigre) Richard, whose appearance belied his nickname ("Tiny" in English). The invitation Richard issued to every Hells Angel in Quebec and in Halifax was not to be refused. All of them, including, especially, the North chapter members, were told to attend an important meeting on March 23, 1985, at the Sherbrooke clubhouse. The bunker was a sprawling, red-roofed brick house with dormer windows that stood high and isolated on a hill over the industrial businesses of South Wellington Street, on the outskirts of the city. (Because it was located on the road to nearby Lennoxville, it was also known as the Lennoxville clubhouse.) This was to be a command performance. Missing it, the invite ominously stated, was not an option.

The Hells Angels were about to kill fellow members en masse.

Even for hard-driving warriors like the Angels, accustomed to enforcing punishment on their own, it was a stomach-churning plot. "I can't wait until this is over and we get rid of them," Luc (Sam) Michaud, one of the South chapter members, said to Lessard and two other bikers, according to later testimony. "I can't sleep. My nerves are shot."

Not all the Laval bikers were to be killed on the spot, with no pity or recourse. Lessard planned to spare three of them because they could be useful. Gilles (Le Nez) Lachance, Richard (Bert) Mayrand, and Yvon (Le Père) Bilodeau, once the Popeye leader known as "Gorille," would be given grisly roles to play in the bloodbath to come; Lachance would then be given the opportunity to join the Sorel chapter, while the others would be told to retire—or be killed. But six of the North chapter men would have to be executed, including Yves Trudeau, Lessard's old partying buddy. According to later court testimony, Lessard told Gerry (Le Chat) Coulombe, an eager prospect for the Hells Angels' South chapter, that Trudeau had killed sixty people—a much higher number than the hitman would ever admit to—and that he feared the serial assassin, known for turning his weapons against fellow Angels if so ordered, would come after him.

And so preparations for the massacre began, methodically and meticulously. No detail was too small or insignificant. For starters, George Beaulieu bought sleeping bags for the expected corpses at a sporting goods store in Sherbrooke that he had frequented over the years. He paid cash because he did not want a bill of sale to be drawn up, presumably because he knew the purchase could be easily traced back to him. The owner of the store would later say it was unusual, even rare, not to make up a bill to accompany a purchase. But he acquiesced; he knew better than to question it.

Coulombe, the lowly gofer trying to become a full-patch member of the Sorel chapter, was assigned many of the other preparatory tasks, without knowing until later the true dread purpose of the party. He was told to rent rooms at a local motel for the "guests" who were coming in from out of town. Then he got a very specific set of instructions from Normand (Bull) Tremblay, a full-patch Angel he dared not question: pick up an already rented truck, deliver it to a Sorel shopping center, and leave a box in the truck that contained bottles of Javex and Mr. Clean, a pair of gloves, a parka, and a knife. "There was nothing to sign for, nothing to pay," Coulombe later testified. "All I had to do was pick it up. He told me to wear gloves and make sure I didn't touch anything."

Once back at the Sorel clubhouse, Coulombe was handed pistols and revolvers wrapped in rags to take to the clubhouse where the meeting was to be held.

But on March 23, the designated date of the meeting, things went awry from the start. Most members of the North chapter did not show up. It was not that they expected trouble; they just weren't interested and were busy doing their own thing. Undaunted, Lessard declared that the meeting would take place the next day, Sunday, March 24. Again, he ordered everyone to attend. This time, most did.

When the handful of Laval members walked into the clubhouse, they were faced with an army of at least forty-one bikers from the Sorel, Sherbrooke, and Halifax chapters. Gilles Lachance, one of the North chapter members who was lucky enough to be spared, would recall hearing guns and fighting as he entered the bunker's vestibule. He froze as Jacques (La Pelle) Pelletier, a member of the Sorel club, pointed a gun at him and told him that if he was quiet, nothing would happen to him. Lachance was silent as he stepped into the room beyond the vestibule, where he got a full view of the executions. The scene seemed like something from a horror film: three members of the North chapter—Jean-Guy (Brutus) Geoffrion, Jean-Pierre (Matt le Croisseur) Mathieu, and Michel (Willie) Mayrand—lay motionless on the ground. Unbelievably, Michel Mayrand's own brother, Richard, witnessed his sibling's murder and did nothing about it. Richard was a loyal Angel and, having been taken off the hit list by Lessard, he sided with the killers, doing nothing to save or help his dying younger brother.

A fourth victim, Laurent (l'Anglais) Viau, was haplessly using his arms to fend off an attacker wielding a gun. He, too, would fall. Lessard approached the dying man to explain why he and his fellow bikers had to be executed: "You sniffed too much," he said, in reference to cocaine. What's more, they had been involved in Trudeau's bombing of the apartment building on de Maisonneuve Boulevard; Viau had been seen talking with Allan Ross and Trudeau at Dunie Ryan's funeral, where the plot was hatched. Lessard, ever the businessman, had frowned on the bombing as excessive. It had brought a lot of unwanted police heat on the club. The North chapter boys had also extorted money from their brethren in Halifax, Lessard continued. And finally, no one had ever liked Mathieu, the "double-crosser," in the first place. That, he concluded, was why they had to die.

Coulombe, meanwhile, was on guard duty outside the clubhouse. He heard shouting and then the sound of bullets. "I was in my car, keeping watch, when I heard gunfire," he later testified. The nervous prospect, who had helped prepare for the massacre, now at last grasped the purpose of his errands. This was why he had been told to rent the van and make sure not to get his fingerprints on it. This was why he had picked up Javex and other cleaning materials. As a full-patch wannabe, he had consciously ignored all the muttered conversations between higher-ups in the South, Sherbrooke, and Halifax chapters over the past six weeks or so. He had done what he was instructed to do, stood where he was supposed to, always waiting, unquestioning and obedient. Now he understood. But he did not dare move from his post just outside the slaughterhouse.

All of a sudden, he saw Guy-Louis (Chop) Adam, the Laval chapter's secretary, burst out the front door, chased by several bikers wielding guns. "There was more gunfire. Chop fell to the ground," Coulombe recalled. The shooters aimed and hit their target no less than seven times. Adam collapsed, bleeding out and unmoving.

By the time the bloodletting was over that night, five Hells Angels lay dead. A pathologist would later rule that they died from cerebral hemorrhages and cranial fractures caused by multiple bullet wounds. Reflecting on the bloodbath many years later, Réjean Lessard would say: "For sure, it was extreme to kill five men, but it was like that—it was the law of an eye for an eye."

Inside the bunker, the surviving North chapter members, who had been told they would be spared if they followed orders, were instructed to strip the dead men, move the bodies, and wash away the blood that had splashed, sprayed, and seeped everywhere. On the cleanup crew were a frightened Gilles Lachance and Michel (Sky) Langlois, the former Popeye who had followed Trudeau into the Hells Angels. They took the sordid task in stride, wrapping the victims in chains to secure their limbs, rolling them into the sleeping bags that had been purchased, carrying the corpses out to the blue van that Coulombe was watching over, and piling them inside. The dead men's effects—their clothing, wallets, and whatever else they were carrying—were stuffed into a steel barrel and set on fire until only ashes remained.

While the cleanup was being done, Coulombe, accompanied by one other biker, followed the truck in his car as it drove away with the bodies. They went slowly, obeying speed limits as they made their way on back roads toward Saint-Ignace-de-Loyola, on the banks of the St. Lawrence River, 135 kilometers to the northwest. When they arrived about two hours later, it was still too light out to dump the bodies. The three men whiled away the time by stopping at a restaurant for a meal. Finally, they determined it was dark enough to go to work. They backed the van up to a dock on the river, and Coulombe moved a bit farther away to keep watch and ensure no one came by as his two companions dumped the sleeping bags, now weighted with concrete blocks, in the river.

There was a *plop* as each bag hit the water.

The culling was not complete. Some Laval chapter members remained missing. One was Michel (Jinx) Genest, who, ironically, was in the hospital recovering from an assassination attempt not by his own pals but by the Outlaws biker gang. Lessard sent the hapless Lachance to visit Genest, to describe the carnage and give the recovering biker a stark choice: join the South chapter or be killed. Was there really a choice? Genest immediately opted to join. But Lessard was not through with him; he would soon force Genest to prove his loyalty.

For his part, Lachance was running scared. To keep him in line during the hospital visit, he was accompanied by two South chapter members. Then he was given orders to empty out the North chapter clubhouse of everything of value. On Monday, March 26, he arrived at the heavily fortified—and now eerily empty—bunker in Laval. Lachance stripped it clean, seizing anything biker-related, including cash, drugs, and six Harley-Davidson motorcycles.

While in the neighborhood, he ran into Ginette Henri, the North chapter's accountant, who had lived with Jean-Pierre Mathieu for the past seven years. Understandably, she was worried. She hadn't seen her boyfriend since he'd left their home around noon two days earlier, even though he had promised to meet her at his mother's house that evening for a baptism.

Lachance was in a tough spot. What was he supposed to tell her? "Oh yeah, I saw your boyfriend's bullet-riddled body, and then we dumped it in the river?" He chose to be diplomatic and evasive, telling her Mathieu and four other Laval members had been "dishonorably" expelled from the Hells Angels. He believed that, in a not-so-subtle way, he was telling her they were dead; it was the only way to be ejected with dishonor. But Ginette Henri didn't know that. And she herself would soon become a target of Lessard's systematic cleanup.

The Quebec bikers were now justifiably worried that their brethren in the rest of the country would be shocked and unnerved once word leaked of the in-house slaughter. The bikers were known for—indeed, they were proud of—their penchant for violence. But never before in the history of the Hells Angels had so many full-patch members been killed by their own. So on March 27, Lachance flew to Vancouver to try to allay the concerns of the British Columbia Angels, which outside of Quebec constituted the most powerful HA chapter in the country. Lachance was accompanied by three Hells Angels who belonged to chapters other than the ill-fated Laval one, perhaps to monitor what message he delivered. But it was his presence that was key. The idea was that Lachance, as a former member of the now decimated North chapter, could speak from personal experience about how selfish and unruly its members had been, and that would make the news more palatable. It worked.

His dirty work done, upon his return to Quebec on March 28, Lachance took all of his Hells Angels property—rings and necklaces and badges—to Yvon (Le Père) Bilodeau, who had been "retired" after helping to clean up the mess of blood and bodies a few days earlier. A badly shaken Lachance told his buddy that he, too, had decided to quit the bikers. Asked why, he said: "I saw the reason on March 24."

Two other bikers had been targeted but managed to miss the carnage: Régis (Lucky) Asselin, who may have caught wind of the deadly plan, and Yves (Apache) Trudeau, who had cofounded the now dishonored North chapter and was perhaps the most notorious cocaine user of them all. Lessard had specifically wanted him eliminated because he feared the out-of-control assassin might come gunning for him.

By this time, the bikers' most accomplished assassin had forty-one kills under his belt, and he had managed to escape the biggest massacre in Hells Angels history. Where was Trudeau? And what would the professional killer do to avoid being killed himself?

PART TWO

"THEY WANT TO KILL ME"

9.
A TIMELY REFUGE

As his Laval comrades were being ambushed and shot to death in Sherbrooke, Yves (Apache) Trudeau, who had done more than his own fair share of killing for the money he needed to support his coke habit, was safe from the gunfire, over two hundred kilometers away, in the middle of a pine forest.

By then, his addiction was costing him at least $25,000 a week, and he had checked himself into the Maisonnée Oka, a treatment center in a bucolic rural setting northwest of Montreal. That a no-nonsense killer had the strength of character to confront his own addiction—if Trudeau's actions were genuine and not just a show—was remarkable enough. What was even more surprising was the timing of his decision, for he found refuge only a week before the massacre took place. Had Trudeau somehow gotten word of the murderous plans? He was mostly a loner, so it was unlikely. But maybe he was growing increasingly suspicious, knowing how angry his fellow bikers were with him over the bombing, which had dominated headlines and brought unwanted scrutiny to the club. Or maybe it was plain good luck and good timing. Either way, the serial killer had been spared being killed himself. So far.

The nonprofit drug treatment facility, which opened its doors in June 1982, billed itself as a personal growth center for people with addictions. It featured short-term stays and used a treatment model based on the principles of Alcoholics Anonymous. In other words, addiction was treated as a disease, not a personal failing, and while there was the possibility of recovery, it would require constant monitoring and support outside the institution, because there was no cure.

Not the kind of rehab program that was likely to appeal to a gangster who had shown little remorse and few regrets.

In what must have been an arduous routine for the impulsive and selfish biker, Trudeau's days would have been filled from early morning to night with activities that stressed service and self-knowledge. Some days, he would have been one of the first to get up, to prepare coffee for everyone else. He may have been on cleanup duty after meals, and he would have had time both in one-on-one meetings with counselors and medical professionals and in group sessions with other residents. There was time dedicated to self-reflection, and maybe an opportunity for a walk in the woods. Contact with the outside world was curtailed; visitors were limited to once a week.

As it turned out, this was not the first time the dedicated Hells Angels killer was rethinking his affiliation with and loyalty to the gang.

It was a hot and quiet summer night in Montreal in 1984, a few months before the turmoil of the bombings and murders that were to come. A young Montreal cop was on the night shift with his partner, surveying the streets from an ambulance-like patrol van. Mario Dumont was tall, with broad shoulders and a brush cut. He'd been looking for excitement when he joined the force at the age of twenty, and his first assignment, at a station in Montreal, was too quiet and residential for his taste. So when he was transferred to Station 33, at the corner of Saint Dominique and Ontario streets, on the east side of downtown, he was excited. To prepare for patrolling on tougher turf, he even bought himself a bulletproof vest; something the police department did not automatically provide back then because it did not deem the extra protection necessary. "This was where the action was," Dumont recalls. "This was where I'd be able to show my stuff. But my wife decreed I needed to stay safe."

That night, Dumont and his partner were parked on Hôtel-de-Ville Avenue, observing the flow of traffic and pedestrians along Saint Catherine Street East. It was after midnight, and all seemed routine: one car after another passed, interspersed with pickup trucks and transit buses; pedestrians laughed and chatted on the sidewalk. This area was part of the city's fabled Red-Light District, sandwiched between the grungy central bus station and the strip clubs of Saint Lawrence Boulevard, colloquially known as "The Main." It was in the early stages of gentrification but was still largely undeveloped, with just enough empty storefronts and seedy bars to make it dangerous, at least in the early hours of the morning, when much of the city was asleep.

All of a sudden, Dumont spotted a long green car—a Buick, maybe—reversing against traffic for a block, then backing onto De Bullion Street, where the driver turned off the lights and sat waiting. Was he lurking? Hiding? Why wasn't he getting out? "What's this?" Dumont said, turning to his partner. Then both men spotted police cruisers with their lights and sirens on a few blocks to the west. Clearly the mysterious driver wanted to remain inconspicuous. But why?

The cops put on their own flashers and drove toward the green car. Carefully, Dumont got out and approached, calling out as loudly as he could, "Don't move!"

The driver rolled down his window and politely said, "Bonsoir, Monsieur Agent." He was a slight man with longish brown hair, dark eyes, and a thin beard. Unprepossessing and polite, even well-spoken, he wore a T-shirt and jeans, and he kept his hands on the wheel, as if he knew the drill.

"Good evening," Dumont replied, standing at the driver's side window. "Your driver's license and registration, please."

"Of course."

The man did not ask why the patrol officer was asking for his papers. He probably figured it was for illegally backing down a busy road. But he did not seem at all worried.

Dumont returned to the patrol van, where he ran the license and registration through the police computer. A routine check, nothing more. But it did not take long for interesting results to come up: Yves Trudeau, born February 4, 1946, a member of the Hells Angels—the police knew that much. There was an outstanding warrant for his arrest, though not for any of his murders. The police were still blissfully ignorant of the serial killer lurking in the shadows of the biker world. No, Trudeau was wanted for unpaid fines, probably parking tickets. "Please inform the Sûreté du Québec if Trudeau is picked up," the message concluded.

The young policeman went back to the car. "Monsieur, there is a warrant out for you for unpaid fines, but if you have the cash, you could pay them right now and go," Dumont explained.

As it turned out, Trudeau, who made tens of thousands of dollars for killing people and spent just as much on drugs, did not have enough cash on hand to pay the fines, which amounted to only about $300. Uncomplainingly, he allowed himself to be handcuffed and escorted to the police van, driven to Station 33, and placed in a cell. Ever the professional, Trudeau was not a hothead ready to explode against the cops. He may have been cold-blooded and vicious when it came to paid killings, but he knew how to pick his battles.

On the way to the police station, he made friendly conversation with Dumont and his partner, showing them his tattoos, especially a large one that covered much of his upper left arm and depicted a Hells Angels skull with black holes for eyes, with the date of his induction into the gang and a blank space below for the date when, he hoped, he would be retired with honor.

At the station, as he handed over his personal effects, he pulled out a handwritten letter that stated he was a member in good standing of the North chapter of the Hells Angels, complete with the names and contact numbers of its other members and an empty space at the bottom for a date in the future when he left on good terms.

"It was his plea to his chapter to be allowed to quit in good standing," says Dumont. "In hindsight, it was clear he was thinking of quitting the gang long before he checked himself into Oka in March of '85."

Why? Trudeau never shared his thoughts with the friendly police officer. Was he getting tired of killing? Unlikely, since he had more than thirty murders under his belt by then and another nine to go in the coming months. Was his drug habit taking its toll? Was the letter a backup escape plan in case things got too hot?

As Dumont puts it, "Personally, I felt his retirement would be six feet under the ground if his request to leave in good standing was not granted."

No one knew the reasons behind the letter—perhaps not even Trudeau. But it showed that his loyalty to the gang was fraying, a factor that would become important in the tumultuous events soon to unfold.

That night, Trudeau spent about ninety minutes quietly waiting in a holding cell until a friend showed up at the front desk with enough money to pay the fines and get him out. In the weeks that followed, Dumont wrote out an incident report, sent it to the SQ as requested, and didn't give the encounter another thought. Only much later, when Trudeau became an infamous figure on TV screens and newspaper front pages, did Dumont realize how close he had come to what could have turned into a deadly encounter with an assassin. "When I saw it, I thought someone was watching over us that night. He showed us respect. We didn't scare him, and he didn't scare us. It was like, in his mind, he had to be nice because we were just doing our job," Dumont says. "It would be dishonest to say I wasn't a bit shaken, though. It's all in the timing, right? And I must say, I was glad I was wearing my bulletproof vest that night, just in case."

As part of his treatment at the drug rehab center in Oka's pine forest, Yves Trudeau would have spent much of each day thinking and talking about timing and what might have been, the principles of forgiveness and making amends, part of the twelve steps in the Alcoholics Anonymous playbook. At first, because of his seclusion, he would have remained in the dark about what had happened to his brethren in the Lennoxville massacre. As yet, there were no reports about the slayings in the media, and in any case, access to newspapers, TV, and radio was heavily restricted in addiction recovery programs, if it was allowed at all.

It's certainly possible that he could have caught wind of the killings in the immediate aftermath. Someone might have called or gotten a message to him another way. But a week after the killings, he learned for sure what had happened from a visitor who dropped by on the Maisonnée Oka's designated day for outside guests. Normand (Biff) Hamel made a chilling appearance as an emissary from the plotter of the Lennoxville massacre, Réjean Lessard, to deliver a message in no uncertain terms to the man who had escaped biker vengeance.

It must have been a striking contrast at the quiet, isolated addiction center, where most visitors were worried spouses, children, or friends coming to see their troubled loved ones. Here was a burly biker with a goatee—though no doubt dressed in "civilian" clothes—coming to see another sullen and dark biker.

Tall and muscular, Hamel cut an imposing and threatening figure. After serving time in prison on drug charges in the late 1970s, he had begun his biker career as a member of a white supremacist gang called the SS in the early 1980s. Then he graduated to the big time, becoming a prospect for the troubled North chapter of the Hells Angels in 1985. But he had chosen a bad year—and a bad chapter—to join.

As a rookie in the chapter targeted for elimination, Hamel was not immediately slated to be killed. At the site of the Lennoxville murders, he was given a stark choice at gunpoint: join the Sorel chapter or walk inside to join his fellow Laval bikers in the execution line. It was not a hard decision. Hamel was given a gun, told to stand guard outside the clubhouse, and ordered to cut down any of his former buddies who tried to escape. So Lessard knew Hamel would be the perfect person to carry his message to Trudeau, able to flesh out just enough grisly details for the hitman to realize his worst fears had come true.

Hamel informed Trudeau that he had been declared "dishonorable," and that he had to immediately erase all of his Hells Angels tattoos and forfeit his motorcycle. In other words, Trudeau had been marked for death. Although bikers were known to have retired from the gang with "honor," the hitman knew no one was allowed to walk out simply by getting rid of tattoos—and certainly not someone who had, in effect, been declared a persona non grata.

For Trudeau, the message must have been shattering. He had turned thirty-nine in February and had spent almost half his life—seventeen years—as a member of a biker gang: first the Popeyes and then the Hells Angels. It was all he had known for his adult life. They were, for all intents and purposes, his family. But for all the mythology of "Hells Angels Forever" and the brotherhood of the bikes, Trudeau knew better than anyone that a fault line of betrayal ran deep within the ranks. There was a fierce camaraderie, to be sure, but it could quickly turn fickle and sour.

Built like a military organization, albeit one that acted outside the law, the gang had strict rules, all of which Trudeau had broken. He understood all too well what the punishment was for that. Indeed, he had killed at least two former comrades, including Paul April, who had been his partners in the murders of other gang members. And he wouldn't have been surprised to learn that five of his North chapter cronies were now lying at the bottom of the St. Lawrence River, their bodies weighted down by cement blocks. It was business. He would have done the same.

So as Hamel recounted the gory outcome of the mass slaying, Trudeau had to be wondering what he could do to reverse the decision to declare him dishonorable. He would not have panicked; that wasn't his style. He made money from killing and understood how that world worked. Rather, he would have coolly considered his shrinking options and decided that the first thing to do would be anything the South chapter asked him to, in order to get back into their good graces.

Anything at all.

10.
THE HITMAN BECOMES A TARGET

Although he had orchestrated the execution of five men, Réjean Lessard was far from finished wiping out the North chapter. He had forced Michel (Jinx) Genest—the North chapter member who had survived the massacre only because he was in the hospital—to join the South chapter or be killed. Now Lessard wanted to test Genest's loyalty. The man who had been spared the hail of bullets had to put a bullet into another biker.

After he was released from the hospital, Genest was ordered to kill Claude (Coco) Roy, a North chapter prospect who was close to the five murdered bikers, because, according to later police testimony, Roy "talked too much." On April 7, Genest, accompanied by Normand (Biff) Hamel, arranged to meet Roy, ostensibly to close a drug deal, in Unit 103 of the drab Motel Idéal in Saint-Basile-le-Grand, on Montreal's South Shore.

The only deal the Angels were interested in was Roy's death. He was beaten mercilessly in the motel room and his body dumped in the same spot in the St. Lawrence as the five others. In an added gesture of fealty to his new chapter, Genest handed over five bags of cocaine that Roy had been carrying at the time of his murder.

Lessard planned to test Yves Trudeau the same way: prove your loyalty by killing people associated with your beloved North chapter.

A week after Hamel's visit at the rehab center, Trudeau checked himself out. As instructed by Lessard's emissary, he covered up his HA tattoo with black indelible ink—a less painful way to comply with the gang's order to remove them. He went straight to the brutalist gray cement garage in Laval that had served as the North chapter bunker. There, he saw that it had been stripped of everything it had contained, including his motorcycle and, most annoyingly, $46,000 he had hidden away.

He called Hamel to ask about the bike and the money.

"Forget the cash," Hamel advised him. "It's gone."

It's unlikely Hamel knew that the ninth step in the Alcoholics Anonymous program Trudeau had abandoned was about making amends. Still, he made it clear that Trudeau might be able to patch things up with a furious Lessard if he made amends, of a sort, by doing what he had always done best: killing. If Trudeau agreed to kill two people the South chapter leader wanted dead, he might get his bike—and his life—back.

His first target was Ginette (La Jument) Henri, whose nickname meant "The Mare." She had been Jean-Pierre Mathieu's girlfriend, but more importantly, she had been the now-defunct chapter's accountant. She knew all its secrets, including where they hid their drugs. Henri had been asking around about her missing boyfriend. A nervous Gilles (Le Nez) Lachance had told her that Mathieu had been discharged from the club with "dishonor," but that would only have worried her more.

Lessard was pretty sure Henri would never talk to police, but he couldn't know for certain. Either way, he feared that the drugs hidden by the North chapter could be found and become evidence in a case against the gang. It was best to deal with the problem by getting rid of the accountant.

Trudeau had in the past shown no reluctance to kill women—girlfriends, wives, and one mother—whose only transgression was associating with his targets. But he was reluctant to risk getting caught, and when he began his surveillance of Henri, he noticed a police presence the likes of which he had never seen before. They were showing up everywhere, hovering, knocking on the doors of everyone related to the five North chapter men who had gone missing. So he backed off.

With the cops sniffing around, asking questions, and getting tips, the Lennoxville massacre would not remain a secret for much longer.

The police raids on Hells Angels clubhouses were massive, swift, and devastating, if only in the short term. On Wednesday, April 10, they barged into chapter headquarters throughout the province, from Chicoutimi in the Saguenay region to Sorel on the South Shore. More than four hundred officers from the Sûreté du Québec and local forces were involved, along with police dogs trained to sniff out bodies, blood, and drugs. Over four days, hundreds of handguns, shotguns, and rifles were seized, along with knives and even swords, about $150,000 in cash, bulletproof vests, police scanners, baseball bats, and ammunition, not to mention drugs worth an estimated street value of $6 million. But they found no bodies.

"Police say they were acting on a tip that six members had been killed March 26 or 27," newspaper reports said. The cops may have had the number of dead and the dates slightly wrong, but they were on the right track. They even had the names of most of the victims: the *Montreal Gazette* reported that police believed the dead included Laurent (l'Anglais) Viau, Jean-Pierre (Matt Le Croisseur) Matthieu, Michel (Willie) Mayrand, Guy-Louis (Chop) Adam, and Claude (Coco)

Roy. Investigators were only missing the name of the final victim, Jean-Guy (Brutus) Geoffrion, the North chapter's chemist-in-chief, and they were misinformed about Roy, for he had not been killed in Lennoxville with the others, but a couple of weeks later in that sad little motel room in Saint-Basile-le-Grand.

Still, the police knew a mass killing had taken place. They just could not find any proof.

Brandishing semiautomatic weapons and using bulldozers, they smashed their way into the Lennoxville clubhouse. For several days, they dug through the woods behind it, aided by three search dogs. Yet they found no graves, just a flannel shirt with a bullet hole through it.

"It was nothing but a publicity stunt," said one angry member of the Sherbrooke chapter. "It's bullshit. Suppositions don't go nowhere." But he refused to say where the missing men were.

Friends of the missing bikers clung to hope they were alive and were skeptical of reports of their death. "I'll believe it when I see the bodies," one man told reporters.

On April 15, police finally called off the search. The men were not buried anywhere near the Sherbrooke clubhouse.

The police arrested more than eighty bikers during those initial raids on the clubhouses across the province, but it was a perfunctory sweep meant to harass and threaten more than anything else. All but six were let go with no charges.

In the early morning hours of April 10, for example, the police nabbed three bikers from Sherbrooke and two of their girlfriends, charging them with possession of restricted weapons without permits. But Superior Court judge Louis-Philippe Galipeau ordered police to release them, calling their detention illegal because they had not appeared in court within the required twenty-four hours after their arrest.

Trudeau was also arrested during the massive sweep, but his detention merited just fourteen words in a lone newspaper's lengthy account of the raids: "In Montreal Sessions Court, Yves Trudeau, 39, was charged with possession of a restricted firearm" was all the *Montreal Gazette* reported. It was the first time his name had appeared in the media, and he was treated as just another low-level biker. No one in the police, the press, or the public had an inkling of who he really was, much less what he had been doing for the past fifteen years.

The police indicated their investigation was just beginning. "The charges and seizures are only secondary," SQ Constable André Blanchette told reporters in a briefing after the raids. "This is a murder investigation and we're after murder indictments. We haven't found what we're looking for. But we'll continue to search until we find the bodies."

Little did Blanchette and the rest of the police know that the man who could unlock the mystery was sitting in one of their cells. A hitman no one had heard of, who moved through the underworld undetected, leaving only blood and bodies behind.

Five days after Yves Trudeau was arrested, he made bail on April 15; firearms possession was a relatively minor offense. He was safe from the police, for now. But what about the Hells Angels? He watched nervously as the murderous fallout from the Lennoxville massacre kept on building.

Even though the police were circling, Réjean Lessard had lost none of his obsession with getting rid of his remaining targets from the disgraced North chapter. On May 1, 1985, Régis (Lucky) Asselin, who had partnered with Trudeau on several hit jobs, was shot multiple times in the chest, shoulder, and throat as he left his apartment in Bellefeuille, a small town in the Laurentian region north of Montreal. Living up to his nickname, Asselin managed to stumble into his van and drove himself to a hospital in nearby Saint-Jérôme. After a week spent in intensive care when few expected him to live, he survived.

Trudeau, meanwhile, had been given the task of killing two other people tied to the North chapter. He had wisely backed off from murdering Ginette Henri because of the police presence around her. That left his second assigned target: Jean-Marc Deniger, a skinny, bearded, curly-haired drug dealer and associate of the North chapter whose nickname was "La Grande Gueule," or "Big Mouth." According to a heavily redacted police report, on or around May 6, 1985, the thirty-five-year-old was strangled to death with thin, strong ligature, such as a wire. His body was discovered around six thirty that evening, wedged between the front and back seats of a Chevrolet station wagon abandoned in a residential neighborhood just south of Villeray Street in Montreal's north end. Deniger became police file no. 797, with his father, Paul Deniger, identifying his son's mottled, bruised body.

Yves Trudeau could not have known it, but that execution, his forty-second, would be his last job as a free man; he would manage to orchestrate a final assassination from prison, shortly after his arrest.

Trudeau *did* know his days were numbered, though. Sure, as Hamel had promised, he got his motorcycle back after carrying out the assigned contract killing. But he was a dead man walking, one of the few surviving North chapter members and, by all accounts, one of those most guilty of what had so angered the other bikers: snorting cocaine, stealing money, and refusing to follow club rules.

"It's not easy to leave the bikers," notes psychiatrist Louis Morissette, who has interviewed many of them in jail. "If Trudeau said, 'I don't feel like it,' I am not sure that would have worked." Morissette points out that Trudeau's main skill for the gang—indeed, his only one—was as an assassin. "He knows all too well that if he doesn't do that, what's his status in the group? If he can't keep doing what he's good at, the group will be frightened of him."

Trudeau knew he wasn't safe. Not in that world. It wasn't just that he had failed to kill Ginette Henri. More than anyone, he understood that the criminal biker world was cruel and unforgiving, and with the police now involved, Réjean Lessard and the rest of Quebec's Hells Angels were getting even more unsettled and furious. For the rest of his life, Trudeau would always be looking over his shoulder for an assassin. Maybe it would be someone he knew, someone who didn't care as long as he got paid. Someone just like him.

The hunter had become the hunted.

11.

A FATEFUL DECISION

The first decomposing body surfaced on June 1, 1985, floating in the murky waters of the St. Lawrence just downstream from the ferry dock in Sorel, where the South chapter of the Hells Angel was based. It was a grisly sight: a naked heavyset man with matted long hair and an unkempt beard. The only things he was still wearing were his biker boots.

To keep the corpse from being discovered, his killers had wrapped a chain around his legs, secured it with a lock, and weighted everything down with a cinder block. Although their intent was to keep the body hidden in the depths of the river forever, bloating and putrefaction had caused it to rise to the surface and drift, the skin discolored where blood had pooled and stringy hair floating around the head like seaweed.

This was all that remained of Jean-Guy (Brutus) Geoffrion, the Laval chapter's corpulent drug chemist-in-chief and motorcycle mechanic. A fisherman found him on a lazy Saturday afternoon and immediately called the police. Swatches of fabric from the sleeping bag he had been wrapped in were still stuck to his body. An autopsy showed he had been shot twice in the head.

Finally, the police had a body, their first break in a mystery that had stumped them since early April, when they began to hear whispers of the Lennoxville massacre and discovered a Laval bunker that was strangely, scarily empty. Back then, amidst all the raids, the arrests of more than eighty bikers and their coteries, and the seizure of drugs and a panoply of weapons, they were sure they'd find the corpses of the missing men buried in the thick woods behind the Sherbrooke bunker. But as much they had dug, exhaustively doing a grid search with shovels and sniffer dogs, their efforts had been for naught, as was their hounding of the bikers' friends and family. "Do you know where he is?" they asked. "When was the last time you saw him?" They got no answers. People knew better than to talk. Biker rules were commandments, and if they hadn't known better than to break them before the massacre, they certainly did now. No one was going to cross Réjean Lessard and the South chapter, not after what he had orchestrated.

But now, with the surfacing of Geoffrion's body, there was both evidence and a big clue to the location of the rest of the missing bikers: the bottom of the St. Lawrence, filled with muck, fish, and secrets.

There was a delicious irony to the fact that police were hunting for clues in the river. Back in April, soon after the clubhouses were raided in the wake of the Lennoxville massacre, the bikers had launched civil suits that totaled $358,300 for what they claimed were illegal searches and damage to their reputations. "This was nothing but a big police fishing expedition to find a way to arrest and question people," declared their lawyer, Michel Dussault, to the newspapers. "They had nothing on anybody." Now there was a real fishing expedition. In the first week of June, supper-hour TV news programs and the front pages of newspapers were filled with unusual pictures:

an all-out search of the river, complete with motorboats, divers, dogs, and helicopters.

And what the search turned up was gruesome. Over the next few days, the police pulled up four other bodies. All had been stuffed into sleeping bags, some weighted down with cinder blocks, others with heavy metal discs. They were bloated from gas as their bodies decayed. Laurent (l'Anglais) Viau, at five feet, five inches, was the shortest of the victims and remained in his sleeping bag in a fetal-like position, arms folded across his chest.

The last body—that of Jean-Pierre (Matt le Croisseur) Mathieu—washed up on a beach near Neuville, fifty kilometers west of Quebec City, a week later, on Sunday, June 9. Residents found him, mottled, bloated, and light enough for the water to carry him more than 130 kilometers upriver, despite the chains around his legs. As with the others, there were scraps of sleeping bag still attached to his body, like a cloth bandage attaches itself to wounds.

It wasn't only bikers' bodies that were turning up. During their hunt, police pulled up a skeleton from the watery graveyard: all that remained of Berthe Desjardins, the broad-smiling, apple-cheeked wife of André Desjardins, the former Hells Angel who had tried to leave the gang and was suspected of being an informant. Yves Trudeau had executed him, Berthe, and his mother, Jeanne, back in February 1980. André Desjardins's body had washed up on the shores of the St. Lawrence later that same year; his mother's body had been found crumpled, battered, and broken at the bottom of the staircase in her Plateau-Mont-Royal apartment. But Berthe's whereabouts had remained a mystery—until now. It was perhaps a form of bitter justice that her fate would be discovered as part of the search for the slain North chapter bikers, as one of the other recovered bodies was that of Jean-Pierre Mathieu, who had helped Trudeau kill her.

The day after Berthe's skeleton was discovered, Yves Trudeau was trying desperately to stay alive. Beset from all sides, about to appear in court, and with his fellow Hells Angels closing in on him, the killer made a fateful decision.

On June 7, 1985, Trudeau walked into the solemn black-and-gray building in Old Montreal that is known as the Palais de Justice, although there is nothing palatial about it and, at times, little justice. He had been out on bail for two months on a charge of unlawful possession of a firearm. Now, of his own accord, he walked into room 3.06 of the courthouse and pleaded guilty.

Why? As many other bikers had done before, he could have skipped bail and gone into hiding. Or, like many other criminals, he could have fought the accusation in court and hoped for, if not an acquittal, then perhaps a suspended sentence. After all, the charge was a minor one in the greater scheme of things. But it is likely that at this time in his life and in the current biker landscape, Trudeau felt safer inside a prison than on the streets.

Quebec Court Judge André Duranleau gave him what he wanted, sentencing him to one year in prison. He also slapped on an order that forbade Trudeau from possessing firearms when he got out—a definite career killer for a contract assassin. Of course, at the time, the judge believed Trudeau was just another small-time biker who had been nabbed on a small-time charge. Trudeau was handcuffed and led out through the door in the prisoner's dock into the fluorescent-lit warren of corridors that were off-limits to the general public. He then disappeared into Bordeaux Prison, a provincial institution in north-end Montreal that had recently been described as a "paradise for drug dealers."

As Trudeau began his time behind bars, the police were facing a conundrum in trying to solve the Lennoxville murders. True, they finally had the bullet-ridden bodies that proved multiple homicides. But who had pulled the triggers? SQ investigators realized they needed an insider, a turncoat in a world where none seemed to exist. Someone who would describe the inner workings of the Hells Angels, and how the awful decision was reached to ambush and cold-bloodedly kill their own. Someone who was willing to breach the strict and fearsome biker code that governed this band of bloody brothers. Someone willing to tell tales out of killers' school.

But no matter how hard investigators tried, or what they offered as recompense, they might as well have been bashing their heads against the fortified walls of the biker bunkers. According to the bikers' defense lawyers, on April 11, a day after the massive police raids, the authorities promised $25,000 and a new identity to Robert (Ti-Maigre) Richard for information, but he turned them down. Then they made an even more generous offer of $100,000 to Richard Rousseau, one of the Sherbrooke chapter's three founding members. He, too, refused to cooperate.

Both of these bikers belonged to chapters that had carried out the executions. But there was another biker behind bars who police knew had been a member of the targeted North chapter. Would Yves Trudeau be willing to talk?

As he sat in his cell in Bordeaux Prison, Trudeau's mind must have been racing. Just weeks before he was incarcerated, he would have heard the news that one of his former accomplices, Régis (Lucky) Asselin, had narrowly escaped death by dragging his bullet-ridden body to the hospital, somehow surviving a hit. Then, in the days before he stepped into court, Trudeau, like so many other Quebeckers, would have watched in amazement and horror as the police pulled body after body out of the St. Lawrence. Unlike most people, however, he knew the victims. They had been his friends. The Angels he rode with on Harleys. His drinking buddies and fellow coke sniffers. Now they were bloated corpses.

Trudeau knew he could be next. How safe would he be in a prison filled with bikers and other criminals willing to take out a fellow inmate for a small fee or favor? More worrisome was that Trudeau was serving time on a relatively minor charge that carried a one-year sentence. With good behavior, he could be out in mere months. Then again, what if police discovered he was "the Mad Bomber," the Hells Angel secret assassin? He knew it was likely that, with more and more bikers rounded up and questioned, someone would blab that he was behind the bombing at the apartment building on de Maisonneuve Boulevard the previous November—that he had made the bomb, orchestrated the delivery, and triggered it, sending four men to oblivion in pieces. Indeed, a confidential informant with close ties to the West End Gang had already said as much to Montreal homicide inspector André Savard, although Savard's warnings were not heeded. But if that changed, or someone else talked, Trudeau would be facing multiple murder charges that could put him behind bars for the rest of his life.

Worse, Trudeau heard whispers of a $50,000 contract the Hells Angels had taken out on him. In the aftermath of the Lennoxville massacre, they still wanted him dead. Those whispers turned into headlines in the tabloids, which investigators at the time made sure the hitman saw. Now the roles were reversed. The contract killer had a substantial contract put out on *him*, and the Hells Angels were intent on finishing the job. Trudeau took the threat seriously; no one understood the transactional nature of killing better than him.

Although his first kill for the Popeyes had been done out of passion and anger, in retribution for the theft of a motorcycle, Trudeau had changed over the years. He had grown into the job, so to speak. It had become a business, with work to complete and payment to collect. And it had the added benefit of helping to finance his coke habit. Perhaps at times he had killed those he would rather have not—girlfriends with bad timing, a mother who refused to give up information about her son, victims he mistook for his target—but he had no regrets. For Trudeau, murders were just a commodity.

Now it was time for another pragmatic business decision, not to kill, but to save his own life. Trudeau asked to see Corporal Marcel Lacoste of the SQ, who had diligently led the investigation into the bikers' murders.

Lacoste must have been both excited and intrigued by the request, and when he arrived at Bordeaux Prison, Trudeau delivered what the police had longed hoped for: a snitch inside the closed world of bikers. An informant.

"I have killed for them, and now they want to kill me. That's gratitude?" Trudeau is reported to have said, according to crime journalist Jerry Langton. He told Lacoste he was ready to reveal everything he knew about the deaths in Lennoxville, and about the Hells Angels in general. He would talk about how the gang worked and made decisions, its hierarchy, and its rules. In return, he asked that the investigator guarantee the safety of his family—he fully expected there would be attempts to avenge his decision to turn stool pigeon—and that his testimony would not be used against him in future cases.

By going to the police and both becoming the key to solving the mystery of the murdered bikers and providing a road map to how the Hells Angels worked throughout the province, Trudeau was able to get a plea deal and a new identity. As he would later say, "I was as good as dead already. I was supposed to be dumped in the river on the twenty-fourth," referring to the date in March 1985 when his North chapter buddies were slaughtered.

On August 5, Trudeau was transferred from a prison full of potential enemies to a much safer location at the Parthenais Street headquarters of the SQ. On the fourth floor was a cellblock for special prisoners, guarded by provincial police officers who were armed to the teeth.

For Trudeau, turning informant was just another transaction in a lifetime filled with them. As in all his previous transactions, he did not commit until he had done the research. To that end, there was one other person he needed to speak to before he would fully commit to signing on the dotted line. An old acquaintance. A cop who had known Trudeau when he was a young, happy-go-lucky Popeye doing wheelies.

In the summer of 1985, John Dalzell, once the Montreal police department's liaison to the motorcycle gangs that were springing up all over the province, was promoted to duty inspector. His new job meant working the midnight shift out of the department's headquarters on Saint Urbain Street. He was the senior executive on duty at that hour, running point on major crimes that broke on his watch. When things were quiet, he conducted spot checks on individual police stations to make sure they were in good shape, with desks tidy, documents properly filed, and coffee mugs emptied and scrubbed clean.

"I had a car and driver, and when the radio cars that worked each neighborhood spotted us in the area, they would call in to say we were coming," Dalzell recalls. "By the time we got to the station, everything would be perfect and proper. It was funny—you had to have worked in the stations to know that, at three o'clock in the morning, this was not normal. But you went along with the charade."

One late night in August, Dalzell got a phone call from the duty officer at SQ headquarters on Parthenais. "We have Yves Trudeau—Apache—in a cell here," the man said. "He has asked to see you."

"Apache? I haven't heard that name in fifteen years," Dalzell said, surprised. "Why does he want me to come see him?"

"Don't know," came the terse reply. "Apparently, he'll only talk to you."

Dalzell had long since lost touch with the biker gangs he'd worked with in the late 1960s. He was married now and living in Otterburn Park, a suburb on the South Shore of Montreal. Instead of scouring chop shops for stolen motorcycle parts and riding with biker gangs on weekends, he spent his free time coaching football and hockey. Still, he had followed the news about the Maisonneuve bombing. How could he not? It had occurred on his old stomping grounds, practically across the street from Station 10, as if the perpetrator was so confident in his skills it didn't matter that police were in the immediate vicinity. He knew about the raids that had gone nowhere, and the bikers who were freed soon after being arrested. And like everybody else in the province, he had watched as bodies were pulled from the St. Lawrence.

But Dalzell had contacts the public did not, and when he heard through his police buddies that an informant had named Trudeau as the man responsible for the Maisonneuve bombing, he was surprised—even shocked. The biker he had once known, small, secretive, and on the sidelines, didn't fit his image of someone who could build a bomb, let alone kill people. He thought back to the nights he had given Trudeau rides home on the back of his Harley and their careful conversations about nothing much, and to the biker's childlike delight as he reared up on his motorcycle as if it were a horse, managing to hold the wheelie for longer than anyone else.

"He wasn't an assassin, not back then," Dalzell says. "That I can tell you."

Dalzell had his driver drop him off at the entrance to the mid-rise building in east-end Montreal that served as the SQ headquarters. After passing through the security check, he entered the elevator, calm and ready for anything. When an expressionless guard opened the cell door, he went in alone. "Yves," he said. "What's going on?"

"Hey, John," Trudeau replied.

He hadn't changed. He was still the same slight man with slicked-back hair, sharp features, and dark-brown eyes, which now gazed at his visitor steadily. "They got me for the bombing on de Maisonneuve," Dalzell remembers Trudeau saying.

"Yeah, I sort of heard through the grapevine that you were one of the guys," Dalzell responded, wondering where this was heading.

"Well, I want to become an informant."

Dalzell was shocked. He had thought he was prepared for anything, but he certainly hadn't expected this. "Okay, Yves," he said, "but what's the deal? You got to deal to become an informant, and from what I see, you can't deal on the bombing. They got you on that. You can't expect to become an informer with that and plea bargain for a reduced sentence."

"I got stuff to deal. Other stuff."

"What stuff? What are we talking about here, Yves?"

"Assassinations."

"What?"

"Yeah, forty-three assassinations," Trudeau confessed.

Dalzell was stunned. "Forty-three? Yves, forty-three assassinations? I mean, holy shit!"

Trudeau sat calmly as Dalzell processed what he had just been told, trying to reconcile the man sitting before him with what he knew about unsolved murders in the Montreal region. Was this who'd done them? Apache, a little guy who weighed 135 pounds soaking wet? Dalzell took a deep breath. "And the bombing, Yves? Where'd you learn stuff like that? I know that some of the bikers came up through the military, but you?"

"Don't you remember, John? You used to drop me off at home in McMasterville, where C-I-L is. I worked there. That's where I learned. You know about C-I-L and chemicals and bombs, John?"

Back in 1968, Dalzell hadn't known anything about the company. But one of his neighbors in Otterburn Park was a vice president at C-I-L, and he was now well aware of the company's expertise in manufacturing explosives for a variety of clients, including police and the military.

Dalzell was shaken. The man sitting across the table from him was a methodical and unrepentant killer. He looked at Trudeau and asked, "So why did you ask to see me?"

"I want to know if I can trust the SQ," the biker replied. "The only cop I know is you. And you, I trust."

For a moment, Dalzell was at a loss for words. As far as he knew, this was the first time the SQ had been involved in a major investigation of biker gangs. And the potential of such a high-value informant . . . did the provincial force possess the knowledge—the wiliness, the chops, the guts—to cut a proper deal with a man like Trudeau? A *killer* like Trudeau? Then again, everything he had heard about the investigators in charge of the case was good. They were good cops, and good guys.

"Yeah, Yves," he finally said. "I think you can trust them."

He stood up to take his leave. "Goodbye, Yves," he said.

"Thanks for coming, John," came the reply. "Goodbye."

Yves Trudeau, as a twenty-three-year-old Popeye, receives an award from Montreal Police Chief Jean-Pierre Gilbert in November 1969. (Jean Goupil, *La Presse*)

Undated photo of Trudeau. (public domain)

Trudeau with his Harley-Davidson. (public domain)

Trudeau (second from right, first row) with his Laval chapter. The five members killed in the Lennoxville massacre were Laurent Viau (first row, third from right), Jean-Guy Geoffrion (second row, far right), Michel Mayrand (second row, third from right), Jean-Pierre Mathieu (third row, third from right), and Guy-Louis Adam (third row, far right). (public domain)

Trudeau's sister, Suzanne, pictured on the front page of *Allo Police* in June 1986 with a machine gun in her hand and a .357 Magnum in her holster. The quote in the headline about her having been a member of the Popeyes came from an allegation from her brother during a trial, but she denied it. (*Allo Police*)

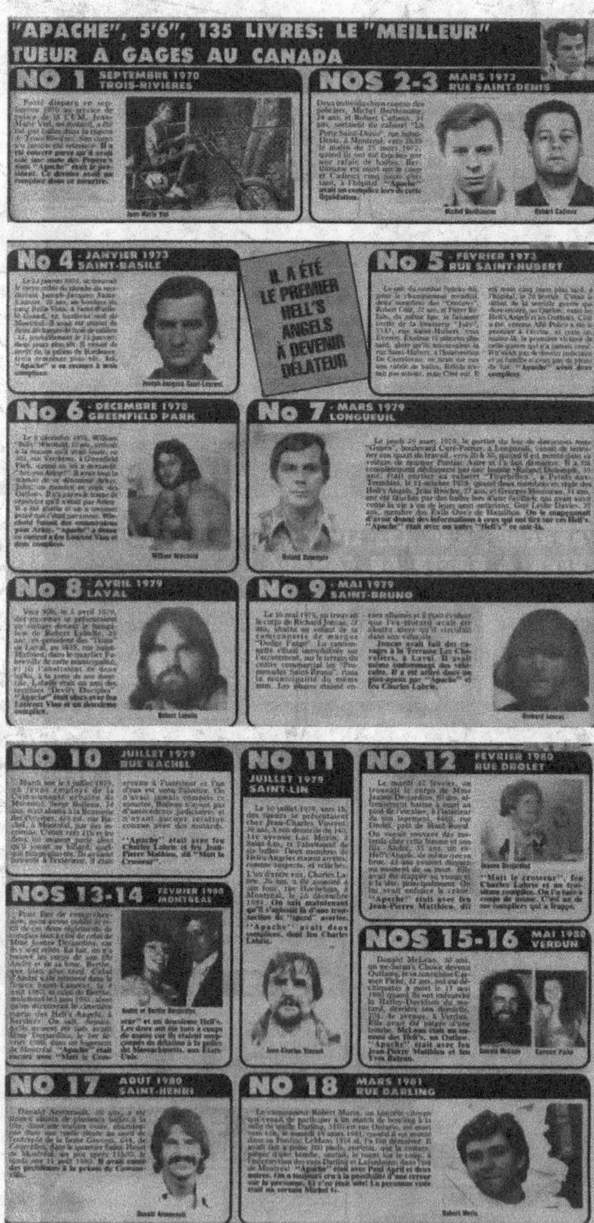
"APACHE", 5'6", 135 LIVRES: LE "MEILLEUR" TUEUR À GAGES AU CANADA
NO 1 SEPTEMBRE 1970 TROIS-RIVIERES
NOS 2-3 MARS 1972 RUE SAINT-DENIS
No 4 - JANVIER 1973 SAINT-BASILE
IL A ÉTÉ LE PREMIER HELL'S ANGELS À DEVENIR DÉLATEUR
No 5 - FÉVRIER 1973 RUE SAINT-HUBERT
No 6 - DÉCEMBRE 1978 GREENFIELD PARK
No 7 - MARS 1979 LONGUEUIL
No 8 - AVRIL 1979 LAVAL
No 9 - MAI 1979 SAINT-BRUNO
NO 10 JUILLET 1979 RUE RACHEL
NO 11 JUILLET 1979 SAINT-LIN
NO 12 FÉVRIER 1980 RUE DROLET
NOS 13-14 FÉVRIER 1980 MONTRÉAL
NOS 15-16 MAI 1980 VERDUN
NO 17 AOÛT 1980 SAINT-HENRI
NO 18 MARS 1981 RUE DARLING

NOS 19-20 MAI 1983 ROSEMONT

NO 21 OCTOBRE 1983 WESTMOUNT

NO 22

NO 23 MAI 1982 SAINT-SULPICE

DES GESTES NERVEUX

NO 24 JUIN 1982 SAINT-SULPICE

NO 25 JUILLET 1982 SOREL

NO 26 JANVIER 1983 RUE SAINTE-ROSE, MONTRÉAL

COMME UN ÉCUREUIL...

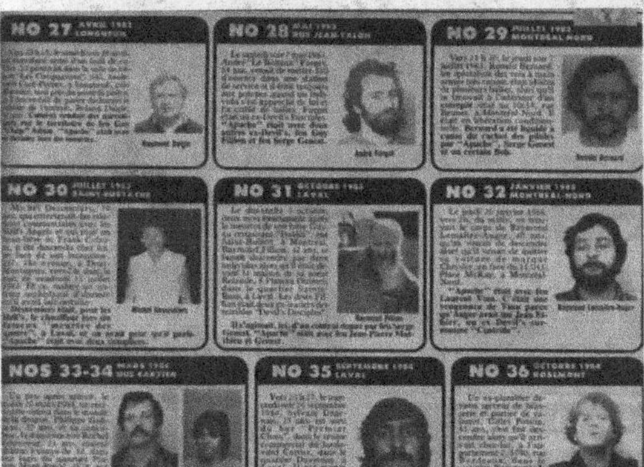
NO 27

NO 28

NO 29

NO 30

NO 31

NO 32

NOS 33-34

NO 35

NO 36

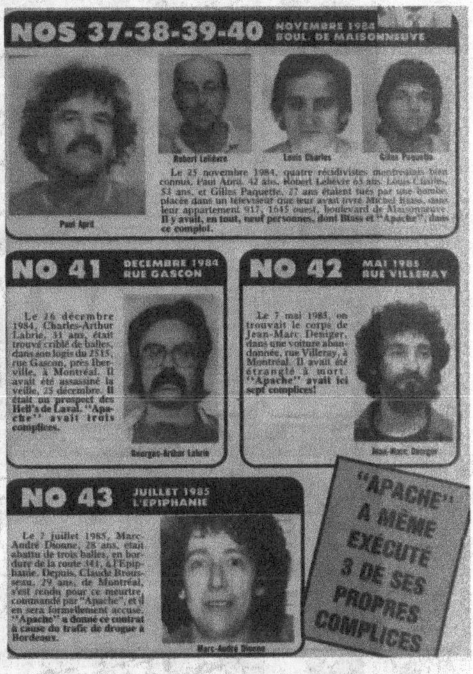
NOS 37-38-39-40 NOVEMBRE 1984 BOUL. DE MAISONNEUVE

Robert Lelièvre — Louis Charles — Gilles Paquette — Paul April

Le 25 novembre 1984, quatre récidivistes montréalais bien connus, Paul April, 42 ans, Robert Lelièvre 63 ans, Louis Charles, 53 ans, et Gilles Paquette, 27 ans étaient tués par une bombe placée dans un téléviseur que leur avait livré Michel Blass, dans leur appartement 917, 1645 ouest, boulevard de Maisonneuve. **Il y avait, en tout, neuf personnes, dont Blass et "Apache", dans ce complot.**

NO 41 DECEMBRE 1984 RUE GASCON

Le 26 décembre 1984, Charles-Arthur Labrie, 31 ans, était trouvé criblé de balles, dans son logis du 2515, rue Gascon, près Iberville, à Montréal. Il avait été assassiné la veille, 25 décembre. **Il était un prospect des Hell's de Laval. "Apache" avait trois complices.**

Georges-Arthur Labrie

NO 42 MAI 1985 RUE VILLERAY

Le 7 mai 1985, on trouvait le corps de Jean-Marc Deniger, dans une voiture abandonnée, rue Villeray, à Montréal. Il avait été étranglé à mort. **"Apache" avait ici sept complices!**

Jean-Marc Deniger

NO 43 JUILLET 1985 L'EPIPHANIE

Le 7 juillet 1985, Marc-André Dionne, 28 ans, était abattu de trois balles, en bordure de la route 341, à l'Epiphanie. Depuis, Claude Brousseau, 29 ans, de Montréal, s'est rendu pour ce meurtre, commandé par "Apache", et il en sera formellement accusé. **"Apache" a donné ce contrat à cause du trafic de drogue à Bordeaux.**

Marc-André Dionne

"APACHE" A MÊME EXÉCUTÉ 3 DE SES PROPRES COMPLICES

The list of all forty-three of Trudeau's killings, compiled by *Allo Police*. The headline reads: "'Apache' the 'Best' Killer in Canada." (*Allo Police*)

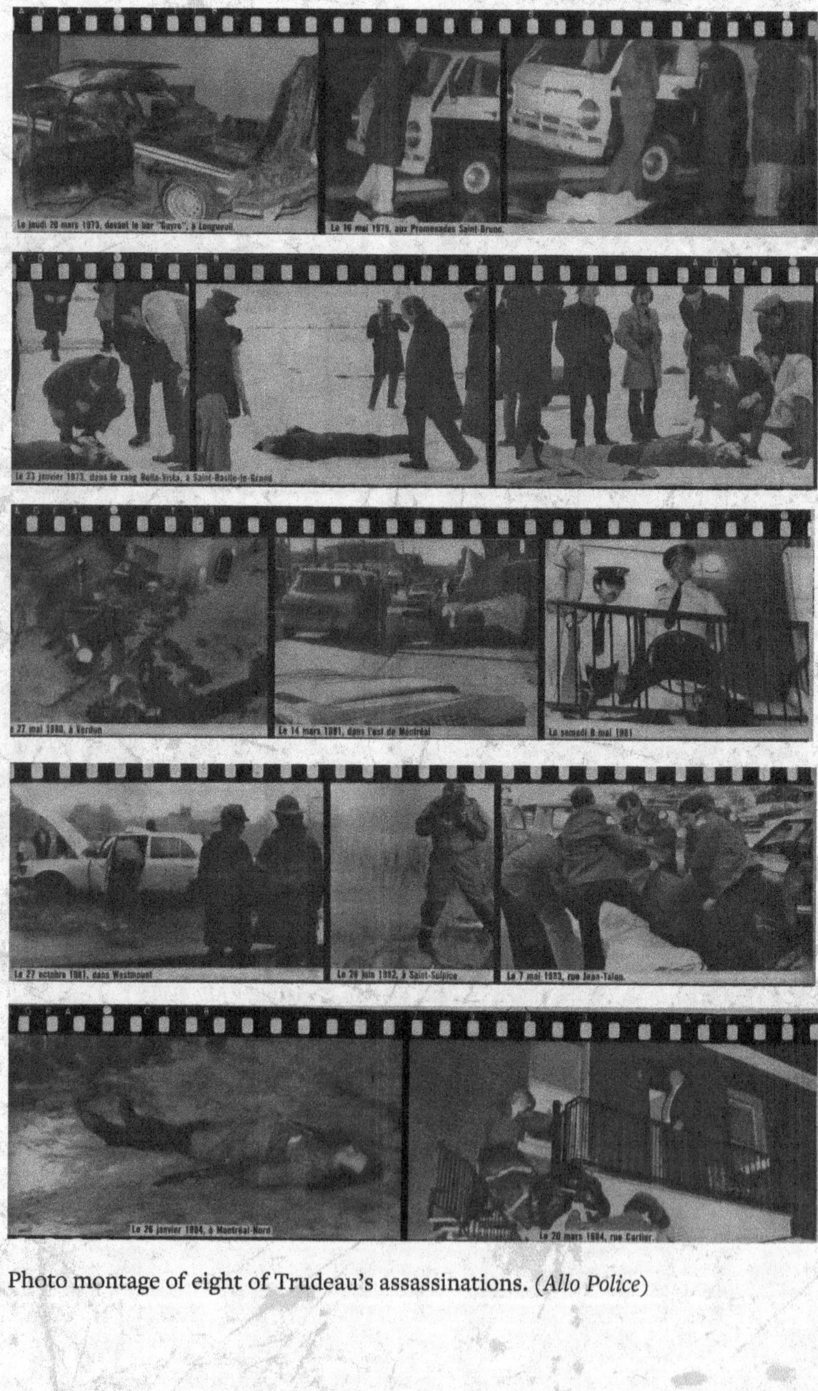

Photo montage of eight of Trudeau's assassinations. (*Allo Police*)

LEFT: Darlene Weichold outside the house where her brother Billy was killed by Trudeau in one of his several murders of innocent people. (Lisa Fitterman)

TOP RIGHT: Billy Weichold shortly before he was killed at age 21. (*Allo Police*)

BOTTOM RIGHT: A teenage Billy holds his younger sister Darlene. (*Allo Police*)

Trudeau escorted by heavily armed police officers as he testifies against his fellow bikers in 1986. This is the last known photo of Trudeau. (*La Presse*)

12.
OUT OF THE SHADOWS

Murder trials are like real-life mystery novels: they are all about who done it. Coroner's inquests, on the other hand, are usually more focused not on the who, but the why. A dam broke and people died; what went wrong? A child in foster care starved to death; how did the system fail them, and how can such a failure be avoided in the future?

Quebec law states that a coroner's inquest must be held into the circumstances of a death when there is reason to believe it occurred from "violence, or negligent or culpable conduct of a third person." Violence was abundantly evident in the case of the dead bikers recovered from the waters of the St. Lawrence. The police had the bodies, they knew how they died, and they had suspicions about who had committed the murders. They needed proof, however, and that meant finding witnesses. But in the secretive world of bikers, with its perverted sense of brotherhood, people did not talk. Police and prosecutors were not ready to make any arrests, much less go to trial.

Their solution? Hold a high-profile coroner's inquest, where the rules are different and, unlike in a regular trial, witnesses can be compelled to testify. Think of it as another kind of fishing expedition, only this time, instead of dragging bodies from a river, the authorities would try to drag the truth out of the bikers.

To pull it off, the provincial government would need more than your run-of-the mill coroner. They needed a judge who knew the law inside and out, who could control a courtroom and fearlessly make decisions despite the bikers jammed into the public gallery sporting skull tattoos, silver knuckle dusters, and threatening scowls.

While Yves Trudeau sat in his jail cell, contemplating his next move, the government was strategizing how best to go after the bikers who had slaughtered his North chapter buddies.

Pierre-Marc Johnson was a savvy politician and lawyer. In the summer of 1985, he was both Quebec's justice minister and the solicitor general; he would go on to become the premier by the fall. He knew the stakes were high. "My role, as minister of justice, is, among other things, to ensure a certain social peace, so I am responsible for shedding light on what happened," Johnson said. It was clear, he noted dryly, that the five bullet-ridden corpses, with cinder blocks attached to chains around their limbs to weigh them down, had not died due to natural causes. So on June 26, he named one of Quebec's highest-profile judges to head the biker inquest: Judge John D'Arcy Asselin of the Quebec Court's criminal and penal division, or Sessions Court, as it was called at the time.

Appointed to the bench in 1977, Asselin was tall and bespectacled, with a military-like bearing, and was commonsensical and unafraid of speaking his mind. He had presided over sensitive cases in the past, even taking on his boss: the previous year, he had declared the former chief justice of Sessions Court, André Fabien, guilty of having cheated provincial tax authorities. (In 1990, Asselin would go on to convict Michel Chrétien, the son of Jean Chrétien, the federal Liberal Party leader at the time, of sexual assault and sentence him to three years in prison.)

Surely Asselin was equipped to handle rough biker witnesses who did not want to be at the inquest. Perhaps. But he never got much of a chance. The bikers' lawyers were experienced criminal defense attorneys who reveled in judicial theatrics and guerilla legal warfare. They sought to thwart the hearings before they ever began. One was Jacques Bouchard, built like a fire hydrant, with a barrel chest, luxuriant gray mustache, and the manner of an attack dog. Another, Léo-René Maranda, given to bespoke suits, monogrammed shirt cuffs, and a pipe, was his gravel-voiced, smoothly eloquent opposite, "a stickler, a man who squeezes between the commas and examines every letter of the law," as one *Montreal Gazette* columnist put it. They knew all too well that this was an inquest like no other. At issue was not how the victims died, as with most inquiries of this nature, but who killed them. Already, nine bikers the police suspected of being involved in Lennoxville killings were being held as what the legal system euphemistically called "material witnesses." They would have to swear a solemn oath to tell the whole truth, even if it meant incriminating themselves and others. If this had been a criminal trial, they would have been within their Charter rights to refuse to take the stand.

As if to emphasize what few rights they had, the bikers, unlike witnesses in any normal coroner's inquest, were being held behind bars and transported en masse to the court. Outraged, the defense lawyers reached for every argument they could think of. They filed affidavits in Quebec Superior Court—the next level up from Asselin's—that Asselin should be disqualified. They hit upon a cogent argument, too, because just weeks before he knew he would be sworn in as coroner, he had issued warrants against five of the bikers that forced them to appear as witnesses at the inquest. In turn, the bikers had challenged the judge for abrogating their Charter rights.

Given that history, the bikers' lawyers argued, how could Asselin now be impartial? The Superior Court agreed, ruling that the judge could potentially be seen as being in a conflict of interest. By the end of July, after just a few weeks of hearing testimony, he was gone.

Undaunted, Justice Minister Johnson immediately replaced his first choice with another Quebec Sessions Court judge, Jean B. Falardeau. By appointing another judge, the minister was sending a stern message that it was imperative someone well-versed in criminal law oversee this unusual inquest. The minister would not be deterred or cowed, not when so many bodies had been recovered from the St. Lawrence. The public had a right to know what had happened. Law-abiding citizens needed to know they were safe from such extreme violence.

Johnson felt confident that the bespectacled and balding Falardeau, sporting a dark mustache and a quizzical expression, could tussle with both the bikers and their lawyers. He had been appointed to the bench only a year earlier, but he had years as a skilled and tough Crown prosecutor.

Once again, the defense lawyers unleashed a flurry of procedural motions and delays. Typical of Maranda's propensity to read "between the commas," they filed another suit in Superior Court, claiming that the judge's appointment as coroner was not legal because he had not resigned from the bench beforehand. And just in case the higher court dismissed that argument, the bikers' lawyers added a twist: Falardeau's appointment was not legal because Johnson had acted unilaterally in naming him. According to their reading of the law that governs coroners in Quebec, the appointment should have been agreed to by the government as a whole, and the National Assembly had not been sitting at the time.

This time, the Superior Court did not buy it. It upheld Falardeau's appointment, arguing that the public's interest and right to know superseded the defense's claims of personal injury to their clients.

Finally, with the legal skirmishes over—at least temporarily—the inquest into the inner workings of the Hells Angels was set to get underway in earnest.

There had been nothing like it in Canada, or really anywhere in the world. A curtain would be raised into the dark and mysterious world of the Hells Angels.

In the late 1970s, American authorities had used an anti-racketeering law to go after a number of California Hells Angels, including the top leader Sonny Barger, but the trial fizzled after seventeen days and ended with a hung jury. Now for the first time, in a small courtroom in Quebec, for weeks on end, the public would get a shocking behind-the-scenes view inside the most powerful yet most secretive outlaw biker gang in the world. More than any other organized crime organization, the HA around the world had been adept at public relations, holding charity toy runs and carousing with Hollywood and rock stars. Sure, they were rascals, but of the lovable rebel kind: hairy and big but cuddly, like the teddy bear runs they held in the United States.

Quite a different story would emerge in the spare, fluorescent-lit courtroom in Joliette, about thirty-five kilometers northeast of the ferry dock where the bodies from the Lennoxville massacre were dumped.

Once Judge Falardeau's inquest got underway, the first witness was Louis De Francesco, a senior investigator on the SQ team. Tall and thin, with thick, blunt-cut salt-and-pepper hair and a penchant for golf in his spare time, De Francesco was a solid and professional witness: understated and unemotional, his revelations were all the more gripping. He methodically ran through what the police had learned about how the five Angels met their end on March 24: four of them were surrounded and forced to lie down on the floor, where they were executed, and the fifth was cut down as he tried to escape.

De Francesco admitted that police, as one news report put it, "did not have a first-hand account of what happened inside the clubhouse or who killed whom"—a stumbling block in any future attempts to obtain convictions. He did, however, name several bikers who he said were "behind the trigger" in Lennoxville, including Réjean (Zig-Zag) Lessard, Robert (Snake) Tremblay, Luc (Sam) Michaud, Yvon (Ro) Rodrigue, and Charles (Cash) Filteau. He also dispassionately listed what the police had seized during raids of various bunkers, including many firearms, although none of them were used in the executions. And he revealed that at least two of those who were being held in prison were believed to have tried to execute a $50,000 contract to kill Régis (Lucky) Asselin, the former North chapter biker who had miraculously survived an assassination attempt the previous May.

The Crown prosecutors were trying to make the case that the nine detained bikers should stay behind bars. But in the end, Falardeau granted bail to all but three of the witnesses: Luc Michaud, Yvon Rodrigue, and Jacques Pelletier, whom the SQ had positively placed at the site of the killings six months earlier.

The police had laid the groundwork, but they were outsiders, desperate to peer into the hidden world of biker gangs. They needed an insider, someone who knew the inner workings of the Hells Angels, with all its madness and mayhem and murder.

Thus, the stage was set for the big show. Who would come into a courtroom filled with journalists and bikers sitting in the public gallery? Who would reveal the secrets of the Hells Angels?

It was time for the hitman to step out of the shadows.

The news first leaked, as many scoops about the bikers did, in a story in the *Journal de Montréal* by veteran crime journalist Michel Auger. A dogged and dedicated reporter with deep sources among the cops and the criminals, Auger revealed that a little-known biker named Yves (Apache) Trudeau had turned police informant. It got people talking. Would he or wouldn't he? Was Trudeau—a founder of the Hells Angels in Quebec, a member of the now-destroyed North chapter—really cooperating with the police, or was the story an SQ plant? *Well*, went the whispers, *what would you do if the HA put out a $50,000 contract on your life, as the tabloids said? Look at the attempt on Asselin's life last May!*

Two weeks later, on the morning of August 27, it was warm outside, and cloudy, when Trudeau arrived at the little courthouse in Joliette in an unmarked police vehicle. The public got its first look at the man known in criminal circles as "the Mad Bomber," "the Mad Bumper," and "Apache." As he emerged from the car, one oxford-clad foot at a time, he was surrounded by plainclothes police officers who kept their jackets open to display the pistols they carried. TV and still cameras captured the image of the star witness for the prosecution, ready to spill secrets about his former brothers in crime. For onlookers, the change in the once scruffy-looking biker was startling. The boots were gone, as was the long hair and sparse beard, and there was not a tattoo to be seen. Instead of a leather vest and jeans, he wore a single-breasted suit jacket of nubby gray tweed with matching gray pants. His short, styled hair, trimmed sideburns, and clean-shaven face highlighted a sharp nose and thin-lipped mouth.

On the surface he looked like a new man, but inside he hadn't changed at all. As with his many kills, Trudeau had done his research, weighing the options and imagining the outcome of every possible scenario before deciding to become the first full-patch member of the Hells Angels to turn on the club in such a dramatic, public way. It was Trudeau being practical, as usual, and saving his own skin. Sure, betrayal was bad news for a biker. But no matter how he tried to work it, the alternative was always worse: *not* becoming a snitch meant a bullet in his head. Or a cord pulled tight around his neck. Or a knife in his back.

It meant he would end up at the bottom of the St. Lawrence like his biker brethren.

But he was also someone who had spent much of his adult life operating in the dark, a skilled stalker and killer who proudly wore both the Hells Angels skull patch and another that declared him a member of the select "Filthy Few," a badge given only to the most dedicated and hard-core among them. Now, as he stepped into the light, the public at large would know his face too. There would be no more hiding, not as Yves Trudeau, not in this province.

Did he feel guilt, shame, or fear as he walked into the courtroom? Did he feel anything as he passed by the angry bikers—guys he had once partied hard with—knowing that he was about to break their code of silence? Knowing that *they* knew what he planned to do? Probably not. For all of his faults and failures, Trudeau was not one to look back and regret his actions. He could not afford to.

Taking the stand, the contract killer swore to tell the truth and nothing but the truth—not something he had done with any consistency for the previous forty years of his life. Right from the start, he admitted he had an agreement that anything he told the inquest would not incriminate him. Then, over the next two days, under direct questioning by prosecutor René Domingue, Trudeau painted a vivid picture of the Hells Angels, filled with what one crime tabloid described as "head spinning" revelations delivered in a flat, matter-of-fact tone. As if what he was describing was routine, like brushing one's teeth or having that first cup of coffee in the morning.

For most members of the public, and probably for a lot of the police, it was their first exposure to the inner workings of the much-feared outlaw biker culture. Trudeau delivered a Hells Angels primer, from A to Z, that encompassed everything from how to become a member through how one could leave the gang—and remain alive. Potential members were called "prospects," he explained; to be considered, one needed to have known a full-patch member for at least ten years and own a Harley-Davidson motorcycle, which would be given up in the interim as surety. For at least a year, the prospect needed to follow a member, learning along the way. The decision about whether the prospect would be a good match for the club, and a positive addition, was made in a vote. Although it wasn't necessary for the prospect to commit murder, if he did and it was good for the club, all the better. And to have killed a rival who had murdered one of their fellow Angels? That was the best of all.

There had to be a good reason, like an accident or an illness, for a member to quit the club, Trudeau continued. And there were just two designations for former members: honorable and dishonorable. That was it, definitive. As far as Trudeau could recall, about ten men had been declared dishonorable. He said, simply: "Some are missing, and some have been found."

Trudeau stunned the inquest, and the public, when he declared that the six bikers killed as part of the cull of the gang's North chapter were not the first to be executed in the province. Indeed, at least twelve others had been summarily murdered in the recent past on their club leaders' orders, largely because they would not fall into line. The individual reasons varied: they may have been forever high on drugs, or incurred heavy debts, or simply given up their Harleys for rides that were decidedly more establishment, such as Cadillacs and Corvettes.

Of the forty bikers who had formed Quebec's first Hells Angels chapter in Montreal in 1977, Trudeau said, only five were still active members; one or two may have been granted an "honorable discharge" from the club, while others had died in motorcycle accidents or in fights with rival motorcycle gangs. Knowing what the gang was capable of made him decide to become an informant; he wanted to start a new life away from all the violence and make sure his family was safe.

Because he was the first to be named to the order of the "Filthy Few," ostensibly for killing in the name of the club, Trudeau claimed, he was the one who bestowed the designation on others in Quebec, including Laurent Viau, Luc Michaud, and Réjean Lessard. "Everyone, really, except for Brutus Geoffrion and Père Bilodeau," he explained. "Yvon Bilodeau had three kids and a wife, and I didn't want Brutus, who was our chemist, to have other potential problems."

When Domingue asked Trudeau how the Hells Angels disposed of bodies, he spoke matter-of-factly of his own experience, like he was talking about taking out the garbage. "We wrap it in a sleeping bag, wrap chains attached to a cement block around the feet, and then toss it in the river. Usually at Berthier," he recounted, referring to the small county along the St. Lawrence not far from the Sorel clubhouse. "Berthier, that was my own cemetery."

The HA's rules to live by were simple, Trudeau continued: "No rape, no burn, no shoot." The first was self-evident; the second meant that one never stole drugs that were destined to be sold; and the third meant no shooting up heroin. An addendum would soon be added by the South chapter: that members should never use cocaine. Period.

This was all fascinating stuff, but it was safe territory for Trudeau: he was talking about generalities, not the specific crimes he had carried out. But then the prosecutor moved on to the blood Trudeau had on his hands.

René Domingue began by asking his witness to describe the act that changed everything for him and the Angels: the Maisonneuve bombing on November 25, 1984, which would result in his own life being blown to pieces and a shocking decision to cooperate with the police.

Yes, Trudeau said, he knew the victims. Yes, they were his friends. And yes, he also knew Dunie Ryan, the leader of the West End Gang, who was ambushed and shot to death at Nittolo's Garden Motel in west-end Montreal on November 13, 1984. Four days later, Trudeau attended the funeral service at St. Augustine of Canterbury, in the heart of the city's Notre-Dame-de-Grâce neighborhood. There, on the steps of the church, he chatted for a long time with his gang-mates and Allan Ross, the West End Gang member who was poised to take over the organization and wanted revenge for Ryan's murder.

"We knew who shot him," Trudeau continued. "So Allan Ross asked me to eliminate the guy who shot him . . . I accepted."

The hitman said Ross promised to pay him $200,000 for the deadly deed, and to forget about the huge amount of money various Hells Angels owed the West End Gang for drugs. For the first time, Trudeau revealed details of the deep debts: "Charlie Hachey owed $145,000, Denis Kennedy owed $165,000, and Laurent Viau had a debt of $185,000," he recalled. "Those three have since died," he added, omitting that he had played a central role in the first two deaths, a revelation that had yet to come out.

Domingue then asked Trudeau to take the court through the clear, cold night when he tore apart the bodies of four people with a devastating bomb that reverberated throughout downtown Montreal. Trudeau delivered the story in a flat, unemotional tone, devoid of guilt or remorse. He had visited his target, Paul April, on the ninth floor, he said, and after noticing that he had few furnishings, offered to buy him a TV and a VCR, as well as a video about the Hells Angels. April accepted with alacrity, so Trudeau went out and bought a TV large enough to hide the explosives inside. Two days later, he called Dunie Ryan's killer to say the gift would be delivered that night by a mutual friend, Michel Blass. "You're going to see how the HA have become so powerful," he told April, knowing the unsuspecting thug would not understand his deadly double meaning.

"I calculated everything," Trudeau boasted. "The thickness of the walls, the position of the elevator. I didn't make a mistake."

The streets were quiet and most of the windows in the apartment building were dark when Michel Blass made his delivery shortly after 4 a.m. Trudeau sat across the street in his car. He watched as Blass, with whom he had killed before, carefully carried the booby-trapped television into the building and disappeared into the elevator. Blass then helped to install and connect the gifts. When he emerged about fifteen minutes later, Trudeau moved his car down the street a bit and waited some more. This time, he was waiting for the men in the apartment to put the cassette into the VCR and hit Play. Then he activated the remote control, and *BOOM!*

"That night, Paul April learned just how powerful the Hells Angels were," Trudeau said, with a chilling calm and the hint of a smirk.

Other Hells Angels had tried to make bombs too, he continued, but they didn't understand the science and technique behind it, and there had been what he called "accidents." He, on the other hand, understood perfectly well how to prepare and calibrate a bomb because of his work at C-I-L years earlier. It was as if he was proud of his expertise, maybe even bragging a bit.

The trouble started, Trudeau told the inquest, when he went to Ross to collect his pay. The West End Gang leader did not have the rest of the money he had promised. Yes, the drug debts were forgiven. But for his fee, Trudeau would have to go to other HA chapters, cap in hand, for the money they still owed Ross: $85,000 from the Sorel chapter and $110,000 from Halifax. Sorel wouldn't pay Trudeau. There was an argument. Finally, the hitman said he was willing to forgive the debt: "You are my Hells' brothers. You can forget the $85,000."

So he was off to Halifax, with Jean-Guy Geoffrion as his translator, since Trudeau spoke barely a word of English. At the Halifax clubhouse, the wheeling and dealing began, and the Quebeckers collected $46,000 as a down payment on the chapter's debt.

Trudeau and Geoffrion returned to Quebec to wait for the rest of the payment. On February 27, 1985, the North chapter bikers were celebrating a fellow biker's birthday when Randy Mersereau of the Halifax chapter showed up with another $52,000. That brought the total payment to $98,000—not the full amount owed, but close enough.

Trudeau was happy, but at the time he had no idea that Halifax leader David Carroll and South chapter president Réjean Lessard were furious at him for the bombing, which brought unneeded police attention, for his debt collecting for Ross, and for using a lot of the money he collected to put cocaine up his nose. He did, however, know how bad tensions were between his cocaine-sniffing Laval club and the other bikers. When asked by prosecutor Domingue what the relationship was like between the North and South chapters at that point, Trudeau answered, "Like cats and dogs." They snarled and pushed at each other, one group instituting new rules to ease the Hells Angels into a new, more responsible business-minded era, and the other unwilling to play.

Trudeau claimed that he had tried unsuccessfully to convince his Laval buddies to get more serious. That was perhaps a stretch, considering that he was a serious coke addict himself. But it was true that even while consuming copious amounts of the drug, he was able to carry out the business of killing. By contrast, Trudeau told the inquest, his fellow chapter members were just party animals. "In Laval, these were guys who were a little bit rock and roll, with drinking and sniffing," he said. "I told them, 'Follow my example, it'll be enough.' But they were sniffing cocaine constantly. It turned them into real vegetables."

And it eventually turned them into murder victims in Lennoxville.

"It's for this that I lost my chapter," Trudeau testified, for the first time showing the slightest bit of emotion. "They did too much of what they wanted to."

Next it was the defense's turn to cross-examine the witness, and Trudeau was lucky that it was mercifully brief. All Léo-René Maranda wanted to know was why. Why had the devoted contract killer for Angels turned snitch?

What was most important, Trudeau responded, was that his family be made safe. And if not for the good fortune of being in the

Oka drug facility, he would have been tossed in the river on March 24 along with his buddies.

Maranda then asked if Trudeau knew of Donald Lavoie, a hitman for the dreaded Dubois brothers, who had made headlines a few years earlier when he, too, had turned informant.

"Yes, I read his book," Trudeau replied, referring to a popular account that had been published the year before. He then critiqued his fellow assassin: "For the most part, the people he killed were good guys," he stated, implying that his own targets had been bad guys, deserving to be murdered. Still, Trudeau calmly told the court, killing was just business, and the two professionals were not rivals. "He was a hitman, just like me, nothing more. It wasn't a competition. I didn't feel superior to him, and he wasn't superior to me."

Trudeau repeated that all he ever wanted to do was to protect his family; that his mother had sold her house and moved elsewhere. "My sister is dealing with this because I'm in prison at 1701 Parthenais. My tattoo is gone. For me, being a Hells Angel is finished. I don't want the symbol and I don't want the motorcycle."

The hitman's final words at his first public appearance were about his personal health—or rather lack thereof. Trudeau testified that he had snorted cocaine only once since undergoing drug rehab the previous March, but that he was still in a sorry state. "That last time, I didn't like it at all, in any way," he stated. "My health wouldn't let me. I have cirrhosis and a stomach ulcer. On the health side, I can't do it any longer."

And that was it. After barely two days on the witness stand, Trudeau was escorted out by armed police, put in a car, and whisked back to his cell.

As court performances go, it wasn't bad. He managed to give a sense of how the gang was run, how utterly ruthless it could be, and why he had decided to testify for the prosecution. But Trudeau had gotten off lightly, with none of the merciless grilling by the defense that would turn his testimony at later trials into shambles. He was spared because the bikers' attorneys knew he was not a key witness to the main focus of the inquest: the Lennoxville slaughter.

Trudeau was not present in Sherbrooke on March 24, so he could not speak directly to what had happened. It would be up to those who were there to describe the bloodbath, the cleanup, and the dumping of bodies that followed. But how could they reveal the secrets of that weekend without implicating themselves in the massacre?

13.
THE TRAP

Barely two days after Yves Trudeau's dramatic debut as a witness for the prosecution, the inquest was rocked when police arrested the man they had been searching for on a coroner's warrant since early July.

Réjean (Zig-Zag) Lessard, the South chapter leader who was the instigator and mastermind of the massacre—its "master of ceremonies," as one investigator put it—had proved a wily adversary, a prominent in-your-face Hells Angel who suddenly seemed to vanish. Over the summer, many of his underlings had been arrested as material witnesses and were facing potential charges of murder. But not him, not yet.

A clean-shaven vegetarian who wore button-down shirts that hid the tattoos carved all over his torso and arms and preferred his fancy car to his Harley, he was a meticulous, careful criminal who knew how to blend in with the general public.

Until September 1, 1985.

It was early afternoon when the police caught a break, not from diligent, relentless investigation, but from sheer dumb luck. A thirty-six-year-old traffic cop was working alone at the corner of Atwater and Notre Dame streets, just north of the Lachine Canal. Jacques Guilbault was watching to make sure vehicles obeyed the lights and turning restrictions. It was an unexciting job and routine: cars turning, lights changing, cyclists in groups or alone, pedestrians in the crosswalk, all in a choreographed dance of stop and start. Then, around 1 p.m., he rubbed his eyes in disbelief as he watched a motorcycle make an illegal left turn onto Notre Dame. Did that really happen? Did the driver of the motorcycle actually flout the law in front of a traffic cop with an identifiable Montreal police vehicle idling at the ready? He switched on the siren and flasher, and the motorcycle stopped about halfway down the block.

When the cop ran the licenses of the driver and his passenger, he made an unnerving discovery. The driver was Richard (Bert) Mayrand, who had watched his brother Michel be gunned down at Lennoxville but had been spared himself because Lessard liked him. And sitting behind Mayrand, looking everywhere but at the cop, was Lessard himself, one of the most wanted men in the province.

The young traffic cop was not prepared to deal alone with two bikers, never mind one who was a suspected mass killer on the run. His training had not prepared him for this. Were they carrying guns? Where were they going? Frantic, he called for backup. Stat.

"That poor cop, he wasn't there to arrest bad guys, or anybody, really. He was there for accidents," says Ken Sweeney, a now-retired Montreal police detective who specialized in gang investigations and was called to the scene. "He was practically hyperventilating." (When Guilbault's wife found out who her husband had arrested, she was so scared, she suggested he would be better off at a desk job than working the traffic beat.)

The backup arrived at the scene within minutes and seized two stolen revolvers and a machine gun equipped with a silencer. It turned out that the traffic cop had stopped the Hells Angels en route to Cazelais Street, in the residential Saint-Henri neighborhood. The rival Outlaws had a clubhouse there, and the two men had planned to spray the building with bullets, one of the last acts in what became known as the First Biker War between the two gangs, which had begun in 1978 for control of the province's lucrative drug trade.

Sweeney did the initial booking for Lessard at a local Montreal police station before handing him over to the SQ, which was spearheading the massacre investigation. While Lessard waited in a holding cell for transport to Parthenais, the detective had the biker strip so photos could be taken. The excuse he gave Lessard was that he wanted proof the Montreal police department had delivered the biker to the SQ with nary a mark of violence on his body, just in case the SQ might not be as polite. In reality, Sweeney wanted the details of the never-before-seen tattoos that covered Lessard from the waist up. It was like looking at a secret language with no key to translate it, an intricate map of death's heads, hearts, knives, and words like "Filthy Few." The photo of the almost naked Lessard was filed into evidence and ended up in the crime tabloids, published with a lexicon—at once a map and dictionary—that explained the meaning of his body's artwork of death.

Then he was transferred, along with Mayrand and Normand Hamel, who had been arrested later the same day in an east-end Montreal duplex, to the overcrowded jail on the top four floors of the Sûreté's headquarters on Parthenais Street.

The three loyal Hells Angels were no doubt angry they had been arrested and worried that they were leading suspects in a murder conspiracy awaiting justice. But what must have infuriated them most was knowing that, just six floors below the jail, lounging in a comfortable, roomy cell protected by police, was the man they considered a traitor, Yves Trudeau.

The killers and the informant were all waiting to see what would happen next at the inquest that each day was looking more and more like a very public police investigation.

In the interim between Trudeau's testimony and the arrest of the three bikers, Judge Falardeau had been keeping busy. He had heard from two pathologists who examined the bodies recovered from the river; both said the cause of death was from skull fractures and cerebral hemorrhaging after being shot in the head. They noted the bodies were covered in tattoos, including one that read "I loved, I suffered and now I hate" in French and another that proclaimed, in English, "The Hells are the best and the rest can go to hell." Falardeau also heard evidence from a crime scene technician who noted that bloodstains recovered from the floor of the blue rental truck matched the blood types of two of the victims, Jean-Guy Geoffrion and Michel Mayrand.

On August 27, Falardeau infuriated the defense when he ruled that, unlike during a trial, the bikers could be compelled to testify, even if they might later face charges in the case. In fact, during a bail hearing five days earlier, prosecutor René Domingue and investigator Louis De Francesco had suggested that such charges were likely.

On September 11, Lessard, Mayrand, and Hamel, all of whom Falardeau had decided must remain in custody for the duration of the inquest, made a brief appearance in the Joliette courtroom, the sound of clanking chains around their ankles announcing their passage into the glassed-in prisoner's dock. They grinned at the bikers in the public gallery, who mugged back.

Twenty-three minutes later, the inquest was suspended as their lawyers moved to another courtroom, before another judge, to argue against Falardeau's ruling that their clients had to testify. They told Superior Court Judge Jacques Dugas that the bikers were as good as charged already; that the Canadian Constitution, the provincial human rights charter, and the principles of common law all protect those who are accused by stating they do not have to, and cannot be forced to, testify at their own trials. Rather than an inquest, the defense insisted, the coroner was overseeing a proceeding that, more than anything, resembled a preliminary criminal hearing, where it is determined whether there is enough evidence to send a case to a full-blown trial.

The Crown disagreed, noting that the articles of law the defense was citing did not apply in this instance because the bikers were not on trial. Technically that was true, though the inquest sure sounded and looked like a trial. But the Crown insisted: if the law protected anyone who might eventually be accused from testifying, then what was the point of holding inquests in the first place?

The Superior Court issued its ruling eleven days later. The Crown won. There was no evidence, the judge wrote, that the law was tipped in favor of prosecutors, who, like the coroner (and judges, for that matter) are appointed by the provincial justice department. The impartiality and independence of a coroner or judge is dependent not on their place in the legal hierarchy, but on the strength of their "moral fibre."

That was it. The defense gave up, deciding it would take too long for an appeal to be heard. And so the stage was set for the inquest's next stage: the testimony of the bikers.

After months of waiting, of the inquest progressing in fits and starts before stalling and starting again, the public would finally get to hear the bikers' side of the story. But what would they say? Bikers were known to be close-mouthed and secretive at the best of times, never mind at an inquest the defense claimed was nothing more than an illegitimate fishing expedition for facts and evidence as a precursor to laying murder charges. How would they handle being sworn in and expected to tell the truth, the whole truth, and nothing but the truth, even if they incriminated themselves in the process? Although the Superior Court ruling emphasized that an inquest is not a criminal trial, so the right of an accused to refuse to testify does not apply, it seemed a stretch that they would candidly tell the truth. Which begged the question: Would the bikers say anything at all?

The skies were clear the next morning as Sûreté investigator Serge Carignan and his dog, Arko, conducted a search of the grounds surrounding the Joliette courthouse and inside the room where the inquest was being held. With bikers in the witness box and in the public gallery, it was wise to make sure no explosives or firearms had been hidden away. Once the investigator called the all-clear, proceedings began.

The first to be called was Robert Richard, Réjean Lessard's burly, bearded right-hand man. He refused to take the stand. He felt the coroner didn't have the power to make him do so, and besides, he claimed, he was suffering from such serious memory loss, he might say things that would embarrass him if he did testify. "I will provide a doctor's note to support this," he told Falardeau, who agreed to put off his appearance until the following Monday.

Then it was Lessard's turn, the man whom police called the mastermind behind the massacre. Like Richard, he refused to take the stand, but he made no claim of memory loss or any other medical condition. Instead, he baldly stated that he did not recognize the validity of the inquest, so would not be sworn in. In swift response, the coroner cited Lessard for contempt and sentenced him to the maximum time possible for such an offense: six months behind bars.

Jacques Pelletier, tall and slim, with light-brown hair parted in the middle and a thick mustache, was the third biker to be called to testify that day. He had been tasked during the Lennoxville carnage with keeping nervous bikers like Gilles Lachance quiet and in line. Although he agreed to be sworn in and answer questions, his memory was crystal clear only when it came to the activities of the

Hells Angels back in the 1970s. Once prosecutor Pierre Sauvé began to skirt around the months surrounding the massacre, his recall clouded over to the point that he seemed to suffer from what one journalist called "profound amnesia."

Sauvé's questions were so slow and careful, the usually even-tempered Falardeau lost his patience at one point. "I'm not here to investigate the Hells Angels in general," he said. "I am here to investigate the deaths of six people who were recovered from the [St. Lawrence] river."

The defense had no questions. After three hours or so, Pelletier was excused from the stand, not having said much of anything at all. The coroner released him from bail conditions that he'd set on August 26, which included not being able to communicate with his fellow bikers and reporting to a police precinct near where he lived twice a week.

The next day, Charles Filteau, who had dark hair, close-set eyes, and a small paunch, was called to the stand. In prison at Parthenais since June because De Francesco had fingered him as one of several bikers "behind the trigger" on March 24, Filteau sat slouched in the hot seat, as far away from the microphone as possible, mumbling his answers.

The prosecutor asked if he had visited the Sherbrooke clubhouse on the weekend of March 24.

"I don't remember."

Was anyone from Sorel, Halifax, or Laval present?

"It's possible."

When was the last time he'd seen the ill-fated members of the North chapter?

"I don't remember."

Filteau claimed there was no hierarchy in the Sherbrooke chapter and members made decisions as one, then contradicted himself when he admitted he was its secretary-treasurer.

Throughout the day, the Crown tried again and again to elicit a straight answer from him about anything, but it was no use. Exasperated but with little choice, Judge Falardeau had to set Filteau free because he had fulfilled his duty as a witness, and that was the only reason he had been behind bars in the first place. The Crown wanted him to remain in prison, but there were no grounds to continue holding him—at least for now.

As the triumphant Angel stepped from the witness box into freedom, other bikers in the room cheered.

On October 1, it was time to hear from the Hells Angel who, perhaps more than any other biker, had been put in a dreadful spot: Richard Mayrand had chosen to side with Lessard and the other killers, and then witnessed the execution of his own brother. But he, too, refused to testify. Léo-René Maranda, his lawyer, suggested his client was overcome by the death of his brother—a ludicrous argument considering he had done nothing to save Michel's life. The judge would have none of it, citing Mayrand for contempt and sentencing him to three months behind bars.

What would the next day bring? More memory lapses, excuses of illness, and jail sentences for contempt? As the bikers closed ranks, the prosecution had its work cut out for it. Would it be up to the challenge?

The next morning, October 2, the doors to the second-story courtroom opened at around eight thirty so people would have time to take their seats before the inquest began at nine. Bikers with subpoenas shuffled in, as did journalists and curious onlookers. Crown prosecutors and defense attorneys were at their tables near the front of the room, ready and waiting. Expectant, even.

It was supposed to be just another day in a bizarre inquest that had dragged on for three months. But suddenly, before Judge Falardeau could enter and get things going, there was a rustle of activity. Turning around in their seats, spectators saw that SQ officers had formed a human wall to block the exit. Making a narrow passage for members of the public to leave the room, they requested that every biker in the courtroom quickly move from their seats into the prisoner's dock. There, they were handcuffed and shepherded out into the passageway reserved for detainees.

The police were springing the trap that defense lawyers had expected from the start.

A prison transport van transported the bikers two hundred kilometers to a court in Sherbrooke, where they were to be arraigned and jailed in the interim.

When Falardeau came in, Domingue informed him that the Crown had filed charges of first-degree murder against twenty-seven Hells Angels, including Lessard and David (Wolf) Carroll of the Halifax chapter, whose meeting in early 1985 had been the spark that set the massacre in motion. The inquest was suspended, with no findings—proving that it had been a fishing expedition all along. A furious Léo-René Maranda wondered why it had taken the Crown and the government so long to recognize what he had been saying from the beginning. This had been a "colossal" waste of time and money, he declared.

But from the point of view of the police and prosecutors—and, arguably, the public—the inquest had not been a waste of time at all. For the first time, in an open legal setting, the violence and ugliness of the Hells Angels had been exposed for all to see. Yves Trudeau had stepped out of the shadows. And the authorities had been able to squeeze out a few morsels of information about what had happened in Lennoxville.

Still, it was one thing to put on a show at an inquest, where the rules favored the authorities. It would be quite another challenge for police and prosecutors to try the Hells Angels in a court of law.

14.

THE CONTROVERSIAL DEAL

From the comfort of his quiet and well-protected cell on the fourth floor of the SQ Parthenais headquarters, Yves Trudeau would have followed the news of the arrests of so many of his former biker buddies for the six killings that took place at Lennoxville and afterward. But what of the forty-three murders he had confessed to? As an informant, what punishment would he be given for those crimes? During his testimony, he had not been asked what he was getting in return for his cooperation. He'd been clear he had no other option, and that he wanted protection for his family. The prosecution had no reason to question any deal that was in the works. And the defense lawyers were too busy fighting the entire inquest procedure as a farce to bother pushing Trudeau for specifics.

It would be five months before a firestorm erupted as the details of his deal emerged. But everyone got a taste of the coming controversy when Trudeau's accomplice Michel Blass made his appearance on the judicial stage as an informant and a dealmaker.

Trudeau had squealed to the authorities that Blass was his key partner in the fatal apartment bombing on de Maisonneuve Boulevard in the fall of 1984. Dark-haired, pudgy, and louche, Blass was an associate of both the West End Gang and the Hells Angels, and it was he who had delivered the jerry-rigged television set and helped set it up in the living room. In mid-September 1985, police moved in to arrest him.

The younger brother of the infamous armed robber and killer Richard Blass, Michel had his own lengthy criminal record, including a 1976 conviction for manslaughter. But over the summer of 1985, Blass had to be worried that he would be the next target. With so many of his biker pals arrested and Trudeau turning snitch, he must have known word would get out about his role in the bombing. Would any friends of the victims come after him? Would Allan Ross, the West End Gang leader who had put out the contract, order Blass killed, just as he'd had others executed to keep them permanently silent about crimes he was involved in?

Friday, September 13, turned out to be Blass's unlucky day—or his lucky day, depending how you look at it. In the dark of night, he was arrested. It probably saved his life. After all, that week, the *Journal de Montréal* had run a story that asked in its bold headline: "Who Will Get Michel Blass—the SQ or a West End Gang Killer?" As he walked out of a nondescript apartment building in Montreal North, Blass got his answer. Surrounded by police, he didn't put up a fight. Like Trudeau, he knew he had no choice; it was arrest or death by assassin.

Blass agreed to become an informant, hoping that would help him avoid a lifetime behind bars on a multiple murder rap, where he would always be looking over his shoulder for a shiv, a bullet, or a fatal beating. To cement the deal, the police quickly made an unusual request of their newly minted informant: Would he wear a wire when he met with his lawyer, a well-known defense attorney named Réal Charbonneau?

Charbonneau had been on the police radar for some time. He had been convicted the previous year of obstruction of justice when he counseled a client not to testify at another coroner's inquest, and was ordered to pay $5,000 to a drug rehabilitation facility in recompense. Now the authorities suspected the lawyer was up to more dirty tricks to foil the justice system.

Blass immediately agreed to spy on his lawyer. In a sense, the request went beyond the pale, for any communication between an accused and his lawyer was, and still is, considered privileged—it's a relationship based on implicit trust. Police and prosecutors are not allowed to listen in on such conversations. But in this case, as part of a criminal investigation, one party, Blass, knew the meeting was being recorded. So in strict legal terms, the wire was unusual, and perhaps unethical, but it was not illegal.

The police equipped Blass with a sophisticated $5,000 recorder, hidden in the back of his trousers, and a mike attached to the inside of a shirt sleeve. In another meeting, the killer also had a bodypack taped to his torso that transmitted his conversation with Charbonneau to police in real time. When the lawyer came to visit his client at the SQ's Parthenais jail, the recordings captured everything. As police suspected, the lawyer crossed the legal line, presenting Blass with an untruthful affidavit to sign in which his client denied any role in the bombing *and* exonerated the West End Gang's Allan Ross.

Twelve days after Blass was arrested, it was his lawyer's turn. On September 25, as Charbonneau was leaving Parthenais after meeting with another of his clients, he was arrested and charged once again with obstruction of justice.

The disgraced lawyer went on trial in February 1986. In a strange reversal of roles, Michel Blass, his former client, was now the chief witness against him. But as would happen with Yves Trudeau over the course of many trials in which he would testify, it was the informant, not the accused, who got the worst of the grilling on the witness stand.

In return for his cooperation with police and prosecutors, Blass had been allowed to plead guilty to twelve reduced counts of manslaughter, rather than first-degree murder, in connection to deaths going back to 1974. Although he was sentenced to life in prison, because "manslaughter" is the legal term for involuntary homicide, he would be eligible for release after serving a mere seven years rather than the twenty-five years the Criminal Code mandates for premeditated killings.

At Charbonneau's trial, the additional perks of Blass's deal came out in embarrassing detail. He would remain for several years on Parthenais's fourth floor, in a cell equipped with a color television and a telephone, and be paid $25 a week. For the rest of his sentence, he would spend two years in an unspecified provincial prison and another two years in a halfway house.

Charbonneau's defense lawyer, the diminutive, dignified, and highly respected Jean-Claude Hébert, blasted Blass for being untrustworthy, a murderer with a long criminal record who spoke of killing as if it were of no more consequence than shoplifting. He argued that Blass could be "coloring" his testimony to get early parole.

"We can see for ourselves," admitted Sessions Court Judge André Bilodeau. "It's a nice gift." Despite his distaste, though, the judge made it clear he had no power to rescind any deal.

Blass's testimony, along with the recordings, was enough to sink Charbonneau, who admitted in court that it was Allan Ross's lawyer, Sidney Leithman, who had put him up to the scheme. After some procedural delays, Charbonneau was found guilty and sentenced to eighteen months in jail.*

Still, neither Blass nor the justice system emerged unscathed. Jean-Claude Hébert's relentless cross-examination, his disdain of the informant's deal, and his warning that Blass had a blatant interest

* *Although the Quebec Court of Appeal ordered a retrial, it never took place because Leithman, Charbonneau's principal witness, was assassinated in May 1991. In Charbonneau's case, this meant the conviction was vacated.*

in tailoring his testimony to earn early parole opened the gates to public criticism of police and prosecution tactics when it came to negotiating justice with informants.

And Blass was just the opening act. When Yves Trudeau returned to the public stage with his performance as an informant against the Angels, all hell would break loose.

The news of the Lennoxville massacre, the fishing of the bodies out of the river, and the spotlight on the bikers' inner workings at the coroner's inquest had helped bring the Hells Angels into the public eye as a crime menace in a way they never had been before. As if to emphasize the new danger, in a report issued in September 1985, the RCMP's criminal intelligence service labeled biker gangs as the most serious organized crime threat in the country, eclipsing the Mafia and Cosa Nostra in Montreal and Toronto. Its report cited thirty outlaw gangs in Quebec that had 350 members altogether, with 90 belonging to the Hells Angels. It warned that the gangs had become more sophisticated, investing illicit profits from drugs and loansharking into legitimate businesses, conducting counterintelligence investigations on police, and even trying to soften their image with slick campaigns that supported local charities.

Meanwhile, behind the protected walls at SQ headquarters, Yves Trudeau was painting a much more detailed—and scarier—picture of the Hells Angels for the police. He was a fount of underworld information for Sûreté investigators; along with the forty-three killings he admitted to personally participating in, he gave his handlers details on forty other murders and a further fifteen attempted murders. He also dropped lots of names, eighty at least, some as accomplices and some he claimed were involved in other murders.

Finally, the SQ had an informant who seemed to know what he was talking about, a founder of the Hells Angels in Quebec, a longstanding biker whose knowledge seemed to extend into every area of the gang's business. Investigators knew it was impossible to break into that world without someone on the inside, which meant someone willing to break laws and even kill.

The police and prosecutors could have ended their collaboration with Trudeau there, using the insider intelligence he provided as a road map to launch their own investigations. Instead, they chose a different, riskier route. They wanted Trudeau to be their star witness and testify publicly at a series of murder trials. Trudeau agreed, but he needed a lot more in return—more than the guarantee of safety for his family. The complete deal has never been divulged, but academic researchers later found four photocopied pages, typed in tiny black script and divided into three sections. The first section stated that Yves Trudeau would plead guilty to forty-three counts of manslaughter; the second, that the prosecution would recommend a life sentence; and the third, what the punishment would actually be and how it would be administered. Like Blass, as long as Trudeau remained on his best behavior, he could be out in seven years.

Seven years. That amounted to less than two months for each murder he had committed or orchestrated.

For his first four years in detention, from 1985 to 1989, he would remain on the fourth floor of Parthenais, guarded by police and taken out to appear as a witness. In 1990 and 1991, he would be transferred to another prison and granted work leaves. After he finished serving his time, the next two years would see him installed in a halfway house, and then in 1994, he would be released into the community under a new name.

The agreement required that the SQ keep his family safe and, once he was released, keep him safe too. In other words, police protection at taxpayers' cost.

Once the agreement was signed to everyone's satisfaction, the police were ready to parade their star informant into court for the first time. Not a coroner's inquest, with its special rules, but a real criminal courtroom, where justice is supposed to be handed out impartially and fairly. On February 28, 1986, at Montreal's Palais de Justice, filled with armed members of the Sûreté's special weapons and tactics team, Trudeau pleaded guilty to forty-three counts of manslaughter.

That, for the curious onlookers and the ever-critical journalists, was the first hint about the extent of the deal. *Manslaughter?* That was usually reserved for people who killed someone by accident. The plea suggested that Trudeau's callous assassinations—twenty-nine by shootings, ten by bombs, three by beatings, and one by strangulation—had not been of his own volition. Yet he had done the killing himself in most of them and confessed to being the getaway driver, lookout, or master planner in a few others.

Claude Parent, Montreal's chief prosecutor, seemed uncomfortable with the deal, or at least with taking responsibility for it. He read each of the forty-three counts aloud, the names, dates, and locations, in a monotone, with none of the usual prosecutorial flamboyance and flourish. Afterward, he took the unusual step of making it clear that the deal was not the Crown's decision; instead, word had come down from the justice ministry to make it so.

The police knew it was a hard sell. SQ media officer Denis Hachez attempted to explain the rationale for the deal by suggesting investigators were hamstrung because, without Trudeau's confession, they had little evidence to prosecute him for any of the murders. Other than Blass for the apartment bombing in November 1984, the force had no witnesses able or willing to finger Trudeau; the people at his crime scenes tended to turn up dead. "We didn't have much to go on," Hachez said. Besides, he added, Trudeau had provided investigators with information on other murders that would conceivably allow them to close cases that had been on the books for years.

The spokesman's efforts were for naught. Over the next few days, more details about the deal and the hitman's life in prison leaked out in the crime tabloids, then in the mainstream media. Trudeau may not have received cash for plastic surgery to change his face, or for a new passport, the newspapers reported, but an annual stipend of $10,000 would be paid into a trust fund for him over four years. Every week while he was in jail, he would get $35 for incidentals such as cigarettes. He had a roomy cell with a color television and cable, a shower and a bath, and steak and sodas on the menu. Toss in the escorted leaves he enjoyed every two weeks or so to visit his family, dressed in a dark hoodie pulled down low over his eyes as he left the institution so he would not be recognized by those tempted to follow (news that came out at the inquest, during testimony by one of the SQ constables assigned to protect him), and it is easy to understand the universal outrage, fury, and disgust.

This was plea bargaining in which justice was shown not to be blindly equal but something one could haggle over as if it were a product on the market. The SQ was putting its trust and the weight of its evidence in the hands of a man who made a living by murdering. As Hachez had awkwardly noted, there was nothing to corroborate his claims.

The critics pounced, and hard. Predictably, the loudest voices came from the bikers' defense lawyers. "You buy what is convenient for you to get, not what is the truth," spat Léo-René Maranda. His colleague Jacques Bouchard went even further, stating that if the informants were willing to kill, they would have no problem perjuring themselves. "These witnesses are like puppets for the police," he said.

Such protestations were to be expected from the Hells Angels' attorneys. But other, more neutral parties from within the justice system were also disturbed by the deal. Serge Ménard, at the time a Montreal criminal lawyer and the vice president of the Bar of Quebec, noted that, while police had to use such methods to solve crimes in a civil society, few plea agreements were as spectacularly shocking as Trudeau's. The future provincial justice and public security minister also warned there was a danger that people who cheat, steal, and kill as a way of life might lie to get better deals, and he urged that such agreements be made in more transparent fashion—after the information was corroborated and proven in court.

The media had a field day with the revelations of Trudeau's perfidy and his perks. "'Apache' the 'Best' Killer in Canada," screamed the cover of *Allo Police* on March 16, 1986. Inside, on page three, it listed the most prolific killers in Quebec: Michel Blass, at twelve; his brother Richard, with twenty; Donald Lavoie, the hitman for the Dubois brothers, with twenty-eight; and then Trudeau, who had "43 Murders in 15 Years!" Another headline proclaimed, in bold black capital letters, "EXPLOSIONS, LIQUIDATIONS, CONTRACTS, REVENGE—HE ALSO HAD THE NICKNAME 'MAD BUMPER.'"

The harshest condemnation came from the *Montreal Gazette*. In a vicious editorial, it asked: "Shrugging off slaughter?" The editorial continued, "Consider Yves (Apache) Trudeau, a thug who admits to killing 43 persons, far more than Billy the Kid, Clifford Olson or John Gacy were ever accused of slaughtering. As measured in blood, it is hard to think of a more vile person that Quebec has produced. He was sentenced to life imprisonment, but the chance of parole means he may be free in seven years. You can get a longer term killing someone with a car—accidentally."

The public furor reached a boiling point on March 11, when journalists at the National Assembly in Quebec City corralled a visibly uncomfortable Herbert Marx, the provincial justice minister, bombarding him with versions of the same question in French and English. Should the police buy information from criminals? Should the government sanction it? What about the victims and their families?

Making deals with criminals was not a question of principle but rather a "fact of life" that authorities could not ignore, the minister replied. "Nobody is getting off scot-free for crimes they've committed," he said, adding that he was considering legislation that spelled out what kind of deals police could make with criminals who helped them solve crimes.

The government never did introduce such legislation.

It would soon be up to the public, along with the police, prosecutors, and politicians, to decide for themselves if it all had been worth it. Would what many thought was a scandalous deal actually pay off?

Yves (Apache) Trudeau was about to appear in a courtroom, not as an accused killer, but as a witness for the prosecution.

15.

"HE WAS LYING"

Yves Trudeau's career as a witness had started, perhaps not surprisingly given his track record as a cold-blooded killer, with a bold, even brash pantomime of murder.

It was a preliminary hearing in Sherbrooke on January 27, 1986, for thirteen of the Hells Angels accused of killing their own at the Lennoxville clubhouse. The courtroom was large, with a bullet-proof plexiglass cage that had been specially built to contain the prisoners. Trudeau sauntered in as a star, cocky and coiffed, surrounded by armed police officers, their eyes swinging left and right as they watched for flashes of metal or sudden movements. Everyone in the public gallery had been searched and had gone through a metal detector, but with bikers, the authorities knew not to drop their guard.

As Trudeau made his way past the prisoners' box, he slowed down. He looked straight at those he knew would have killed him if they had the chance and smiled slightly, his thin lips stretched to bare small teeth, taunting them with his very existence and willingness to tell tales. To press the point home, he pretended to be cradling a machine gun and crooked his fingers as if shooting it, mowing them all down one by one. This was payback—and revenge.

Although Trudeau briefly took the stand, there was a publication ban (as there usually is at a preliminary inquiry), so no details of what he said emerged. But the machine-gun stunt was the first hint of how badly things could go. Trudeau was all show and little substance, a man unable to contain his feelings in public, a witness who could not hide his violent streak from jurors. It was an inappropriate, even inauspicious start for an informant who was supposed to be the greatest catch the SQ had ever landed. In theory, he should have provided a powerful glimpse into the dark, bloody world of the Hells Angels. He was perfectly placed to become a teller of tales: a longtime member of the Popeyes who had helped found the Hells Angels in Canada; a man who had murdered on their behalf and witnessed a slew of crimes.

Thankfully for the prosecutors, the Lennoxville murder trial was put off until the fall. Trudeau's first real test on the stand would come in another trial—this time for a murder he had personally ordered and directed.

"Tell me, Mr. Trudeau, are you wearing your witness costume today?"

So began the caustic cross-examination of Yves Trudeau in the first murder trial for which he was the principal witness. It was June 1986, less than a year after he'd cut the deal with the Sûreté du Québec to become an informant. In the previous cases in which he had appeared—at the coroner's inquest and then at the preliminary hearing for those charged in the Lennoxville massacre—his testimony was peripheral, limited to speaking about the bikers' code and lifestyle. He had not been a witness to the murders on that fateful weekend.

This trial was different. In the prisoner's dock sat Claude Brousseau, twenty-nine, a Hells Angels affiliate accused of first-degree murder in a killing that Trudeau had told police he had controlled from beginning to end. The victim was Marc-André Dionne, a hapless drug dealer. His was the last of the forty-three murders Trudeau admitted to when he agreed to become a police informant. Remarkably, the serial killer had managed to pull off his final job while behind bars. So his testimony, and his credibility as a killer turned prosecutorial star witness, was central to the case. It was time to see whether the government's pact with the devil would yield dividends.

"Well?" prompted defense lawyer Daniel Rock, pushing for an answer to his question on Trudeau's attire.

An uneasy Trudeau stared back, as if trying to get Rock to back off. The lawyer didn't rise to the bait, letting silence fill the room. The seconds ticked by as Trudeau fidgeted in the witness box. Finally, after five seconds, Trudeau icily replied, "Yes."

In the courthouse in Joliette, about seventy-five kilometers north of Montreal, the jury sat riveted as Rock ran his eyes over Trudeau, up, down, and up again: at the suit and tie, the clean-shaven face, the short hair, parted on the left, that looked feathered and blow-dried. He wanted to implant in the minds of the jury that the man sitting before them in a respectable business outfit was not what he appeared—not by a long shot. After all, it was a rare witness who had to wear a bulletproof vest under a tailored jacket and be escorted by police in plainclothes, their guns tucked into side holsters, easily accessible in case of an emergency, like an attack on the witness's life.

Rock knew the gritty details of Trudeau's killing spree could come later. For now, it was enough that the jury understood the essence of the witness who sat before them. He was a stone-cold killer playing the role of a suited and coiffed penitent citizen. Rock wanted them to know that beyond a reasonable doubt. No matter how much the police and the Crown tried, they could never hide Trudeau's true nature.

For Crown attorney Maurice Parent, the case must have seemed like a slam dunk: just three drug dealers who had a falling out that ended in murder. Trudeau, the Crown's star witness, got his pal Claude Brousseau, the defendant, to kill Marc-André Dionne, the victim. Dionne, a twenty-eight-year-old with a gap-toothed smile, a mop of curly brown hair, and a penchant for partying, was Trudeau's final assassination.

Patiently, the prosecution walked Trudeau through his account of what happened. He had met Dionne in March 1985, when both were undergoing drug recovery in Oka, the rehab stint that had kept Trudeau away from the Lennoxville massacre and saved his life. The two men crossed paths again at the Montreal courthouse while awaiting trial appearances, and then for a third time while serving their sentences in Bordeaux, the provincial prison in north-end Montreal. Trudeau was there doing his stint for illegal possession of a firearm.

The hitman explained to the jury that Dionne was being released from the prison on weekend passes, so on the face of it, he was a perfect candidate to bring illicit drugs back for other inmates. In effect, he was a drug mule. He might be cursorily searched upon his return, but the benefits were well worth the risk. Trudeau took charge of the logistics. He instructed Brousseau to procure a supply of cocaine and hashish, then meet with Dionne and make sure it was carefully hidden in Dionne's clothing before he headed back to Bordeaux.

It didn't work out as planned.

The first time, in mid-June, the bumbling Dionne returned without the drugs, saying he had been at a party and used them. Inmates waiting for their fixes were furious and wanted to make Dionne an example for those who didn't follow instructions. Remarkably, Trudeau, the hitman who, over the years, had thought nothing of offing his chosen targets for the slightest offense, counseled patience. "Let's give Dionne another chance," he said. "He's going out again this coming weekend. Let's see what he does."

When the next weekend rolled around, Dionne was instructed to meet Brousseau and pick up the drugs. This time, he was a no-show. Upon his return to prison, he sheepishly explained that he got caught up at a party and did not have the time to make the rendezvous.

That was it for Dionne. You didn't fail Yves (Apache) Trudeau twice in a row.

Trudeau testified that he called Brousseau from the prison pay phone with explicit instructions. "He has pulled a fast one on us two times now. Make him disappear."

The death warrant issued, the plan was for Brousseau to pick Dionne up at the entrance to Bordeaux. Trudeau instructed his buddy to make sure Dionne was a goner, because he'd promised other inmates the deed would get done. Brousseau protested that he didn't have the weapons to accomplish the killing. Not a problem, the hitman assured his partner. Trudeau told Brousseau to go to the Taverne de Faubourg at the corner of Ontario and Cartier streets. The dive bar was just south of La Fontaine Park, where the Popeyes had set up the club's headquarters all those years ago. "I had friends there who owed me," he told the jurors. "They would give Brousseau what he needed."

Trudeau continued his detailed testimony. On Sunday, July 7, he got a phone call. "Okay, I did what you asked," Brousseau told him. "You'll never see him again. He has been dispatched."

The next day, Dionne's body was found in a quarry in L'Épiphanie, a small town fifty kilometers northeast of Montreal. Trudeau testified that he confirmed the death the following Wednesday, July 10, when he read a story about the grisly discovery in the *Journal de Montréal* and was driven to call Brousseau again. "You practically did it in my own backyard," Trudeau joked. "That's the street where I live, on Route 341 in L'Épiphanie."

Then the man in the witness stand uttered words that prosecutor Maurice Parent probably wished he had kept to himself: "To kill was never a pleasure," the assassin said coldly. "It was a necessity."

Although chilling, Trudeau's testimony was clear and concise. He had laid out the murder plot in step-by-step detail. But prosecutor Parent knew the jurors were not likely to take kindly to, much less entirely believe, a self-confessed murderer. To bolster Trudeau's credibility, and the Crown's case, Parent called the hitman's live-in girlfriend and his sister to corroborate his story.

The girlfriend, Jeannine Keagle, did not have much to say, save that Brousseau showed up at her home the night of the killing and told her what happened. Suzanne Trudeau, always close to her big brother, caused more of a stir. Dressed primly and respectably in a skirt, blouse, and sensible shoes, with her auburn hair tamed and neatly combed, she told the jury she had accompanied Brousseau to the Taverne de Faubourg on the first weekend in July. There, they met one of her brother's "friends," as he had instructed. The man, whose identity she never learned, took them to his home nearby and handed Brousseau a .22 rifle, with which he would kill Dionne. Suzanne told the jury she even went with Brousseau to a Canadian Tire to purchase bullets for the gun, although she couldn't remember where the store was. Then, on the Sunday night, Brousseau dropped by to tell her the deed was done. Dionne would never again embarrass Yves Trudeau.

The prosecution was done with Trudeau's sister, hoping she came off as a more innocent and therefore more credible witness to the events. But then it was defense lawyer Daniel Rock's turn with her. He was a skilled criminalist who was used to complicated cases and difficult defendants. His clients included a member of Parliament accused of taking kickbacks and a biker charged with killing a Hells Angel associate. Diminutive and balding on top, Rock possessed a quiet theatricality steeped in research and experience that made him seem larger than life, and a voice that bore listening to.

"Do you always dress like you are today?" he began his cross-examination of Suzanne Trudeau.

"Yes," came the answer.

"What do you know about guns?"

"Not much."

"You've never handled a gun?"

"I'm too busy caring for my children," she replied.

"Not even as a hobby? Not even a little bit?"

Her reply was the same: "No."

"Were you a member of the Popeyes?"

"No," she stated firmly. "My brother was. Not me."

At that point, Rock produced a color photograph his client had given him. In it, Suzanne Trudeau was sitting on a motorcycle on a dirt road, one hand curled around the handlebar. The photo, with cranberry bushes in the background, appeared to have been taken in the autumn. Wearing blue jeans and a black vest that showed off well-toned arms, Suzanne's head was turned toward the camera, a slight smile playing across her face. And there, unmistakable, in a holster sitting on her left hip, was a .357 Magnum, while crooked in her right arm was a machine gun, her fingers on the trigger.

After showing the photo to the Crown, the judge, and the jury, Rock continued his questioning. "Is that a machine gun slung over your shoulder? And a pistol at your hip?"

So much for a young, conservatively dressed mother who was too busy caring for her children to think about guns. On the stand, she had denied the allegation her brother had made that she was a member of the Popeyes. Still, the photograph was damning. In the jurors' mind, Rock hoped, it showed that Suzanne aspired to look just as menacing as her brother. Presumably, that made her just as untrustworthy.

The defense lawyer made equally short shrift of another witness the prosecution had brought forward to bolster their case. Lionel Rousseau was a convicted fraud artist who briefly shared a holding cell with Rock's client, Claude Brousseau. He was a typical "jailhouse rat"—a prisoner promised leniency for testifying that he had overheard an alleged confession. It took Rock only a few minutes to get Rousseau, whom he called a "clown," to recant his entire testimony and wonder aloud why he had agreed to come to court in the first place.

These witnesses had not been hard to grill and expose. Rock understood all too well that his real challenge would be attacking and undermining the hitman himself.

Rock knew that his cross-examination of Yves Trudeau would be central to winning his case. He needed to show the jurors that although Trudeau was now before them, eagerly informing on his former friends in the criminal world, it was only because they had wanted to kill him. And Trudeau knew better than anyone how effective the bikers were at meting out their extreme version of justice. All he had to do was glance at his own bleak and bloody CV.

So Rock proceeded to patiently, ruthlessly, walk Trudeau and the jurors through the litany of crime and murder. He started with an armed bank robbery that Trudeau, at the age of twenty-five and as an eager leader of the Popeyes gang, had committed back in 1971 in Saint-Hyacinthe, about sixty kilometers east of Montreal. Back then, the court hadn't bought Trudeau's protestations of innocence, and he ended up serving his first stint behind bars. Trudeau explained that he had to quit his position as a president of the Popeyes while doing time in prison.

Rock then got Trudeau to admit that, once out of jail, he decided, with fellow Popeyes Yves (Le Boss) Buteau and Yvon (Gorille) Bilodeau, who would later become the senior biker known as "Le Père," to found the first Quebec chapter of the Hells Angels.

"What was your role in that organization?" Rock asked.

"I was a sergeant at arms," Trudeau said.

That sounded official, if not harmless. Rock pushed. "To be more specific, an assassin?" he asked.

"Yes," came the hitman's reply.

And so began the slow and methodical questions about each of the forty-three murders Trudeau admitted to playing a role in. Jean-Marie Viel, who had stolen a Popeyes' motorcycle in 1971, was the first; Trudeau pursued him to teach him a lesson about the evil of taking another person's property. The resulting death, he said, was no more than an unfortunate "accident."

"I don't like the word 'murder,'" he told the court, as if it was a question of semantics.

But Trudeau was not an accidental killer. This was the man who was the first in Quebec to earn the Hells Angels' coveted "Filthy Few" badge, rumored to be given when one has killed for the gang. This was a hired assassin who became so proficient, he worked not only for the Hells Angels but also for the Mafia and the West End Gang, which controlled Montreal's port.

Rock went on to show that Trudeau's actions were not accidents, but deliberate and deadly. He concentrated especially on the bombing in November 1984 at the apartment tower on de Maisonneuve Boulevard, which Trudeau had carried out for the West End Gang to avenge the killing of their leader, Dunie Ryan.

Trudeau, seeming almost proud of his handiwork, admitted he had "calculated everything" from the thickness of the walls to the position of the elevator to make sure he eliminated Paul April and his three associates. "I didn't make a mistake. There were four deaths."

"But others were injured," the lawyer countered, referring to the innocent residents in the building.

"That was inevitable" came the hitman's curt reply.

For Yves Trudeau, killing wasn't a spontaneous act of personal rage or revenge; it was business. Death for dollars. Asked how much he got for each contract killing, Trudeau told the court he pocketed anywhere between $5,000 and $200,000, pretty much all of which he used to support his drug habit.

Trudeau's cash flow didn't stop once he traded in his biker leathers for police protection as an informant. Rock questioned Trudeau extensively about the money he got from the government: $40,000 from the get-go, and a further $10,000 a year once he was released from prison, money that he said he would use to start his own business since, given his unfortunate resumé, no one was likely to hire him.

The defense lawyer also grilled Trudeau about his sister, Suzanne, whose machine-gun-toting photograph had been entered into evidence. Trudeau admitted he had paid for her shooting lessons and claimed that, back in the day, she was a member of the Popeyes.

Rock wrapped up his interrogation of Trudeau by emphasizing that, although he professed to be telling the truth in the witness box, he'd had a propensity for lying all of his life. He had deceived his own fellow gang members and had consistently misled the authorities—and the court in this case, Rock argued. Trudeau had testified that his target, Marc-André Dionne, had received prison leave on three consecutive weekends. But according to the Bordeaux employee in charge of issuing the passes, there were only two granted, not three.

Rock asked Trudeau why, in his initial statement to police about Dionne's death, Trudeau never mentioned it was he who had ordered the young man to be killed.

"I stated the truth, but forgot some details," the hitman said.

As if death was just a detail.

It took Rock more than six hours to make his final arguments before the jury. The case was based on a flimsy tissue of lies, he said, from a trickster who prevaricated as easily as he breathed. He lied to relieve himself of any responsibility and to give his interrogators exactly what they wanted to hear. Nothing was his fault—not his killing of innocents due to mistaken identity, not his murder of a contract's girlfriend just because she was there, and not his execution of a mother trying to protect her son. And those innocents injured in the Maisonneuve bombing? "This Apache, he shrugged and said it was inevitable and that he built his bomb to perfection," Rock told the jury.

Hoping he had demolished Trudeau's credibility, Rock turned his attention to the failings of the police. "The evidence they collected in this case is sorely lacking," he said. He cited the crucial weekend passes from prison that the victim, Marc-André Dionne, received; although they were central to the drug trafficking scheme and his eventual death, the police never bothered to check with Bordeaux officials about the number of passes Trudeau's drug mule had been given. It was a small detail, but a glaring example of tunnel vision. "Investigators believed the assassin, Trudeau, and went from there, failing to independently verify what he said," Rock concluded. "This biased the entire investigation."

There are different theories about what it means when a jury is quick to deliberate and return a verdict. Is it a good sign for the prosecution or the defense? The only thing certain is that they see the case as open and shut.

In this case, featuring Trudeau's first appearance as a government witness, it took the jury only two hours to reject his testimony and acquit his alleged accomplice, Rock's client Claude Brousseau. And that included the time it took for them to have their last free lunch together.

In the aftermath of his debut as a government witness, the headlines in the crime tabloids and the mainstream newspapers made it clear that everyone saw it as a black eye for the justice system, but first and foremost, as a blow against the notorious Yves Trudeau. "First Defeat! The Principal Informant of the Hells Angels Loses His First Match!" stated one. "First Test of the Informant 'Apache' Trudeau Before a Jury: A Friend of the Hells Angels Is Acquitted of Murder," blared another.

To be fair, Trudeau was shouldering the burden for a legal trainwreck that was not entirely his fault. Nowhere did the media mention that it was, in fact, the Crown that lost its case, or the police that failed in their investigation. The loss was down to Yves Trudeau.

Richard Desmarais, the editor-in-chief of the influential *Allo Police*, tried to raise and broaden the stakes. In a hard-hitting editorial under the headline "Grave Error," Desmarais questioned the wisdom of using witnesses like Trudeau—people who have committed heinous crimes—to bring biker gangs and other crime groups to justice when their credibility is central to a case. He warned what it could mean to the other trials at which Trudeau was supposed to be the key prosecution witness. "The career of the informant, Yves (Apache) Trudeau risks becoming very ephemeral following the acquittal of Claude Brousseau, the first such individual to face a trial before a judge and jury because of sworn statements of an ex-member of the Hells Angels," Desmarais cautioned.

Looking back years later, defense lawyer Daniel Rock puts it more bluntly: "How could anyone trust him? You only had to look at him to know he was lying."

That did not bode well for Trudeau's testimony in the cases to come.

16.
A RARE VICTORY

When it came to taking on the Hells Angels, the bungling by authorities was proving downright embarrassing. Yves Trudeau's first attempt to help prosecute outlaw bikers had been a flop.

The justice system had looked even more hapless in February 1986, when Montreal had hosted the Salon de la Moto, a popular motorbike show held each year at the sprawling downtown convention center. One of the officially sanctioned exhibitors was the Hells Angels, with no less than seven kiosks under a huge red-and-white banner that boldly read: *The Hells Angels, The Big Red Machine.*

The display was even more galling because the space had been rented by Michel (Sky) Langlois, a founder of the Popeyes and a prominent member of the HA's South chapter, in charge of gang expansion. He had been rounded up in the summer of 1985 along with many of his fellow Angels for his role in the Lennoxville massacre; a newspaper photo showed him under arrest, his hands cuffed and attached to a chain that locked around his shackled feet. Released shortly afterward on his own recognizance, Langlois had skipped bail. The next newspaper photo of him showed the handsome biker front and center at the motorcycle show, insouciantly posed on a gleaming Harley as if for a fashion shoot. His hair was carefully mussed, his beard close-cropped so that it was not quite a five o'clock shadow, and he sported blue-tinted glasses, a black leather jacket with an HA patch, and jeans. It was a bold display of arrogance by a Hells Angel wanted by the police, a public taunt that stated: "Come and get me—if you can."

By the time twenty SQ officers arrived at the scene, he had fled. "We missed him by a hair," said police spokesman André Blanchette. "He was there when we checked out the gang's booth at the convention center, but when we returned for the arrests, he was gone."

Langlois managed to board a plane for Europe, where he hid out for two years before returning to Quebec and turning himself in to authorities. After all that, he got just a slap on the wrist for having helped to clean up after the massacre.

It was understandable that the government was desperate for things to go better when the trial against four men accused of murder in the Lennoxville massacre opened in Montreal in the fall of 1986.

The trial got underway with the heaviest security the province had ever seen. At the Montreal courthouse on September 14, 1986, there were security checks for everyone entering and an armed police presence in the largest courtroom. The four accused were shackled and handcuffed behind a bulletproof plexiglass cage big enough for thirty people, which had been specially built at a cost of $30,000.

Standing accused of murder were Réjean (Zig-Zag) Lessard, the key plotter behind the Lennoxville massacre, and three of his associates: Jacques (La Pelle) Pelletier, Luc (Sam) Michaud, and Robert (Ti-Maigre) Richard. Yves Trudeau, supposedly the government's biggest catch in its war against the Hells Angels, had appeared at their preliminary hearing with his machine-gun stunt. At the main trial, however, he was a nonentity, either because he had not been an eyewitness to the events in the case or because he had proven unreliable on the stand—or maybe both. This time, the prosecution's case rested on the testimony of two other bikers turned informants. Gerry (Le Chat) Coulombe, the former South chapter prospect, was cooperating with police because he was scared he would be next on the kill list, while Gilles (Le Nez) Lachance, a member of the North chapter whose life was spared, could not forget the bloodbath he had seen. Unlike Trudeau, both were witnesses to what happened that day and afterward. They knew firsthand how brutal and callous the Hells Angels could be, and the lengths to which they were willing to go when members didn't play by their rules.

Prosecutor René Domingue was worried, knowing that the bikers, enriched from the drug trade, had more resources than the state. "They had better sources of income," he recalls. "And it all boils down to what is your budget. They were able to pay the best lawyers."

The Hells Angels would use some of that money to try to buy off the jury.

Unlike Yves Trudeau, Coulombe and Lachance performed well on the stand. Coulombe was up first. An avid reader and history buff whose personal collection included Nazi and US Civil War memorabilia, he made a colorful and convincing witness. He had been an unquestioning gofer in the leadup to the massacre, booking rooms at a local motel for bikers from out of town and picking up the rental truck that would be used to transport the bodies.

He told the jury how he went from eager devotee of the Angels to fearful recruit with a target on his back. At first, he explained, he thought he'd found a home with the South chapter. "Beer cost nothing, chicks cost nothing," he said. "There was always a bed for you." But in July 1985, four months after the massacre, he was called to a meeting at the South chapter's headquarters in Sorel that no one else seemed to know about. He worried that, rather than getting his longed-for Hells Angels patch, he would be killed as an inconvenient witness. He imagined being ambushed with bullets to his head and ending up in the St. Lawrence, just like the five bodies he had helped dispatch in March. So, when he was roused from a fitful sleep on the morning of July 27 by armed police officers, it did not take him long to decide it was in his best interest to cooperate with the investigation. In return, he was given a new identity and a tax-free living allowance of $500 per week—a much less glamorous deal than Trudeau had secured.

To be sure, Coulombe, a former self-declared "minister of war" for the defunct biker gang known as the SS, was not an ideal witness. His criminal record included drug trafficking, assault, contempt of court, breaking parole, and stealing car batteries. He'd been a debt collector with a nasty Doberman pinscher he was willing to use to get people to pay back what they owed, and he'd once smashed in the windows of a car that belonged to the mayor of Baie-Comeau, a city 680 kilometers northeast of Montreal. But looking sedate with his wire-rimmed spectacles and speaking in measured tones, he was a calmer presence on the stand than Trudeau. And unlike Trudeau, he was not a Hells Angels leader or killer, just a flunky who followed orders because he yearned to be admitted to the gang's inner sanctum.

Over a week, Coulombe slowly and patiently took the jurors back to the massacre in March 1985: the unprecedented decision to wipe out almost an entire chapter of misbehaving bikers; the meticulous preparations and planning; the deafening noise of machine guns; and the messy dumping of the bloodied corpses. He had been ordered to keep watch outside in his car; although he heard gunfire inside, he didn't see anything until Guy-Louis (Chop) Adam came running outside, pursued by Robert (Snake) Tremblay. Adam was cut down in short order.

Coulombe and another biker followed the rental truck filled with bodies to the dump site in the St. Lawrence River, traveling along back roads that were mostly gravel. But when the gravel changed to asphalt, the truck's rear door flew open; Coulombe could see full sleeping bags and cement blocks. His car sped up to frantically signal the truck's driver to pull over so that the corpses didn't fall out and litter the highway.

Though he was absent, Trudeau was never far from the proceedings. Coulombe said Réjean Lessard, who insisted Trudeau's body count was well above the forty-three murders he officially confessed to, was frightened the serial killer would one day come after him—frightened enough to tell Coulombe that Trudeau was on the hit list of Laval members to be eliminated.

Defense lawyer Léo-René Maranda pushed Coulombe about why he had failed to mention Trudeau's name when he had testified back in the summer of 1985 at the coroner's inquest into the massacre. Was it because he knew then that Trudeau was a police informant too?

Coulombe never answered directly, but he tried to paint himself as something more than just a snitch. "I'm not an informer, I'm a witness," he insisted.

He may have been a fearful collaborator with authorities, but Coulombe still respected the biker code and did not want to be labeled a snitch.

Then it was Gilles Lachance's turn. In return for testifying for the prosecution, Lachance, known as "Le Nez" because of the size of his nose, had been given round-the-clock police protection, a $200 weekly living allowance, and $40,000 for surgery to change his appearance, including a nose job. The change was so startling, one newspaper described him as coming to court "dressed to the nines and looking like a movie star."

Lachance had done five years in prison on a manslaughter conviction before being released in 1980 and signing up with the Angels. A member of the coke-addled Laval chapter at the time that it was wiped out, he was spared on March 24 because he was not a "sniffer" like the others (he snorted coke maybe twice a week, tops, he said) and immediately swore fealty to Lessard's South chapter.

The SQ had issued a warrant for Lachance as a person of interest in the massacre, finally arresting him in February 1986 near Mont-Laurier, about 240 kilometers northwest of Montreal. But the charges were soon dropped when he agreed to unburden himself for the prosecution. Lachance told police he could not get the images of what he had seen during the massacre out of his mind. Now, in a hushed courtroom, he shared those images with the jurors.

Lachance testified that on March 25, he was calmly perched on a stool in the Sherbrooke clubhouse's kitchen when he heard fighting in the hall beyond. Suddenly, Jacques Pelletier appeared across the counter from him, aiming a .32-caliber automatic weapon at his chest. "Raise your hands and don't move," Pelletier said. As if it had been choreographed in advance, a biker from the Halifax chapter quickly moved in behind Lachance, holding a gun to his head. Lachance stayed still, head down, arms raised. He heard Laurent Viau, the North chapter president and one of the main targets of the slaughter, cry out in anger and fear: "No bloody guns in the clubhouse!" Then there were shots, lots of them, and Viau cried out no more. When the gunfire ended, Lachance was escorted into the hall and the room beyond, where he saw Viau and Michel Mayrand writhing on the floor, moaning as they died. Jean-Guy Geoffrion, the chapter's "chemist," was not moving at all. Nor was Jean-Pierre Mathieu.

The job of stripping the victims and cleaning up the mess of body parts and blood fell to the three men who had been spared: Richard (Bert) Mayrand, Yvon (Le Père) Bilodeau, and Lachance, who testified that "Z," as Réjean Lessard was familiarly called, had other jobs for him too. The next day, Lachance visited Michel (Jinx) Genest, who was recovering in the hospital after an assassination attempt by another gang, to tell him the North chapter had been destroyed and, if he wanted to live, he needed to join the South chapter, as Lachance himself had done. Genest would also need to prove himself by killing Claude (Coco) Roy, a North chapter prospect who had been outside when the massacre occurred; Lessard feared Roy had too big a mouth to be allowed to live.

Lachance further testified that he flew with two other members from the South chapter to Vancouver, to explain to the west coast bikers why the North chapter had to be disciplined in such an extreme way; the idea was that his presence would help, since he was a former North chapter member who could attest to its members having spiraled out of control. Lachance felt guilty that he was being used as an errand boy to justify the slaying of his chapter pals.

But most of all, he told the jurors, Lachance hated that Z made him accompany Normand (Biff) Hamel to visit Trudeau in the Oka rehab center to deliver the message that the hitman was no longer a member in good standing; that he must forfeit his motorcycle and erase any Hells Angels tattoos. The task scared him. *Trudeau* scared him because he knew what the hitman was capable of. But Lachance did what he was told, all the while determined to quietly leave the gang for good. At the end of March, he gathered up everything he owned that was related to the Hells Angels and dropped it off at Bilodeau's home. He was quitting his beloved Angels.

"Why?" came the question in the courtroom.

"I saw what happened on March 24," Lachance replied.

In their final arguments to the jury, the defense lawyers had harsh words for investigators, charging that they were inept and negligent in how they went about gathering information and corroborating evidence. But not once did they deny that their clients were present when the murders took place; instead, they argued that they could not be convicted based on the testimony of witnesses as unreliable and sketchy as Coulombe and Lachance.

For his part, prosecutor René Domingue said the defense argument reminded him of the old story of a man who killed his wife: "His lawyer argues that the man's wife isn't dead. If she is dead, he didn't do it. If he did it, it was self-defense. If the jury doesn't believe it was self-defense, then he was drunk or under the influence of drugs. And if the jury doesn't accept that, he pleads insanity."

The jury took its time sifting through the often graphic evidence. Two weeks went by without a verdict. Despite the overwhelming evidence, the jury seemed deadlocked. Then came a shocking revelation. The judge received a note from one of the jurors that proclaimed: "I was bought—Hells Angels. Juror No. 8." It would turn out that Mario Hamel, a mechanic, had been bribed by a childhood friend who was a member of the HA. He was immediately struck from the jury, charged with obstructing justice by accepting a bribe, and placed in protective custody.

Finally, two days later, on December 3, the verdict came down. Lessard, Pelletier, and Michaud were found guilty on five counts of first-degree murder, while Richard was acquitted.

It was the first major legal victory for the government against the Hells Angels. But it came without any help from Yves Trudeau. Coulombe and Lachance, both of whom had received much less generous packages from the government in return for their testimony, had delivered what Trudeau so far had failed to: credible and convincing evidence.

Could Trudeau, who had been so adept at fulfilling assassination contracts, still fulfill his part of the deal with the justice system? He would have four chances to redeem himself in murder trials over the next year and a half.

17.
"ZERO CREDIBILITY"

The messy business that saw the justice system making deals with despicable killers was not restricted to the biker world. Many people were shocked that Yves Trudeau would do so little jail time for killing more than forty people, but their anger was tempered by the fact that most of his targets were fellow criminals. Clifford Olson, the self-described "Beast of British Columbia," sparked even more outrage because all of his eleven victims were children.

Around the time that Trudeau was reaching the peak of his murder spree, in the early 1980s in Quebec, Olson was beginning his own at the other end of the country. He lured girls and boys between the ages of nine and eighteen, subduing them with alcohol and drugs before torturing and sexually assaulting them. Then he murdered them and disposed of their bodies. Although he was arrested in August 1981, the police had little evidence to nail him for most of the murders. So they struck a notorious cash-for-bodies deal: in exchange for Olson confessing to the eleven murders and showing the RCMP where to find the bodies of those not yet recovered, the authorities agreed to pay $10,000 per victim into a trust for his wife.

Even though Olson was sentenced to life in prison, the relatives of his victims were overcome with grief and fury. They filed a lawsuit demanding that the trust fund be declared fraudulent and the money given to them instead, as compensation for their loss. But their battle, which wound its way up to the Supreme Court of Canada, failed, securing Olson his bounty.

Typical of the public outrage was an August 1986 *Montreal Gazette* editorial that argued the payment to Olson was "repugnant," prompting "fears that criminals might get the message that crime can pay." Still, the newspaper concluded that, however distasteful, "the discretionary power that police now have to make such deals may be useful in highly exceptional cases. Unless police abuse that power, let's keep it." The *Gazette* cited the case of Yves Trudeau as an example of governments "compensating some criminals handsomely." It reminded its readers that Trudeau was to get $10,000 a year for four years and "the steaks-and-colour-TV treatment in prison." But, the newspaper argued, "unlike Mr. Olson, Mr. Trudeau is testifying against many other persons, thus helping to unravel the fabric of organized crime. This technique has proven successful in cracking down on the Mafia in the United States."

The *Gazette* seemed to be suffering from short-term memory loss. Just a few months earlier, in March 1986, when the details of Trudeau's cooperation with authorities first emerged, the paper had denounced the "sweet deal" as "questionable," arguing, "it is hard to think of a more vile person that Quebec has produced." The *Gazette* also overlooked the fact that, in June 1986, Trudeau's first attempt to help police "unravel the fabric of organized crime" had failed miserably in the Brousseau murder trial.

Still, the message of the editorial was clear and undeniably logical: government pacts with devils like Trudeau were justifiable if there was some payoff for the public and the justice system that saw other killers put behind bars.

Again, the question was, could Trudeau deliver the goods?

In early March 1986, a squad of heavily armed SQ officers arrested Hells Angel Régis (Lucky) Asselin in the small town of Dolbeau in Quebec's Saguenay region. According to what Trudeau told police, Asselin had helped eliminate Sylvain Dagenais, a pushy drug dealer who was killed in September 1984, the second of two related murders. The first had occurred the previous June, when Robert Thomas, a tough guy who had been attempting to insinuate himself and his drug business into nightclubs in Laval, was shot to death as he left his home in Montreal's east-end neighborhood of Rosemont. Dagenais was killed three months later when Trudeau detonated a bomb that he and his partner Michel Blass had placed under the driver's seat of their target's Camaro while it was parked in front of a Laval nightclub.

Based on information provided by Trudeau and Blass, on March 11, 1986, in addition to Asselin, the police arrested Bruno Zanetti, the owner of a Laval strip club called Les Déesses (The Goddesses); the club's manager, Carol Dufour; and Jean-Charles Laliberté, its grizzled doorman.

Laliberté's case was separated from the others because the Crown hoped he would turn on them. He refused, and, in late 1986, he was the first of the four to be tried before a Quebec Superior Court judge and jury. They listened as more than seventy witnesses—the most important of whom were Blass and, to a lesser extent, Trudeau—wove a story that placed the doorman in the plot from the get-go.

Blass, brash and confident, recounted that Laliberté had attended an initial planning meeting at a Chinese restaurant, and that it was Laliberté who came out to the parking lot of Les Déesses to give him two .45-caliber revolvers and $8,000 as a down payment for the job. Blass found Thomas easily enough, staking out his apartment and following him for a while before gunning him down. Next on the hit list was Dagenais, a tough twenty-five-year-old who allegedly specialized in extortion and debt collection, and had developed a morbid predilection for sleeping on top of a coffin. Perhaps that was appropriate; after the murder of Thomas, his partner in crime, Dagenais must have known his days were numbered. But Blass had trouble finding Dagenais. That was when Asselin and Trudeau entered the picture, Blass testified.

When it was Trudeau's turn on the witness stand, he told the jury he had been hired on September 21, 1984, because of his expertise in building bombs. Upon locating Dagenais's Camaro five days later, they wasted no time in killing him. Trudeau described crouching in Blass's truck as he carefully prepared the remote-controlled bomb, made with six sticks of dynamite. Hours later, Dagenais was dead. He and Blass decided to have a drink to celebrate the kill, Trudeau concluded.

For Laliberté's lawyer, Christiane Filteau, one of the few women practicing criminal law at the time, the case was initially daunting, if only because it was one of her first. Until then, she had been a quiet second to the much more experienced, colorful, and voluble lawyers at her firm, Sidney Leithman and Robert LaHaye, well known for their successful defenses of Mafia figures, West End Gang members, and bikers. With her bosses busy preparing to defend Zanetti, Dufour, and Asselin, she had been given only a few months to prepare for Laliberté's trial. "I didn't sleep much, that was for sure," she recalls. "It was me, the young female defense lawyer, against two contract killers, one of whom had admitted to participating in forty-three murders, with my client's freedom at stake."

Blass, with his prompt, assured replies to her questions, proved an adept adversary. So Filteau tried to undermine the circumstantial evidence. Although he had no criminal record, Laliberté did admit during cross-examination by the Crown that he had known Blass for years. The two men had hunted together and had gone fishing on repeated occasions—but that did not mean they had plotted together to kill two men. Indeed, shown a photo taken years earlier during a fishing expedition, in which he held a .45-caliber revolver, Laliberté rejected the Crown's suggestion that it was the gun that killed Thomas. How could that be proven from a dog-eared old Polaroid?

Trudeau, on the other hand, was much easier to demolish. In the witness box he suffered memory lapses, mumbled, and answered "I don't remember" more often than not. "It became a refrain," Filteau says. Once again, Trudeau had proven to be a dreadful witness.

The jury of seven men and five women began to deliberate on Wednesday, December 17, 1986. Two days later, they appeared divided, unable to reach a verdict. On Saturday morning, the judge asked them to try one more time. An hour later, they managed a consensus.

Laliberté was escorted into court, shaking, shuffling, and sweating. Minutes later, tears of relief were running down his face. Not guilty, the jurors had ruled.

"The Informants Lose Another Match!" screamed a tabloid headline. "The Doorman of Les Déesses of Laval Acquitted of Two Murders."

"Michel Blass and Apache Trudeau had zero credibility," Filteau says. "They were revolting men."

18.
"MERCENARIES OF PERJURY"

Yves Trudeau had blown his first two court appearances. Would he fare any better the third time?

Next up for Trudeau—and his fellow informant Michel Blass—was the joint trial of Bruno Zanetti, Carol Dufour, and Régis Asselin. It began in March 1987 and lasted nearly three months. This time, Trudeau and Blass went toe to toe with the more experienced and polished criminal defense attorneys Sidney Leithman and Robert LaHaye. Again, the lawyers deployed the tried-and-true tactic of trying to make the prosecution witnesses look more guilty than the defendants. Taking a page from Daniel Rock's playbook, they subjected the informants to probing, detailed questions about their sordid pasts, asking them to recount the details of each of the murders they had committed. In Trudeau's case, they made him describe his actions as a leader of the Popeyes and his role in founding the first chapter of the Hells Angels in Canada.

In his final arguments, LaHaye did not mince words. "These men are mercenaries of perjury," he said. "They are dumb scoundrels who wanted only to serve themselves and sold their testimony for 1,001 privileges in prison, trying to put our clients in prison for crimes they themselves committed. They have used the sacred oath that we take before testifying to send into the shadows people who they denounce as being accomplices of *their* own previous crimes."

LaHaye stressed that, between them, Blass and Trudeau had been involved in no less than fifty-five murders, which they had managed to transform into pleas of manslaughter in return for their testimony, despite inconsistencies on details such as a description of the interior of the strip club, where contracts were allegedly finalized, payments handed over, and toasts raised to a job well done. "These two killers have found a new power," LaHaye continued. "They lie for their own benefit."

The jurors agreed and acquitted the accused.

Trudeau had testified at three trials since June 1986, and had blown each one. The headlines were bold black echoes of those that had appeared before. "Apache Trudeau and Mike Blass Lose Another One!" blared one. It continued, "Jurors Don't Trust Testimony from Turncoats, Lawyer Says After Trio Acquitted of Murders."

The authorities had kept Trudeau away from the high-profile prosecutions of the men accused of the Lennoxville murders, perhaps not trusting their own star witness. He had made a brief appearance at one preliminary hearing, but did not merit a single mention in news reports about the 1986 trial that saw convictions against ringleader Réjean Lessard and two other Angels.

Perhaps prosecutors hoped Trudeau would fare better when, in April 1987, they went after David (Wolf) Carroll, the charismatic leader of the Halifax Hells Angels, and three of his Nova Scotia partners, accusing them of taking part in the culling of the North chapter. The Crown asserted that Carroll had helped trigger the massacre when he was angered by having to hand over money to a coke-sniffing Yves Trudeau. He was then, by all accounts, involved in the plotting of the Lennoxville massacre and was present during the murders themselves.

The Crown was forced to rely on mainly circumstantial evidence, basing its case on the fact that during a police raid on the Halifax chapter's clubhouse, investigators seized expensive motorcycle parts they traced back to the five murder victims. So prosecutors were counting on the testimony of three biker informants: Coulombe, Lachance, and Trudeau. Coulombe, who was outside the Sherbrooke clubhouse keeping watch during the murders and saw little of the actual killings, repeated what he had said at the earlier trial. Lachance offered a possible explanation for the bike parts showing up in Nova Scotia, noting that an agreement had been reached to divide the North chapter's assets among the remaining clubhouses, including Halifax. Since Trudeau wasn't at Lennoxville, he was not called to testify; all he could have contributed was the story of his trip to see Carroll on Valentine's Day, 1985—not even six weeks before the killings—to collect money as part of his payment for the Maisonneuve bombing.

Thirty witnesses and 110 exhibits later, the Crown rested its case. The bikers' lawyers, Léo-René Maranda and Jacques Bouchard, were so confident of victory, they declined to even present a defense. They gambled that the jurors either would not believe the informants or would consider their evidence too weak to convict Carroll and the other Nova Scotians of conspiracy to commit murder.

They were right. On June 17, 1987, after nearly seven days of deliberation, the jury acquitted all four outright.

Upon their acquittal, Carroll and two of his buddies (the third, who was doing time on another charge in Nova Scotia, would later be set free there) walked out of the Montreal courthouse silent and triumphant, wearing jeans, Hells Angels T-shirts, and slight smiles, their eyes hidden behind sunglasses. Ignoring the scrum of reporters and cameras, they took refuge in Maranda's office a few doors away, awaiting their ride to freedom. It arrived in the shape of a flashy black Jaguar driven by Robert Richard, Réjean Lessard's former right hand and the lone biker acquitted in the murder trial the year before that sent three others from the South chapter to prison. They jumped in and were gone.

It was not the last time David Carroll would escape justice.

Since turning informant in 1985, Trudeau had failed miserably in his appearances on the witness stand. He had a fourth and final chance in January 1988, when Régis (Lucky) Asselin, who was living up to his nickname, went on trial yet again for murder.

This murder dated back to July 1983. Michel Desormiers, whose sister was married to Montreal Mafia boss Frank Cotroni, was shot five times on the doorstep outside his home: three times in the head and twice in the back. The killing of such a high-profile crime figure was a mystery to authorities until Trudeau included it among the forty-three assassinations he had participated in. For the hit on Desormiers, he said, he had worked with Asselin and another biker. Now Asselin faced first-degree murder charges in a seemingly open-and-shut case.

Asselin's lawyer, Martin Tremblay, knew that his client, a hardened biker, was not someone the jurors were going to like. So he did what all the good defense lawyers had been doing: he put Trudeau on trial instead.

Known in the tabloids as "The Little Lawyer from Alma," Tremblay was short and slight, with thick, unstyled curly brown hair and a folksy manner befitting a lawyer from a small town in Quebec's Saguenay region. He provided a master class in showing the inconsistencies in Trudeau's testimony, and he trusted the jurors to fill in the gaps rather than telling them outright what they were not hearing.

Like other lawyers had done before him, Tremblay asked Trudeau to laboriously detail each of the forty-three murders he had admitted to participating in. Wasn't he a founding member of the Hells Angels? Wasn't he a member of the Filthy Few, boasting of his murders for the gang? Was it hard to kill? What did he get from the justice department to become an informant? It was a sure-fire recipe for taking the witness down; invariably, the trials went downhill from there.

Over the course of a few minutes, Trudeau could be rude and surly, then a smirking know-it-all. It was never clear whether his answers were the truth or just what he thought the prosecution wanted to hear. In the end, it didn't matter. The jury may not have liked the accused, but it was the character of the informants testifying against them—Trudeau and, to a lesser extent, his buddy Michel Blass—that made all the difference.

During his final arguments, Tremblay was in constant motion, gesticulating and speaking quickly and clearly. Trudeau and Blass were odious killers and truants, he charged, monsters who had killed together, informed together, and now, for the foreseeable future, lived together on the exclusive fourth floor of Parthenais in highly protected cells reserved for turncoats. "I did not hesitate to introduce you to my client, Régis Asselin, who told you about the bullet lodged in his thigh, the result of Yves Trudeau accidentally shooting him in the Hells Angels clubhouse," Tremblay continued. "If you believe him—if he created a shred of reasonable doubt in your mind—you have no choice but to acquit. On the informants' side, we find killers who today are paid by the police to incriminate others. With the favors they have received, and are receiving, do you not believe they have an interest in lying and committing perjury?"

The jury did. "Lucky and Conan Acquitted," blared the *Allo Police* headline on January 31, 1988. ("Conan" was the nickname for Asselin's co-accused in the case, biker Jean-Marc Nadeau.) "Another Victory for the Little Lawyer from Alma, This Time Against the Hells Informants!"

It had been a dreadful run for Yves Trudeau: in five murder trials from June 1986 to January 1988, he had failed each time to convince jurors that he was telling the truth. His former allies, despite the serious allegations against them, walked away unscathed.

After the trial that ended in acquittals for Zanetti, Dufour, and Asselin, defense lawyer Robert LaHaye used the column he wrote weekly in *Allo Police* to pen a scathing letter to Blass and Trudeau. "Dear scoundrels and trash," he began. "Since the start of the 1980s, you have been reproducing, swarming and stuffing yourself with compliments, honours and privileges in police departments and 'suites' on police premises. And, in return for these boundless favours on which you have never ceased to feast, like cockroaches and leeches in stinking carrion, you show your gratitude to those who will beatify you by perjuring yourselves, from one year to the next, from one court to the other, against innocents. Your sudden 'conversion' is matched only by your playing to your most base of motivations: to assure your security and survival, to protect yourselves against the denunciation of your fellow men and, at the same time, to satisfy your personal hatred and desire for revenge."

The column continued, asking what price Trudeau and Blass had to pay for being Judases. Not much, it appeared. Rather, they were *paid* thousands of dollars and given privileges such as their own televisions and telephones, visits with loved ones, and other treats. "As soon as cross-examination exposes you for what you really are . . . your masks quickly fall and you appear in your true form: killers and hitmen to those in the great mercenary pantheon of all-purpose witnesses, prostitutes of testimony for whom the oath has no value and for whom the truth is changeable."

In conclusion, LaHaye urged Blass and Trudeau to "crawl back into the rotting decomposition of their trash bins" as "Lady Justice" triumphed over their lies.

Certainly, LaHaye's angry penned outburst was self-serving. His clients, affiliated with a strip club, might themselves have appeared unsavory. Still, for the jury, any risk posed by freeing these men was trumped by their fear and distrust of the prosecution's star witness, Yves (Apache) Trudeau, who had failed so disastrously in one trial after another.

PART THREE

"I SEE IT AS A PUNISHMENT"

19.
SAFE BEHIND BARS

Yves Trudeau had been an ineffective and at times disastrous witness for the prosecution. But he had fulfilled his end of the bargain he had made with police and prosecutors when he testified against his former cronies. Now the justice system had to deliver on its promises.

For four years, Trudeau sat in his cell on the fourth floor of the SQ's Parthenais headquarters, watching his color television, following the news, and enjoying visits with family. This was as luxurious as life in prison could be in Quebec, with favors, steak dinners to his heart's content, and the knowledge that he was safe. He was allowed "family visits," though what that meant is unclear. It is not known what happened to Jeannine Keagle, who was described as his live-in girlfriend when she appeared briefly at Brousseau's trial in June 1986. In 1985, a few stories in media outlets such as the *Montreal Gazette* and *La Presse* made mention of an unnamed wife and children, and John Dalzell, the former motorcycle cop who gave the biker rides home on the back of his Harley, vaguely recalls chitchat about family. But Trudeau was always tight-lipped about those closest to him.

It was his nature—and the knee-jerk defense of a hitman who knew firsthand what could happen to loved ones.

After four years, he was transferred to a provincial prison outside Quebec to serve out the rest of his sentence. A small, unprepossessing man, his presence and personality had once been defined by his renown as a killer and his membership in a biker gang that never shied from violence. But at least he was still alive. Like Trudeau, Régis (Lucky) Asselin had been targeted for execution. He had escaped earlier assassination attempts and two murder raps, thanks in part to Trudeau's inept testimony. At 10 p.m. on February 2, 1990, Lucky's luck ran out when he walked out of a bar in Saint-Hubert, on Montreal's South Shore, into a hail of bullets.

If Trudeau heaved a sigh of relief that he hadn't suffered Asselin's fate, he must have laughed out loud at the irony of what was happening to Allan Ross, the West End Gang leader who had hired him in 1984 to avenge the death of Dunie Ryan.

On October 7, 1991, Ross was arrested in Fort Lauderdale, Florida. Justice for the man known as "The Weasel" had been more than five years in the making. As part of their plea bargain, both Trudeau and Blass had fingered Ross as the man who had ordered the Maisonneuve bombing. Yet he was never arrested for the murders, or even for his well-known drug trafficking operations. True, there was no other evidence—no wiretaps or written communications—tying Ross to the violent act. All police had was a surveillance photograph that showed Ross talking to Trudeau and the Hells Angels at Dunie Ryan's funeral, which wasn't proof of much at all.

What no one knew at the time was that Ross had a secret weapon to help keep him out of jail: high-powered protection inside the upper ranks of the police. Ross's go-to defense attorney, Sidney Leithman, was a criminal lawyer who may have been more criminal than lawyer. Short and stocky, Leithman often sported aviator glasses and a gold pinky ring that had been a gift from the West End Gang. His roster of clients included Mafia dons and Colombian cartel chiefs. And on Ross's behalf, Leithman had corrupted the head of the RCMP's Montreal drug squad, Inspector Claude Savoie. Money changed hands, at least $200,000, and in return, through the lawyer, Savoie provided Ross with information about ongoing investigations.

Things got murkier when, in May 1991, Leithman was gunned down on his way to work in his Saab convertible. Though undoubtedly a gangland slaying, his murder remains unsolved to this day. The death forced Ross to deal directly with Savoie. Because he wanted to travel to his favorite vacation spot in Florida, where he was also running a major drug importation business, he asked the RCMP inspector to find out what, if anything, American authorities had on him.

When Savoie called Dave McGee, the federal prosecutor in North Florida who had been building a case against the West End Gang leader since 1986, McGee was furious. "Savoie calls out of the blue asking us all these questions, and he's asking questions he should not be asking," McGee says. "He's trying to find out information on a grand jury indictment which is secret. It is sealed by a court. He was trying to use his status as a Mountie to get information from federal agents in Florida."

Foolishly, Ross decided to chance the trip. "He was arrogant," McGee says. "He thought he could get away with it because he had gotten away with it so many times. We got our guys in Montreal watching him to alert us when he actually does come down. And sure enough, he came to Florida. Huge mistake."

Ross was arrested as soon as he landed in Fort Lauderdale and charged with smuggling thousands of kilos of cocaine and hundreds of tons of marijuana through the United States and into Canada. It was hugely embarrassing to the Canadian justice system that a powerful Montreal drug kingpin was arrested and jailed not in his own country, but in the United States.

McGee's indictment also accused Ross of conspiracy to murder as part of building up his drug empire. Back in 1985, Ross's unstoppable streak of vengeance for Dunie Ryan's death led him to have his own hitman David Singer, who'd killed the third man involved in Ryan's murder, executed in Florida. One of the men involved in that plot had fingered Ross when he was arrested in 1990 on a drug charge.

Back in Canada, the story took a dark twist two months after Ross's arrest. The CBC's investigative TV show *The Fifth Estate* had been looking into the connections between Savoie and Ross. So were the RCMP. On Monday, December 21, 1991, the day before *The Fifth Estate* was set to broadcast its revelations, Savoie shot himself with his service revolver at RCMP headquarters in Ottawa just as Mountie investigators were coming to question him.

Dave McGee, as a veteran organized crime prosecutor, was shocked by the revelations of the West End Gang's corruption of such a high-profile Mountie. "What access to information that gave Allan Ross!" he says. "That was astounding. I mean, I've seen lots of corrupt cops in the United States, but I've never seen anyone at that level. That was something. That was extraordinary."

Equally extraordinary was the security that surrounded Ross's trial when it got underway in Gainesville, Florida, in the spring of 1992. Given the Canadian's propensity for violence, the Americans stationed snipers on the courthouse rooftops and deployed dogs to sniff out bombs.

To convince the jury that Ross was a global drug trafficker, McGee needed to expose his track record. "As a part of the proof in a case like this, you always want to demonstrate the violence in an organization," he explains. And who better than Yves Trudeau to provide evidence of The Weasel's killer instincts? McGee asked Ken Sweeney if he could get Trudeau to come down. The Montreal detective had been investigating the West End Gang for years and was assigned to help the Americans prosecute Ross. He contacted the SQ liaison with the Montreal force, who in turn contacted the handler in charge of Trudeau while he was in prison. "The answer was no, because psychologically it would not be good for the inmate's integration and mental health," Sweeney recalls.

Sweeney tried to soften the bad news by telling McGee that Trudeau was "a horrible person" with a horrible track record on the stand. "It's good you don't have him, because no one has ever been convicted based on his testimony," the detective explained. "Juries hate him more than the accused!"

McGee smiled and said, only half-jokingly, "You don't understand. I don't want him as a witness. I want him as an exhibit." As McGee later explained in an interview, "I didn't think Trudeau was going to tell the truth. I wanted to put him on the stand as an exhibit. Like, 'Ladies and gentlemen of the jury, here's the guy that did it. How many people did you kill?' I have questions about the deal he got up there."

As it turned out, McGee didn't need Trudeau. Over six weeks, more than a hundred witnesses, at least fifteen of them gang informants of various kinds, were paraded through the court. At one point, as he was being led out of the courtroom, Ross saw a Montreal police detective who was testifying against him. According to author D'Arcy O'Connor, Ross muttered, "Your new TV and VCR is on its way." American court officials interpreted the comment as an attempted bribe, but Sweeney set them straight, explaining it was far more serious: it was a threat referring to the fatal bombing Yves Trudeau had carried out for Ross.

On May 15, 1992, the jury found Ross guilty of conspiring to import and traffic in at least ten thousand kilograms of cocaine and more than three hundred tons of marijuana from 1975 to 1989. The judge sentenced him to life imprisonment with no chance of parole and fined him $10 million.

That was not the end of Ross's legal nightmares. In October 1993, he was found guilty of conspiracy for ordering the hit on David Singer. In what could only be described as judicial overkill, the judge sentenced him to thirty years in prison on top of his multiple life sentences. Allan Ross was going to die behind bars.

The irony was that not long after the former West End Gang leader was hauled away in chains to a high-security American penitentiary, the man he had hired to kill his enemies walked out of jail a free man. Yves Trudeau had come to the end of his seven-year prison term. He was set to enjoy life on the outside—on parole, hidden under the witness protection program, but essentially a free man.

20.
A BLOODY LEGACY

It is not known exactly when Yves Trudeau was paroled, or even from which province. But sometime in 1994, when he was released under a new identity, the Sûreté du Québec began its job of watching over him for the rest of his life. That was its responsibility under the plea agreement, and a necessity since he had been given a life sentence for his crimes despite having served such a tiny portion of it.

Forced to live a quiet life, Trudeau settled in the Valleyfield area, sixty-five kilometers west of Montreal, on the south shore of the St. Lawrence River—the waterway he'd used as his own personal cemetery, tossing in victims like they were garbage, and where his friends' bullet-ridden bodies had been dumped. The former assassin had little training for any legal trade, other than one that paid minimum wage. He ended up driving a transport bus for a seniors' health-care facility and taking care of its residents: helping them go to the bathroom, pushing wheelchairs, opening doors, and helping unsteady feet negotiate steps. After a life filled with expensive drugs, violence, and a "family" of like-minded men, perhaps he found it boring and frustrating. There is no indication he followed up on his statement to a journalist during a break at one trial: that he would work with youth to ensure they did not follow in his footsteps.

The man he became was a ghost, living far from the action. But his bloody legacy lived on. Trudeau must have watched with amazement, and perhaps a bit of envy, as the Hells Angels launched an unprecedented biker war that raged unabated for eight years, from 1994 to 2002. Although he never directly participated in it, he had in many ways sown the seeds for its unyielding violence, having shown bikers over his fifteen-year career as a contract killer that they could deploy bombs and bullets with near impunity.

And while Trudeau had operated in the shadows, the Quebec biker war was even more scary because it was waged in full view of the public, with utter disregard for the lives of innocents who might be caught in the crossfire—what Trudeau had, in testimony, called inevitable "collateral damage."

Following in Trudeau's footsteps, Maurice (Mom) Boucher took the assassin's fifteen-year killing spree and his brazen confidence that the police would never catch him to the next level, becoming Canada's most famous—and most feared—Hells Angel.

Boucher grew up in Montreal's tough, poor Hochelaga-Maisonneuve neighborhood. A grade nine dropout, by the time he was in his early twenties he had racked up an increasingly violent record of crimes that included shoplifting, break and enter, armed robbery, and then the sexual assault of a woman while holding a knife to her throat. It was during this period that, like Yves Trudeau years before him, he found fellowship in a gang of like-minded "brothers," a white supremacist motorcycle gang in east-end Montreal called the SS.

The Lennoxville massacre in March 1985, which spelled the end of Trudeau's career in the Hells Angels, opened the door for Boucher. The slayings and all the subsequent arrests, trials, and convictions depleted the ranks of the Quebec Hells Angels. The massacre also left a power vacuum, with Réjean Lessard and several of his henchmen serving serious time in prison. It provided the perfect opportunity for a new, charismatic, and dangerous leader like Boucher to rise through the ranks.

Boucher was suitably impressed with the ruthlessness behind the Lennoxville massacre; his only criticism was that Lessard had not eliminated the North chapter altogether. He leapt at the chance to join what he considered a glamorous crime organization with an international reputation. His fellow SS member, Normand Hamel, who had rallied to the HA a few months earlier, sponsored Boucher's membership, and on May 1, 1987, Maurice Boucher became a full-patch Hells Angel in the Sorel chapter.

Bespectacled and barrel-chested, he earned the nickname "Mom" because, just like an overbearing mother, he was always watching his men to make sure everything was okay. As the new leader of the Angels, Boucher picked up where Trudeau had left off, getting rid of rival bikers, starting with members of the Outlaws, whom Trudeau had frequently targeted. In September 1989, an Outlaws clubhouse was firebombed; the following year, the president of the Montreal Outlaws was gunned down in a drive-by shooting, while his top lieutenant was killed with three bullets to the head. By 1990, the Outlaws were essentially wiped off the criminal map, and Boucher turned to his most powerful rivals in the biker world: the Rock Machine.

Sitting in his jail cell, four years into his sentence, Yves Trudeau must have smiled. Boucher, whose name translates to "butcher," was finishing what he had begun.

Boucher unleashed a biker war the likes of which the world had not seen before. By the time it was over, in 2002, at least 162 people would be dead—more than the carnage in Chicago during the Al Capone years or any Mafia war in New York or Italy.

At stake was control of an exploding drug trade and its ever-increasing riches. To keep control of most of the profits, Boucher and his closest allies set up the all-powerful Nomads chapter, going against a long-standing tradition among the Hells Angels around the world. It was customary for chapters to be local or regional, with the location emblazoned at the bottom of the HA vests or jackets. But Boucher's Nomads, as the name implied, could roam and rule anywhere, and all HA bikers in Quebec had to pay tribute to them. Along with Boucher, two of the most prominent Nomads were men Yves Trudeau had dealt with extensively: David Carroll and Normand Hamel.

Taking a cue from Trudeau's successful run as "the Mad Bomber," the Angels and their enemies turned to explosives as one of the most effective ways to spread death and terror, with no less than 84 bombings during the war and an additional 120 cases of arson. Bikers stole dynamite from mines and construction sites or got their hands on C-4 explosives, and they perfected ways to detonate their weapons remotely. At one point, bombs were going off almost weekly in Montreal.

Yet as the bodies piled up, the authorities seemed remarkably unconcerned. Oh sure, there were the usual pronouncements about public safety and crackdowns. But no serious investigations or specialized police squads were formed to take on the bikers. "I'll tell you honestly, the department didn't give two shits," admits André (Butch) Bouchard, a Montreal cop who had taken on the Popeyes and rose up the Montreal police department's ranks to become head of homicide in 2000. "They're killing each other. I give a hell if some guy pops somebody who just got out of jail? No. We didn't give a shit."

Bombs went off in homes, cars, and clubhouses and on the street. Sometimes they went off by accident, or they didn't explode at all. Three Rock Machine members were killed as they planted a bomb outside the clubhouse of a Hells Angels' affiliate group; when one of the targeted bikers fired a shotgun at the bombers, the bullets detonated the charges. On another occasion, an enemy of Mom Boucher parked a truck jammed with dynamite near a restaurant where Boucher was eating. The vehicle was towed away by unwitting parking authorities before the bomb could be detonated.

As happened with Trudeau's assassinations, innocent civilians were all too often caught in the biker war frenzy. A thirty-four-year-old father of two was filling up his car at a gas station in Saint-Eustache, just north of Montreal, when two men drove up in a van and sprayed him with bullets. The rival gang member they were targeting apparently had a car of the same make and color, and some of the same numbers on its license plate.

In the Saint-Leonard neighborhood in north Montreal, two hitmen entered a car rental agency looking for a manager named Serge, who was a member of a biker affiliate group. When another employee with the same first name introduced himself, they opened fire with their .357 Magnum handguns, killing the wrong man.

The costliest mistake—not only because of the loss of another innocent life but also in terms of the resulting political fallout—occurred in August 1995, when a drug-dealing biker was killed by a car bomb in his Jeep outside a bunker on Adam Street in Hochelaga-Maisonneuve. It was a hot summer day, and an eleven-year-old named Danny Desrochers was walking along the same street when a piece of metal the size of a baby's little finger sliced into his skull. He died in a coma four days later.

"I'm convinced today that the person who pressed the button to have the bomb explode saw children across the street," says a furious André Bouchard. "There was no way he could not see the children across the street."

What exploded next was outrage, as photos of the cute blond boy appeared on TV screens and newspaper front pages around the world. "People are asking why this is happening. They're not living in Beirut," the embattled Montreal police chief, Jacques Duchesneau, declared. Under fire, police and politicians finally took action and set up a joint police strike force known as Carcajou, or Wolverine, bringing together the Sûreté du Québec, the RCMP, and the Montreal police.

Naming the squad after a sharp-toothed animal known for its viciousness turned out to be appropriate, but perhaps not in the way authorities expected.

What should have been a show of law enforcement's unity and strength collapsed into police rivalry and back-biting. Instead of exposing the bikers and their murderous war tactics, Wolverine highlighted the incompetence of the SQ, helping to explain why, in past years, the provincial police force had done such a poor job of handling their star informant, Yves Trudeau. The SQ was careless about its confidential snitches inside the biker gangs and jealous of the informants run by other police agencies.

For their part, the Montreal police didn't trust the SQ. "They'd steal your information, take credit for your busts, and lie to you about their own informants," recalls one angry Montreal police detective who worked with Wolverine. The Montreal police chief eventually pulled all his men out of the Wolverine squad.

Things only got worse for the beleaguered SQ when, already rocked by allegations of wrongdoing, it came under withering criticism from a special government inquiry known as the Poitras Commission, set up in 1996 to look into the police force's dysfunction. The commission's final 1,700-page report was scathing, describing the SQ as incompetent and unprofessional, and accusing some of its officers of obstruction of justice, evidence tampering, and threatening witnesses. It also revealed that the hapless force even had the temerity to plagiarize a report on organized crime written by its rivals in the Montreal police.

The inquiry focused on SQ missteps that occurred a decade after Yves Trudeau's arrest; there was nothing about him in the report. Nevertheless, it indicated that the police force that handled such a key informant was not at the top of its game.

With the police forces fighting amongst themselves, Boucher decided to elevate his war against the police and the justice system. Having largely succeeded in wiping out rival biker gangs like the Outlaws and the Rock Machine, the HA leader set his sights higher. By the late spring of 1997, he wanted to attack anyone who he believed threatened his illicit empire: judges, politicians, police chiefs, and even journalists.

He began by getting a biker named Stéphane Gagné and several accomplices to kill two people chosen at random who worked in the prison system. In June 1997, they shot and killed Diane Lavigne, a mother of two grown children and an eleven-year veteran guard at Bordeaux Prison, as she was driving home from work. Barely three months later, in September, they gunned down Pierre Rondeau as he was driving an armored prison transport bus to the Rivière-des-Prairies detention center in north-end Montreal. He was the father of a teenage boy.

Police and prosecutors caught a break when Gagné was arrested and agreed to testify against Boucher. To much fanfare, the Hells Angel leader was arrested and charged with murder. Everything would hinge on the testimony of the informant whose biker nickname was "Godasse," or "Old Shoe." In many ways, Stéphane Gagné was a watered-down version of the more infamous informant who had preceded him. But where Trudeau was cold and calculating, Gagné was typical of the aspiring "hang-arounds" who were desperate to get into the good graces of the Hells Angels and don the official Death's Head jackets; he had even named his son Harley David. As a teen, he had eked out a measly criminal career pushing drugs, then graduated to car theft and break-and-enters before operating crack houses and shooting galleries.

A professional hitman he was not.

Still, when the murder trial against Boucher opened in November 1998, Stéphane Gagné was pretty much all the prosecution had, much as the justice system had been forced to rely on the equally unlikable Yves Trudeau in the biker trials a dozen years earlier.

And just like Trudeau, Gagné was a disaster, at least in his first stint on the witness stand. In a mumbling monotone and at times incomprehensible joual (French slang), he recounted under the prosecutor's guidance how Boucher had recruited him for the murder of the guards and congratulated him after the killings. But then the skilled and shrewd defense lawyer, Jacques Larochelle, did what others before him had pulled off with Trudeau: he grilled the government's star witness to make him even more detestable in the jurors' eyes—and by implication less credible than the accused killer who sat in the prisoner's dock behind bulletproof glass.

"All the company you kept, your whole life, was spent with criminals like yourself, is that correct?" Larochelle began.

"Yes."

"You shared their values, you adhered to their lifestyle, and you were satisfied with being a criminal?"

"Yes," came the sullen reply from the witness box.

"During this entire time, you evidently had no respect for authority?"

"No."

"No respect for other people's property?"

"No."

"No respect for the truth?"

"No."

Larochelle ended his legal dissection by asking Gagné why he turned informant. "Not only did you talk to avoid twenty-five years in prison, you also wanted to talk so that you would not be killed?" he asked.

"Yes."

"Which of the two was more important in your mind?" Larochelle pushed.

"Staying alive," came the simple reply.

It was all eerily similar to how lawyer Daniel Rock had demolished Yves Trudeau on the stand during his first appearance in 1986 as the primary witness in a biker murder trial.

The result was the same too, with the jury deliberating just three days before they pronounced Maurice Boucher not guilty.

Delighted and perhaps even a bit surprised, the triumphant Hells Angels leader stormed out of the courtroom a free man and, to many, a hero. That very night, he went to a boxing match at Montreal's Molson Centre, where some of the audience greeted him with a standing ovation. Police commander André Bouchard happened to be there, working as a ringside judge. "We heard an uproar, and as I turned to my left, it was like Moses had parted the water, and who did we see coming through the crowd—Mom Boucher in full colors, escorted by his henchmen," Bouchard recalls. "What broke my heart was seeing hundreds of people actually give him a standing ovation as if he was a rock star."

Maurice Boucher's knockout punch to the justice system was short-lived. The first year of the new millennium turned out to be a rotten one for the Hells Angels leader. In April 2000, his close friend and fellow Nomad, Normand (Biff) Hamel fell victim to biker bullets. Hamel had survived an earlier attempt in 1995 by the rival Rock Machine when two of their members were arrested and charged with plotting his murder. This time, he was not so fortunate. In a daylight attack worthy of Trudeau, Hamel was ambushed in a suburban parking lot while he and his wife were taking their son to a medical appointment. Unarmed, he tried to flee but took two bullets in the back.

Hamel was the most senior Hells Angel to be eliminated in the biker war. From the safety of his South Shore refuge, did Yves Trudeau mourn a fallen comrade? Or was he glad that the biker who in 1985 came to threaten him at the Oka addiction center had himself become a fallen Angel?

In October 2000, Maurice Boucher got more bad news: an appeals court dismissed his earlier acquittal on the charges of murdering the two prison officials and he was arrested again. While in jail, he witnessed what at the time was the biggest roundup of Hells Angels in Canadian history. Operation Springtime 2001, as it was called, saw the arrest of more than 140 bikers, practically every Angel in Quebec, including all but one of Boucher's elite Nomads. More than a decade after the Hells Angels had unleashed a wave of violence in the province, the police had finally gotten their act together. Using an informant named Dany Kane, who was burrowed deep in the biker hierarchy, they had gathered a massive amount of wiretaps, video surveillance, bank records, and witness statements, enough to shatter the Hells Angels, at least for a short while.

Boucher would finally meet his nemesis in the form of France Charbonneau, a prosecutor known for her steely calm. Yves Boisvert, a leading columnist for *La Presse*, called her "the incarnation of justice in Quebec." Charbonneau had been the near-silent second prosecutor in the earlier botched trial against Boucher, and unlike the other Crown lawyers in the Montreal office, she was determined to fight on. "How could we not appeal?" she later explained. "Let the bikers think they had won? No. I pushed because I felt the Crown did not have its day in court."

Charbonneau got not just one but several days in court in March 2002, when the second murder trial of Mom Boucher began. Once again, the biker's defense lawyer was the smooth and capable Jacques Larochelle. But this time, Charbonneau made sure her main witness, Stéphane Gagné, would shine rather than shatter on the stand. She prepped him—a lot. She patiently walked him and the jurors through his eyewitness account of Boucher's plan to murder the guards as a kind of terror strike against the justice system. Most important, she backed up what Gagné was saying with corroborating evidence from police files: a wiretap here, video surveillance there, phone records, a document, another witness statement when needed. Even the smallest detail helped. When Gagné testified that he was with Boucher on December 5, 1997, as they drove to Sorel for the twentieth-anniversary celebrations of the Quebec Hells Angels, she had a police video showing the men arriving in Boucher's Dodge Ram and making faces at the cops, just as Gagné had said. To back up his story about obtaining surveillance and getaway vehicles for the murders, she had tapes of phone calls made to a car dealer friendly to the bikers.

The goal was to show the jurors that, whatever they thought of the witness, they could be confident he was telling the truth because his story could be verified and amplified in other ways.

It worked. After eleven days of deliberations, the jury rendered its verdict. On May 5, 2002, almost fifteen years to the day after Maurice Boucher had joined the Hells Angels, the jury pronounced Canada's most infamous biker guilty of one count of attempted murder and two counts of first-degree murder. He was sentenced to life in prison. The double count for the killing of the two prison officials was important because, under Canadian law at the time, "life" in prison didn't necessarily mean life. Under the so-called faint hope clause, after just fifteen years a prisoner serving life could apply for parole, although it was far from guaranteed. But that loophole was not available to anyone convicted of two or more murders, which meant Boucher would not be eligible for full parole until twenty-five years after he was taken into custody.

As the man who pulled the trigger in the two prison guard killings, Gagné should have gotten the same sentence Boucher did: life in prison for two homicides and no parole for at least twenty-five years. But in exchange for Gagné's testimony, the prosecutor agreed to drop the murder charge for the killing of the second guard, which meant that, under the faint hope clause, he would have a shot at parole in fifteen years.

What a difference it was from the comfortable deal Yves Trudeau had orchestrated for his forty-three murders. And the other notable difference between Trudeau and Gagné? The wannabe Hells Angel actually did his job on the witness stand. This raises a troubling question: Why did Stéphane Gagné, who was not as smart or as smooth as Trudeau, succeed as a witness when Trudeau had failed so badly sixteen years earlier?

21.
WHAT WENT WRONG

Living a quiet life under police protection, Yves Trudeau must have sighed with relief that he had been spared the punishment visited upon his former biker allies. Maurice Boucher would spend the rest of his life behind bars. In the wake of the Springtime 2001 roundup and subsequent trials, some of his Nomad partners were hit with sentences of at least twenty years. Others got a decade or more in prison.

Trudeau knew that he had also gotten off lucky compared to other informants: he was alive. Dany Kane, the informant who had infiltrated the Hells Angels for the police, committed suicide in the summer of 2000, never witnessing the massive arrests that his work accomplished. The Angels put out a jailhouse contract on the life of another snitch, named Aimé Simard, a killer who agreed to testify against other bikers. In 2003, he was stabbed 187 times by fellow inmates wielding homemade knives in the federal prison where he was being held.

And while Trudeau got out of jail after only seven short years, Stéphane Gagné still faced the prospect of decades behind bars, even though his testimony had been much more effective. What went so wrong with Trudeau's sweetheart deal and poor testimony?

To be fair, not all of the blame can be laid at the feet of the contract killer. For starters, it was a different time. By the time France Charbonneau stood in the courtroom in 2002 and used Stéphane Gagné to convict Maurice Boucher, prosecutors had benefited from more than a decade of biker trials, many of them failed, some successful. They gained experience and confidence, and picked up valuable tricks and skills. Charbonneau also led the way by preparing her witness and securing backup evidence, which prosecutors had failed to do when Yves Trudeau was taking the stand.

The police, or at least some of them, were more savvy when it came to the bikers too. The scandals in the 1990s had revealed the incompetence of the SQ. But at least by then there were officers devoted to handling organized crime and outlaw biker gangs, including a veteran interrogator, Robert Pigeon, who managed to turn Stéphane Gagné and helped make him a convincing informant. In Trudeau's heyday of the late 1970s and the early 1980s, the SQ had little knowledge of or experience with bikers. The police force was provincial in every sense of the word, concentrated in the smaller towns, villages, and farming communities outside big cities like Montreal. Most of its officers were more accustomed to monitoring highway traffic than to bringing drug traffickers to heel. With no specialized knowledge or squads set up to deal with the gangs, they had to scramble to play catch-up when the Lennoxville massacre thrust the extent of the Hells Angels empire into the public eye.

"The SQ was getting involved in those things for the first time and learning from it," recalls Ken Sweeney, the Montreal police detective who also tackled the gangs. "I think most would be willing to say they made mistakes but wouldn't want to air them in public. When you go back to the eighties and the start of the bikers being criminalized, you couldn't get into that world without dealing with that kind of person. The mistake they made was in thinking Trudeau had value as a witness. They rewarded him for that value even though that value wasn't there."

Instead, the police and prosecutors should have used Trudeau for insider information. He should have provided the template for a criminal road map for investigators to follow as part of their own criminal investigation. "If they had used him as an intelligence asset, not as a cooperating witness, that would have been better," Sweeney concludes.

There was a wider problem too. Sweeney points out that when the authorities in Canada use informants to make their cases, there is no real framework to control it one step at a time, as is done in the United States. Agreements in Canada are drawn up beforehand and signed by all parties so that the deal stands no matter the outcome. South of the border, the system is a straight-up quid pro quo in which would-be informants must give up names and details that investigators go off to corroborate. If the information provided is useful and leads to convictions, then and only then will a prosecutor go before a judge to ask for a reduced sentence.

Sweeney recalls how that worked when he got involved with a cocaine dealer who turned informant. Paul Larue, a Sherbrooke bar bouncer and drug trafficker, was arrested in Vermont in 1993 when the American and Montreal police cooperated to run a sting operation. Sweeney was on hand when the US authorities busted Larue, and he offered Larue a Mento mint in the back of the police cruiser, an act of kindness that the criminal, facing a lifetime behind bars in a US federal prison, would not forget. A few weeks later, Sweeney got a call from the Americans: "They said, 'He wants to talk but he will only talk with you. We don't know what he has. Will you come down?'"

Sweeney was accustomed to dealing with criminals who wanted to become informants. When Larue told him he had "stuff" to trade, the veteran cop did not mince words. "You know how it works," he said. "You don't just take your clothes off and expose yourself. You have to get naked, and they want your first layer of skin. So you have to give me *everything*."

Larue stunned Sweeney with his answer: "I'll give you Robert Flahiff."

Flahiff was a jovial Quebec Superior Court judge who had previously been a criminal lawyer and counted Larue among his clients. According to Larue, between 1989 and 1991, Flahiff laundered $1.7 million of the cocaine dealer's money through a Swiss bank account.

In terms of information, this qualified as a blockbuster. But the Americans didn't rush to give Larue a favorable deal and get him on the witness stand; it was more than six years before he got a break on his thirty-five-year prison sentence. First, Sweeney reported what he had been told to the US attorney's office. Then the US attorney's office notified the RCMP, which conducted an investigation and charged Flahiff in June 1997. He was found guilty two years later and sentenced to three years in prison. Only then was Larue brought before a judge, who heard what he had done and lopped ten years off his sentence. In other words, the Americans made sure their informants delivered the goods before granting them any reward.

In Canada, the authorities had learned the hard way that their deal with Trudeau was a one-way street. He got all the benefits; the justice system got very little in return.

Still, even accounting for the questions concerning the police and prosecutorial work in Yves Trudeau's heyday, there remains an intriguing mystery: If Trudeau, back in the mid-1980s, had been handled as Stéphane Gagné was in the second Mom Boucher trial in 2002, would he have been a salvageable informant? Or was he so irredeemable, so compromised, maybe even so patently evil in the eyes of most jurors, that nothing could have saved him?

It wasn't that criminals with long and bloody histories could not make good informants. Donald Lavoie was a long-time hitman for the vicious Dubois brothers in Montreal in the 1970s and early 1980s. When he turned himself in to police in 1982—on the run once he learned his employers now wanted him dead—he admitted to killing at least fifteen people and planning the murders of no less than twenty-seven. Like Trudeau, Lavoie had been a cold-blooded assassin. But unlike Trudeau, he came off as credible, honest, and self-reflective. Even remorseful. "I didn't have no choice for thinking. I was ordered," Lavoie said in a TV interview. "Every day, I try to forget about it but I can't. I think, especially, about the innocent. Some people were innocent. Some people deserved it. They were killers." He continued, "The first time I committed a murder, I found it so easy—a man's life was so easy to take away. Today, I'm sitting here thinking about it, asking myself why I did it, and I can find no damned answer."

Unlike many of Trudeau's statements on the stand, much of Lavoie's testimony was corroborated by police work. Once, the killer said, he'd made his victim dig his own grave first, using only the flame from a lit candle to show his progress. Afterward, Lavoie took that same shovel, smashed the victim's skull in, sent him toppling into the grave, and tossed the candle in for good measure. "When police went to dig up the body, the candle was there too," Ken Sweeney recalled. "He had that kind of memory for detail."

Lavoie succeeded where Trudeau had failed, as did other witnesses, like Gerry Coulombe and Gilles Lachance, who were with the bikers alongside Trudeau and turned against their former friends. Their testimony helped convict, not acquit, other killers. There was something about Trudeau that made him not just less likable, but less credible to jurors.

Killers who testify against other killers on the witness stand are not expected to be angels. But for jurors to believe them and buy in to the prosecutor's case, informants need to show a modicum of humility and remorse. Yves Trudeau did not. He was on the stand what he was on the streets: cold and calculating. A killer who considered his métier a business.

"When you see someone like that, you think he must be pathological," says Dr. Louis Morissette. "But in psychiatry, 'pathology' has a very precise definition. I don't think he corresponds." As a forensic psychiatrist, Dr. Morissette has met and examined infamous criminals such as convicted serial killer Karla Homolka and biker leader Maurice Boucher. He says the lack of empathy Trudeau displayed in killing so many people does not in and of itself make him pathological. "For example, his criminality is not very diversified. We don't have enough information to know if he was a manipulator, a big talker, a pathological liar," he says. "Within the bikers, those who are closer to being psychopaths are at the top of the hierarchy. Apache never rose in the hierarchy, he never became a leader."

That doesn't make Trudeau any less loathsome. He was "evil in the sense that he found his value in violence and power, because to kill someone is taking control," concludes Dr. Morissette. "In Trudeau's story, we have elements of that: he found his value in taking control over others."

In the end, whether or not Trudeau fit the medical definition of pathology mattered little on the witness stand. As Ken Sweeney, the Montreal police detective, warned Florida prosecutor Dave McGee: "Apache really was a horrible person, and a horrible witness. He was the worst, a nightmare for the prosecution and a dream for the defense."

Just how horrible he was would soon become even clearer. Trudeau was poised to emerge from the shadows of his secret life on parole in a way that would make headlines all over again.

22.
A FINAL CRIME

It seemed to be a standard, if all too sordid, sex crimes case. When prosecutor Sonia Paquet looked at the file on the sexual abuse of a minor by the former employee of a senior citizens' residence north of Montreal, she didn't think it was unusual. It was March 2004. Though still a rookie in the Saint-Jérôme prosecutors' office, she had seen it all before. The details could have come from any of the dossiers piled high on her desk, a litany of charges of domestic battery, incest, sexual assault, and drugging, each one horrific and maddening.

In this particular case, a man named Denis Côté faced ten counts of sexually abusing a boy between September 2001 and February 2004. The perpetrator was a fifty-seven-year-old who had been laid off from his job at a seniors' home in 2000, the year before the abuse started. The police photo showed a man with sallow skin, thin lips, and a sparse, grizzled beard staring blankly at the camera. His face was unremarkable, his expression at once unreadable and resigned. The abuse was alleged to have occurred in a number of different jurisdictions around Montreal: in Laval and Saint-Eustache, north of the city; in Saint-Louis-de-Gonzague, a village about sixty kilometers southwest; and in Saint-Jérôme, where the case was filed. There were transcripts of police interviews with the traumatized boy, and dates and graphic descriptions of each assault.

After reviewing the case notes, Paquet was preparing to take it to court when there was a knock on her office door. It was the detective who had made the arrest.

"Sonia, there's something we discovered in the course of our investigation that you need to know," he said.

"And what is that?" she asked.

"Prepare yourself, because the accused has been living under an assumed name. We've checked and checked again to confirm that his real name is Yves Trudeau. He was a biker and a killer, a Hells Angel known as 'Apache.'"

The name was familiar to Paquet, but she was a recent law school graduate who had only been prosecuting for two years; she had to think before it came to her like a flash of newspaper headlines in big, bold type.

A founder of the Quebec branch of the Hells Angels biker club.

A killer who was supposed to die in the Lennoxville massacre, but escaped because he was in detox for a cocaine habit.

An informant who disappeared into police protection after a plea deal that caused a furor when it was made public.

In the mid-1980s, Paquet had been concerned more about her grades and her peers than the news of the day, no matter how sensational. But she had vague memories of outrage when news of Trudeau's deal with the justice ministry broke. Paquet now recalled the disturbing details: the confession to forty-three murders, the much-debated plea bargain, the light sentence, and the killer's eventual disappearance into the police protection system under an assumed name.

Denis Côté.

How many people had met Trudeau under his pseudonym and

not thought twice? How many people had he worked with, how many fragile seniors had he wheeled, bathed, or transported, who had no idea what he had done, or what he was capable of doing?

The plea deal had been debated again and again among Paquet's colleagues and around dinner tables, in the National Assembly and newspapers, on talk radio and TV. It was held up as an example of both the powerlessness of police to investigate dangerous biker gangs without inside informants and, given that none of the cases Trudeau testified in as a principal witness resulted in a conviction, the futility of making such deals.

As far as Paquet knew, the case before her marked the first time in Quebec that a police informant living under an assumed name had been charged with such heinous crimes. The publicity of such a high-profile trial would have unsettling consequences for all the parties involved: it would force the young boy to relive the alleged trauma, and Trudeau's life would be at risk once his true identity was exposed.

Paquet didn't fool herself into thinking the arrest and charges could be kept under wraps. Instead, she prepared for a crash course on how to handle such a controversial case. She knew television cameras and microphones would be thrust in her face before and after each court appearance. And the journalists would ask questions for which she had no answers.

For the moment, though, there was nothing for Sonia Paquet to do but wait. Trudeau was having trouble finding an attorney willing to represent him. Criminal defense lawyers may defend murderers, drug dealers, and rapists, but he was the worst of the worst: at once a killer, a turncoat, and a liar—and now an accused child molester. Although the concept of justice dictated that he be considered innocent until proven guilty beyond a reasonable doubt, any lawyer knew Trudeau would have a tough time escaping the burden of his past. Why would they take on an admitted killer—a *contract* killer—who had been shown to be distrusted by the juries that heard his testimony?

As Trudeau searched fruitlessly for legal help, Paquet wondered whether he would decide to represent himself or insist on his right to representation and have the judge arbitrarily assign him a lawyer. She prepared for every possible scenario. There were a few cases where the accused had argued in court on his own behalf, one of the most infamous being the trial of Agostinho Ferreira in the late 1990s. A waiter who had killed two women and raped several others, Ferreira represented himself, giggling inappropriately as he questioned the victims who had survived. It was excruciating to watch and read about, never mind being in the witness box and having to respond.

No matter what Trudeau decided, Paquet knew there would be a media firestorm when his name was released as the accused.

Sure enough, the news broke on March 19, less than forty-eight hours after Trudeau's arrest. "Apache's Going to Have to Sing a New Tune in Court," screamed one headline. "Hells Angels Hitman up on Sex Charges," stated another. The newspaper stories highlighted his past as the "king of hitmen" and one of Canada's most notorious killers. They noted that his return before the courts placed the provincial justice department and the Sûreté du Québec, who had orchestrated the initial plea deal, in an embarrassing and uncomfortable position. A contract killer who had benefited from one of the most lenient sentences in Canadian history had started reoffending within six years of being released on parole, this time targeting the most vulnerable victim he could find. And he committed these crimes while under surveillance through the witness protection program and the apparently not very watchful eyes of the police.

"Yes, he has benefited from our protection, and he still does," SQ spokesperson Chantal Mackels was forced to admit. "And that's all we can say, because we don't want that security to be compromised."

Indeed, that security was present on the day of Trudeau's arraignment and bail hearing. People had to pass through extra screening to enter the courtroom.

Seated at the prosecutors' table, Paquet waited along with the rest of the packed courtroom for the door leading into the prisoner's dock to open. She had pictured a muscled man who strutted like a peacock. No one had seen Yves Trudeau, under that name, for almost two decades, since his last disastrous appearances in court in the 1980s as a witness who couldn't get the job done. But the man who shuffled through the door, handcuffed and shackled, escorted by two plainclothes police officers, was a shadow of his former self. Rather than the rapacious, cold-blooded monster of public imagination, he was bent and thin, with shrunken shoulders and downcast eyes. This was a man worn down by drugs, by his years in prison, and then by a life in which he always had to pretend he was someone else.

Trudeau remained silent throughout the hearing. His next court appearance was put off to April 29. Then, weak and unsteady, he stood up and shuffled out of the courtroom through the prisoner's door. What was going through his mind? Did it matter?

Paquet collected her files and stood up to walk out of the courtroom and face the media, where she perfected the art of saying "No comment."

By that summer, still unable to find a lawyer, the former hitman decided it would be best to plead guilty. That way, he would avoid a trial and curtail the media coverage that was inevitable because of his notoriety. He threw himself on the mercy of the court, on the grounds that in prison his life would be doubly at risk. Behind bars, snitches and those who sexually abused children were the most hated inmates of all.

When Trudeau appeared in court on July 14, 2004, the room was packed with journalists, including Paul Cherry, the *Montreal Gazette*'s veteran crime reporter, who had covered the bikers for years. He had seen men who were accused of everything from simple assault to premeditated murder, including Maurice Boucher, paraded into the prisoner's dock in handcuffs and leg shackles, as if authorities were broadcasting to the public that their crimes would face harsh treatment. But Trudeau was hidden behind a screen—just a disembodied voice, his face invisible. (Later, outside the courthouse, he was hustled into a police van, protected by a phalanx of officers that blocked any view of him. Once a police informant, always a police informant, it seemed; no matter what he did, the justice department would abide by the letter of its agreement with him. Although he had blown his own cover by breaking the law, he would be kept hidden.)

Cherry listened intently as the man behind the screen stated in a voice that was querulous and soft, even scared: "Your Honor, I'll have to be kept in isolation for twenty-three of twenty-four hours every day."

But if Trudeau hoped the judge would feel sorry for him, he was mistaken. Before being appointed to the Quebec Court bench, Michel Duceppe had been a skilled criminal defense lawyer in partnership with Daniel Rock, the attorney who had, eighteen years earlier, so skillfully eviscerated the testimony of Trudeau and his sister. Duceppe was not likely to take kindly to a confessed killer who had successfully gamed the system.

In his decision, the judge did not mince words. As journalists madly scribbled notes in the large courtroom that had been reserved for the case, Duceppe systematically reviewed Trudeau's long criminal history, including possession of an illegal firearm and armed robbery. He cataloged the forty-three counts of manslaughter, and the innocent victims such as Billy Weichold, the girlfriends killed next to their biker partners, and Jeanne Desjardins, who had valiantly tried to defend her son. Trudeau, the judge reminded everyone, had detonated bombs and used guns, bats, and cords—whatever it took to get the job done. A self-styled businessman who needed to make money to support his drug habit, he lost sight of what was right and what was wrong, if he had ever known in the first place.

"It must be noted that during your life you have killed more people than the Canadian army did during the Gulf War," Duceppe stated from the bench. "Yes, you have worked [since your release] with people who are ill. Yes, you have been taking care of your mother, who today is eighty-four years old. But on four occasions, you sexually assaulted a child [who is now] thirteen years old, when you were in a position of authority and he trusted you. To satisfy yet again your basest instincts, you used ruses, alcohol, and drugs. Today, the youth is disturbed by what happened and is undergoing therapy. You have not respected your obligation to keep the peace, behave lawfully, or refrain from taking drugs."

There was no reason, the judge continued, for the court to consider the hardship Trudeau would suffer by remaining in isolation behind bars. Duceppe sentenced him to four years on each charge, to be served concurrently. This time, Trudeau would not get away with a light sentence. This time, he got the full punishment.

Upon exiting the courtroom, Sonia Paquet had few comments for journalists, other than that justice had been done. But really, there was no need for her to say anything. Duceppe's final words to Trudeau still echoed in everyone's mind: "Definitely there is embedded in you an instinct that is evil."

An evil that was not done yet with the justice system. In four years, Yves Trudeau would make one last startling appearance in a hearing room.

23.
THE DEATH SENTENCE

She stood there, fists clenched, steeling herself. It had been nearly thirty years since that night in December 1978 when Darlene Weichold's life fell apart. The night there was a knock on the door. The night she learned her brother Billy had been taken from her.

For a long time, Darlene had no idea who had aimed a shotgun into Billy's back and pulled the trigger multiple times as he stood in the driveway of the little home he was renting in a Montreal suburb. It wasn't until nearly seven years later that she learned, not from police, but from TV, radio, and the front pages of practically every newspaper in the country, that her brother was one of the people hitman Yves Trudeau had confessed to killing.

Now, on July 15, 2008, Darlene Weichold was getting ready to see Billy's assassin for the first time, at a parole hearing.

The woman in the mirror looking back at her was far from the fourteen-year-old she once was. Over the years, she had tried to rebuild the life shattered by a contract killer. She had married and moved as far away as she could, to the Northwest Territories. She had given birth to three children, the youngest of whom broke her heart even further when he drowned at the age of fifteen, not much older than she was when her brother was taken from her.

The memories came fast and furious. Of when Darlene was a little girl and Billy was taking care of her while their parents were out. She refused to go to bed despite his cajoling, but she finally fell asleep out of sheer tiredness. She awoke in the morning to a roomful of plush teddy bears he had carefully set up in a tableau to surprise her. Of the waterbed Billy had set up for her in his home, and how she found it frozen when she visited with her mom three days after his death because the heat had been turned off.

Of Billy's dogs rushing to his grave and lying there, howling.

Now Darlene's body was thicker, her blond hair shorter, and her brown eyes wary, with dark circles under them like heavy half moons. She knew Billy hadn't been a saint. He liked to party hard. She'd seen him smoke dope, and sell it too. But that was no reason to destroy a life. *No,* she corrected herself silently. *Not just one life, but a whole family's.*

When she closed her eyes, Darlene could see her brother Richard's bitterness, despair, and guilt as he cut himself off from them, and she could still hear her mom, Patricia, crying for days, weeks, months afterward. Patricia's spirit had been destroyed by Billy's death, and it was no surprise when her body broke down too, succumbing to ovarian cancer a few years later.

Darlene had spent thirty years wondering what if? What if Trudeau hadn't pulled the trigger that cold day? What if Billy had lived and had kids of his own?

She hated that Trudeau got to eat steak in prison while Billy rotted in the ground in the windswept cemetery on Montreal's South Shore, all because the killer became a police informant to save his own life. She hated that Trudeau had served only seven years of a life sentence before being released and disappearing into witness protection under an assumed name. And she hated that she'd had to live without answers about her brother's death for so long.

She had not attended any of Trudeau's court appearances. She had run off to Yellowknife as soon as she was old enough, to get away from the whispers, innuendo, and outright accusations that her family was affiliated with hard-core bikers just because Billy had been renting a house from a leader of the Outlaws biker gang. That's where she was, four thousand kilometers away, when, in 2004, she learned that Trudeau had been arrested under his new name for sexually assaulting a young boy and sentenced to four years behind bars. She followed the news from afar, her heart breaking anew for this child whose life would never be the same.

And now, having returned to Quebec, she wanted—she needed—to be present for Trudeau's parole hearing at Archambault, a maximum-security prison in Sainte-Anne-des-Plaines, north of Montreal. Normally, a plea for parole from a self-confessed contract killer and child sex offender would be a dubious bet at best. But nothing had ever been normal about Trudeau's dealings with the justice system. This final encounter would be no different.

Archambault was home to notorious inmates including serial child killer Clifford Olson; Allan Legere, known as the "Monster of the Miramichi"; and Hells Angels leader Maurice Boucher, who was serving his life sentence for the murders of two Quebec prison guards. Trudeau was there not because of his crimes, but because of his health: the prison had a hospital wing. He had been transferred there from a medium-security prison because he needed treatment after being diagnosed with a virulent bone marrow cancer. His doctors said he didn't have long to live.

A panel of the Parole Board of Canada had been convened to decide whether to show him compassion. *How unbelievable is that?* Darlene thought.

Darlene arrived at Archambault with a friend, who came to support her. After passing through the general security to enter the hospital wing, they were ushered into a large, windowed waiting area. She knew she wouldn't get a chance to speak, because the cold-blooded murder of her brother was beyond the purview of the panel considering his case. The deal he had struck with the justice department had ended any possibility that those left behind to mourn would be allowed to express the depth of their loss in court and play a role in his sentencing. Back then, there had been no victim impact statements, and there would be none now. Besides, she wasn't even sure what she would say. Maybe that cancer was an appropriate sentence because it meant he was confined to a bed with nothing to do but think about those he had hurt. Or maybe something like "What gave you the right to shoot anyone, not just my brother? You need to be locked up, with the key thrown away forever. For you, prison was like the Ritz, while the rest of us suffered in hell."

The doors to the hearing room finally opened. It was large, illuminated by fluorescent lights, and mostly empty. Darlene and her friend entered and easily found seats facing a long table at the front. A journalist was there, poised to take notes. Then, through the same door the women had used, attendants pushed a man in a wheelchair. *Trudeau.*

Darlene couldn't look at him. This was the bogeyman who had taken up so much space in her life, yet she knew his face only from photos and video. In those images, Trudeau always appeared cocky, robust, and confident in the government-funded suits he donned to seem respectable each time he entered a courtroom. The man in the wheelchair was a mere shadow of that monster, and if there was the slightest chance she'd feel pity for him, she didn't want to risk it.

Her friend whispered, "I'm going to just take a peek," then reported that Trudeau was just skin and bones, his chest barely moving, and was almost bald. Like a mistake being erased from existence.

Darlene shrugged. She couldn't feel sorry for him. She *wouldn't.*

Trudeau's appearance was also a surprise to Paul Cherry, the *Montreal Gazette*'s crime reporter. Cherry had done his homework, researching Trudeau for days before making the trip out to the hearing. He imagined the dangerous criminal surrounded by guards with guns, a man who even beset with cancer would still pose a threat.

Cherry had attended many parole hearings and knew how the game was played. He had seen prisoners profess regret and swear they would never break the law again; he had watched prisoners accustomed to manipulating others claim that they were suffering from diabetes, or cirrhosis, or any other disease that might get them released. "Then, at the end of the hearing, they jump up, practically the healthiest person in the room," Cherry recalls. Would the same thing happen at Yves Trudeau's parole review?

While waiting to be let into the hearing room, Cherry noticed hospital attendants around a man slumped in his wheelchair. With a start, he realized the man was Trudeau; the attendants simply dropped off the once-notorious contract killer like a piece of baggage. "It was clear that no one considered him a threat any longer. Trudeau was sitting by himself to my right. I thought there was no way this guy could literally hurt a fly, let alone another human being," the seasoned journalist remembers. "I couldn't take my eyes off of him. The monster was gone."

Other than Paul Cherry, Darlene, and her friend, few people were in attendance at the hearing. There were some prison workers—a parole officer and lawyer ready to step in on the ailing prisoner's behalf, if needed—but that was it. Trudeau sat alone, isolated on the right side of the room, the hitman reduced to a shrunken figure without the energy to raise a finger. There were no family members to support him, and he had no friends.

The parole hearing got underway in the early afternoon as the two presiding members of the Parole Board of Canada, Pierre Cadieux and Odette Gravel-Dunberry, took their seats behind the long table. Both were highly experienced in the position, having spent years deciding whether killers, rapists, and other hardened criminals should be let go. Cadieux was a lawyer and former municipal councilor in Rigaud, west of Montreal. Gravel-Dunberry, who had earned a BA in sociology with a focus on criminology from the Université de Montréal, had worked for decades in the fields of crime prevention and victim assistance, had helped develop detention facilities for female offenders, and had served as an assistant warden at Archambault and as warden of La Macaza, a medium-security prison in Quebec's Laurentian region. They were hardly going to be pushovers for a prisoner trying to secure a get-out-of-jail-free card. They knew Trudeau's past. Now they had to determine his future. Still, Cherry got the feeling that Cadieux and Gravel-Dunberry had the same reaction he had upon seeing Trudeau, as if they'd been expecting evil incarnate and instead got this shell of a man on the brink of death.

What followed was unlike anything Cherry had seen before in a parole hearing. Usually, such procedures revolved around dry statistics and debates on the probability that the inmate would reoffend. In Trudeau's case, the parole review did hear the requisite reports: there were details about his participation in a program for sexual offenders, which he had completed in 2007. But the questions soon got more probing and profound.

"What do you think about death?" Cadieux asked Trudeau.

"I see it as a punishment," the killer and child sex abuser replied.

Gravel-Dunberry asked what Trudeau thought about having only a short time left to live. He answered that he wanted to show his mother that he was a good man, despite what he had done in the past. To Cherry, the hitman seemed like a soldier dying on a battlefield, calling out for his mother at the end. It was not for him to judge whether Trudeau was sincere.

But Darlene saw it as an act and a lie—yet another one in a life full of them. She could barely listen as he explained in a raspy voice that he had first joined the Popeyes in the late 1960s because he came from a home where his father was abusive and obsessed with all things regimented and military. The biker gang provided all that, as well as a place for him to explore both his criminal tendencies and his attraction to drugs. Once in, he continued, it was difficult for members to leave: "It wasn't looked upon well by the others. They'd kill you."

Like so many other statements Trudeau had made in legal proceedings, it was a half truth at best. Nobody had put a gun to his head and forced him to kill others. He did it over and over again for the money, for the thrill. Because he could. It didn't matter that, in some of the murders, he did not pull the trigger, tighten the noose, or thrust in the knife; that he was the getaway driver or the lookout. When it comes to first-degree murder, to planned hits and victim stalking, in the eyes of the law, each participant is equally guilty.

In the end, it didn't matter whether the parole board members believed Trudeau's story about trying to please his mother, who was ailing herself and in an institution. They knew they were dealing with a ticking clock: the man before them had mere months, perhaps even weeks, to live. It made little difference whether he was behind bars or on parole. Citing a 2007 psychiatric assessment, they decided there was "no sign suggesting a potential for aggressiveness or acting in a sexually deviant way." Thus, Trudeau was deemed a low risk to reoffend. The board members decided to set him free, but in what they called a "precise and structured way," so he could get treatment at an undisclosed hospital. He was under strict orders not to contact minors or the families of the victims of his other crimes.

It appeared to many that Yves Trudeau had once more gamed the justice system.

"At the end of the day, what comes to mind about Yves Trudeau is the banality of evil," says forensic psychiatrist Dr. Louis Morissette, who never met the killer but studied his life in as much detail as possible. In effect, Trudeau was no different than the Nazi war criminal Adolf Eichmann, one of the architects of the Holocaust, who claimed at his trial in Jerusalem that he was just doing his job. As Morissette notes, Trudeau's excuse for his crimes was that he was asked to find an efficient way to kill people; he was good at it and was asked to continue. "I see him above all as an opportunist," Morissette concludes. "It was a confluence of circumstances."

Trudeau was not strong, handsome, or brilliant. He got lucky: he was never caught for murder, and he barely paid for his crimes. And he could not have survived, much less thrived, in any other environment than a gang as wantonly violent as the Hells Angels, in a city as lawless as Montreal was at the time. They needed him, and he needed them.

But for the victims of Trudeau's rampage, his evil was anything but banal.

Darlene left the hearing in a daze, silent. Had justice really been done by releasing Yves Trudeau to his fate? Like many others, she was angry that the justice system was letting him live out his final days as a free man. But upon reflection, she concluded that maybe the cancer itself was justice for a man who killed as easily as if shopping for a carton of milk and once told a trial that murder was not a pleasure but a necessity in a kill-or-be-killed world. It provided some comfort that her brother's killer would die in in pain, his cancer subduing him, with nothing he could do about it. At the very least, she thought, soon he would be dead and buried.

Just like Billy.

Just like all his other victims.

24.
THE FALLEN ANGELS

Yves (Apache) Trudeau succumbed to cancer and died a few weeks after he was granted parole in July 2008. The exact date is unknown because the once infamous hitman passed away as he had lived and killed for much of his adult life: in the shadows. His death went unnoticed and unmourned. None of the mainstream papers reported on it. Perhaps the crime tabloid *Allo Police*, which had been so eager to chronicle the Hells Angels over the years, might have given Trudeau a fitting send-off, but the newspaper had predeceased him, folding in 2003 after five decades of screaming headlines and graphic photos, often about Trudeau's deadly handiwork.

Many of Trudeau's former associates fared little better, becoming names on a sorry list of deaths behind bars. And the Quebec crime world he left behind would be roiled by rivalries, assassinations, and a dangerous uncertainty.

The leaders of the gangs for which Trudeau had committed murder—the Hells Angels and the West End Gang—ended their long criminal careers dying as old and sick men behind bars.

Allan (The Weasel) Ross was the first to go. Sentenced to life in prison in Florida, where "life" means just that, with no parole, he tried various legal maneuvers over the years to reduce his sentence. Several pleas in U.S. federal court were to no avail. Then, in February 2017, he appealed for early release on the grounds that he was dying of colon cancer. Unlike the sympathy Canadian officials showed the ailing Yves Trudeau, an American judge summarily refused his request. Ross was seventy-four when he died, broken and ailing, on August 21, 2018, in a federal prison in North Carolina that has facilities to treat prisoners with special medical needs.

For his part, Maurice (Mom) Boucher kept up a much more active criminal life behind bars, fending off attacks even as he initiated others. Much of his prison time was spent in the Special Handling Unit, Canada's highest-security prison for high-risk offenders, located in Sainte-Anne-des-Plaines. It didn't offer him much protection. Within his first year in detention, Boucher was attacked twice by a rival gang, once with a knife and then with a homemade bazooka. There was another stabbing attempt in 2010.

In 2014, the media reported that the Hells Angels had expelled Boucher, perhaps blaming him for the police crackdown and new federal anti-gang laws that came in the wake of the unrestrained biker war he had unleashed. But Angel or not, Boucher was not about to put a stop to his criminal career. In 2015, he was accused of stabbing another prisoner multiple times with homemade knives. Later that year, he was charged with conspiracy to commit murder, having passed on messages to Gregory Woolley, a close friend and an experienced killer. The target was a Mafia man named Raynald Desjardins, who had turned against his own mob leaders. It was not the first or the last time the Hells Angels would get involved in the Mafia wars, lending support to one faction or the other. For that crime, Boucher, with his hair gone gray and carrying more weight on his once fit body, stood up in a courtroom in April 2018 and pleaded guilty. He was sentenced to an additional ten years in prison, making 2037 the earliest he could apply for parole.

He didn't make it. On July 10, 2022, the man who had been the most powerful Hells Angel in Canada died of cancer. He was sixty-nine years old.

The five bikers who were convicted of the 1985 Lennoxville massacre and its aftermath would collectively serve more than one hundred years behind bars. Remarkably, they all managed to survive until their release, in part because of some sweet words of remorse to please parole officials, and in part because of a quirky law in Canada's Criminal Code known as the faint hope clause, which allowed convicted murderers to apply for parole as early as fifteen years into their sentences. Timing was on their side. In January 1997, with the country in an uproar over serial killer Clifford Olson's application for early release under the clause, the federal government of Stephen Harper amended it so that anyone convicted of more than one murder would not be eligible. But the change was not retroactive, so that any killer who had done his dirty work *before* then was still eligible for early release. (In 2011, the Harper government, as part of its "get tough on crime" agenda, abolished the faint hope clause altogether.)

The men had never behaved like angels, but after their release from prison, they claimed they were no longer Angels either.

Robert (Snake) Tremblay, the fifth biker to be convicted, in a separate trial after he was arrested in the United Kingdom and brought back, was the first of the Lennoxville killers to be released. He got out in August 2004, after serving nearly eighteen years. "My identity was the [Hells Angels]. I sincerely deplore having taken the life of another person," Tremblay told the parole board, according to the *Montreal Gazette*. "I am very aware that I have to watch out for who I associate with and that I have everything to lose if I return to the criminal world."

In May 2005, it was Luc (Sam) Michaud's turn. Fifty-three at the time, he, too, was penitent, claiming that in prison he had found solace in God, which led the Hells Angels to expel him in 1993. "I sincerely regret participating in that slaughter," he was quoted by the *Gazette* at his parole hearing. "I had no right to decide anyone's fate, even if they were like I was at that time." Sincere or not, these are the kinds of sentiments that help sway a parole board.

Michel (Jinx) Genest, the former North chapter member who had missed the massacre because he was in the hospital, and who had been convicted in a separate trial of killing Claude (Coco) Roy, had to wait twenty-four years before he was let out in March 2010 at age fifty-one. Like the others, he insisted he had left the biker gang while behind prison walls.

Jacques (La Pelle) Pelletier arguably had blood on his hands only indirectly: he had been accused of keeping the other bikers in line as they watched the massacre. Even so, he served the longest of the Lennoxville defendants, not being released until May 2013, when he was fifty-eight. He seemed less repentant, insisting he had done little more than hold a gun on a single biker to keep him quiet. Within months of gaining his freedom, Pelletier was back in prison for violating parole after he was spotted meeting a convicted armed robber affiliated with the Hells Angels, although he was released shortly thereafter.

And what of Réjean (Zig-Zag) Lessard? *Montreal Gazette* crime journalist Paul Cherry, who covered the bikers for years and made a point of attending parole hearings, notes that "Z" had the strangest path to freedom of them all. Lessard had always been a cut above his more uncouth and less educated brethren, the middle-class biker who wore long sleeves to hide his tattoos and preferred his Jaguar over his Harley. In jail, he was different too, forging a path from biker gang to Buddhism. In 1987, Lessard met an inmate who, he said, introduced him to the Eastern religion; by 1989, he had reportedly quit the Hells Angels and isolated himself from most other prisoners, including all of his former gang members. Five years later, he had disavowed all material possessions to the point that his cell was bare.

His ascetic demeanor and penitent behavior was such that in 2008, the Parole Board of Canada granted him day trips outside the prison. The former executioner was now a vegetarian who prayed regularly. "I am not the same man; I have more than twenty years of reflection behind me," he told the board panel, renouncing the violence he had instigated and directed on that weekend of slaughter back in 1985. "Today I know that was unacceptable. It's only in prison that I became aware of what a disaster it was."

Two years later, in 2010, at age fifty-five and having served twenty-four years in a penitentiary, he was described by the parole board as "a model of compliance" whose understanding of his religion "has permitted you to radically change your values and behaviour." He was granted full parole and, by all accounts, has never committed another crime.

Unlike Lessard, Richard (Bert) Mayrand, who was arrested with Lessard in September 1985, never wavered in his support for and solidarity with the Hells Angels, even though he'd watched the gang kill his younger brother, Michel, as part of the Lennoxville purge. He refused a police offer to become an informant; Paul Cherry wrote that Mayrand would never betray the guys who were his real family. Sixteen years later, he was rounded up with almost every other Angel in the province in Operation Springtime 2001 and was one of the few bikers to opt for a full trial before a jury instead of plea bargaining. It was a bad gamble. In 2004, he was sentenced to sixteen years for his role in the biker wars. His statutory release date (in Canada, most inmates are eligible for parole after serving at least two-thirds of their sentence) came up in 2014. But Mayrand was unrepentant. Although he went through the motions of taking part in a "violence prevention program" before his parole hearing, he was honest enough to tell parole officials that he remained loyal to the Angels. He claimed the gang was a victim of a "false image" in Quebec.

The board had little choice but to release him, but imposed strict conditions on his parole. "Your fidelity to the Hells Angels organization is qualified without fail," it declared, according to the *Montreal Gazette*. "You remain loyal and you do not allow that to be criticized."

That wasn't Mayrand's last encounter with the law. In the summer of 2022, he was arrested again, this time charged under Canada's Proceeds of Crime (Money Laundering) and Terrorist Financing Act. The RCMP alleged he failed to declare how much money he was bringing into the country when returning from a trip abroad.

One notorious member of the group who never got caught was David (Wolf) Carroll, who had helped instigate the Lennoxville slayings with Lessard but was never convicted for his role. In the biker wars that followed, his luck continued, as he was the only Nomad not to be caught up in the police sweep that nabbed almost all of the Quebec Hells Angels in Operation Springtime 2001. Although he was charged with thirteen counts of first-degree murder, Carroll was holidaying in Mexico at the time of the raids and fled to Brazil, which has no extradition treaty with Canada. Over the past two decades, there have been unconfirmed sightings of him around the globe, including in Australia, South Africa, South America, and even British Columbia and Ontario. He is believed to have the funds to stay on the run, given that a Crown affidavit in one of the many proceedings against him alleged that he had at least $1 million dollars in a numbered bank account in Antigua. To this day, Carroll remains a wanted man on Interpol's Red Notice list. "Carroll is alleged to have been involved in the murder of thirteen people and the attempted murder of two others," the notice states, adding that he has Hells Angels tattoos on his right arm and back and numerous scars on both arms.

Finally, there remains the fate of Stéphane (Godasse) Gagné, the informant whose 2002 testimony helped take down Maurice Boucher. Gagné also played the Buddhist card to get out of jail early. He had applied for early parole under the faint hope clause in 2016, even apologizing to the daughters of one the prison guards he killed. Parole board members said he sounded "self-centered" and turned him down. Gagné had better luck two years later when he won the right to escorted leaves beyond the prison walls. He claimed he had begun to meditate with a Buddhist monk while in jail. "I don't use violence to solve my problems," he said. "I now know how to manage my emotions. Meditation helps me a lot." The informant, always in danger in a prison filled with angry convicts, noted he had spent four and half years in isolation as protection. "I've lived through all that and fought to stay alive," he declared. "I'm done with criminality. What I did makes no damn sense and was disgusting."

In 2023, Gagné was granted full parole for a six-month test period, given an assumed identity, and made to live under police protection. In January 2024, he was released for good, which made prison guards uncomfortable and angry. Although they acknowledged that is how the system works, they wondered how he, who had killed two of their own, could be allowed to enjoy his freedom under a new name. In a way, it seemed like history was repeating itself. Just as Yves (Apache) Trudeau had done three decades earlier, another assassin for the Hells Angels was allowed to slip away into the shadows.

EPILOGUE

The killers and informants who marked the history of the Hells Angels in the final decades of the twentieth century might be struggling to put their bloody legacy behind them. But as the old saying goes, the past is not dead—it is not even the past. The roots of violence, intrigue, and betrayal cannot be shaken that easily, and it is no surprise that the first two decades of the twenty-first century have seen the same story repeat itself, only with different casts of characters.

In April 2009, more than 1,200 police officers swept across Quebec, arresting almost every member of the Hells Angels and their associates. The crackdown came with a tough-sounding name: Operation SharQc. To this day, it remains the most sweeping roundup of Hells Angels the world over. The men were all charged with conspiracy to commit murder during the biker wars that raged between 1994 and 2002. Once again, the police vowed they were going "to dismantle" the Hells Angels. And once again, their efforts imploded.

When the case began, 156 gang members and their associates were listed on a single indictment. The main evidence came from a lone informant, a twenty-year veteran of the Angels named Sylvain Boulanger. For his testimony, he got a stunning $3 million and immunity for the one murder to which he confessed, according to a later Radio-Canada investigation. Clearly, the authorities were not done making the kinds of controversial deals that had caused such a stir around Yves Trudeau.

It was all for naught. Almost every case fizzled out, crippled by the unwieldy number of defendants, long delays, and prosecutorial misconduct. In 2011, the charges against thirty-one of the accused were thrown out by a judge because the Crown took too long to bring their cases to trial. In 2015, the judge abruptly ended another murder trial against five of the leading bikers because prosecutors had failed to disclose key evidence to the defense. Most of the remaining bikers pleaded guilty to lesser charges.

In the end, Operation SharQc didn't take a bite out of the Hells Angels; instead, the justice system drowned in a mess of its own making.

The major organized crime groups in Quebec can hardly rejoice about the chaos in law enforcement, for they have been reduced to shadows of what they were.

The Irish West End Gang, never much of a structured group to begin with, has more or less ceased to exist, its leaders ailing, dead, or in jail and its once tight control over the Montreal port greatly diminished.

Montreal's Italian Mafia, more established and disciplined, has been on surprisingly shaky ground as well. Vito Rizzuto, the closest thing to a godfather the Canadian crime world has seen, was arrested in 2007 and extradited to the United States, where he was sentenced to a ten-year prison term for three Mafia murders he helped carry out in Brooklyn decades earlier. In his absence, his rivals gunned down members of his family, first his son Nicolo Jr., and then his eighty-six-year-old father, Nicolo Rizzuto. After Vito died of cancer in 2013, his surviving son, Leonardo, eventually found himself a target. In 2023, gunmen opened fire on his Mercedes during rush-hour traffic, putting eight bullets into the car and wounding him. Leonardo Rizzuto has been widely identified in Quebec media as an alleged leading Mafia figure, even though he was acquitted in 2018 of gangsterism and conspiracy to traffic cocaine, and has never faced other Mafia-related charges.

The Hells Angels appeared more stable—at least for a while—under their new leader, Salvatore Cazzetta. Cazzetta had been a friend of Mom Boucher but turned deadly enemy when he became the head of the rival Rock Machine. He survived the biker wars of the 1990s only because he was extradited to the United States to serve a twelve-year sentence for drug smuggling. By the time he got out of prison in 2004 (after serving part of his sentence in Canada), the criminal landscape had changed dramatically. With Mom Boucher in a Canadian jail and Allan Ross of the West End Gang and Mafia leader Vito Rizzuto in American prisons, Cazzetta saw his chance. He joined the Hells Angels—the gang he had hated and fought for so long—quickly rising to lead them as one of the most powerful organized crime figures in Quebec. But he, too, did not last at the top. He was pushed into "forced retirement" in late 2022, a victim of unspecified internal dissent and rivalries, according to the *Journal de Montréal*.

The two major organized crime organizations in Quebec—the Hells Angels and the Mafia—were, if not in disarray, at the very least in difficulty. Nothing reflected the ongoing chaos better than the brazen daytime assassination of Gregory Woolley in the late fall of 2023. In a rogues gallery of Quebec crime figures already filled with larger-than-life (and death) figures, Woolley had carved out a special place. A Black man who had come out of Montreal's street gangs, Woolley gravitated to the explicitly racist Hells Angels and somehow won the respect and trust of Mom Boucher. He became a member of the Rockers, a Hells Angels support gang that helped the bikers wage war with their rivals.

In recent years, Woolley, according to *La Presse* crime reporter

Daniel Renaud, had been forging alliances with the South chapter of the Hells Angels, the club that had planned and carried out the Lennoxville massacre. At the same time, he managed to build bridges with the Mafia, befriending Vito Rizzuto when they were briefly in the same prison. A 2015 joint SQ-Montreal police investigation into a Mafia and Hells Angels drug trafficking ring revealed secretly recorded conversations involving Woolley, which, police alleged, showed that Mafia figures regarded him as their equal.

Being equal also meant being at the top of someone's enemy list. Woolley's large and luxurious home in Saint-Jean-sur-Richelieu, about forty kilometers southeast of Montreal, was the target of a Molotov cocktail in 2022. Then, early on a crisp morning in November 2023, Woolley stepped out of his Lamborghini into a crowded parking lot at a shopping mall near his home with his wife and their three-day-old baby. Shots were fired, a dark van sped away, and Woolley lay dead on the pavement. Luckily, no one else was harmed.

It was an assassination not unlike the many hits Yves Trudeau pulled off. Once again, police labeled it a "gangland slaying." There were few clues and no suspects—and no arrests.

How familiar.

Another Yves (Apache) Trudeau may already be out there somewhere, in the alleys and bars, readying himself as the jockeying for power in the Quebec crime world ramps up yet again.

More bodies on the streets. More opportunities for a young hotshot who wants to prove himself as someone who, for a decent fee, will kill anyone; someone who is careful and cold-blooded, doesn't care who his target is, and has little regard for innocents who become collateral damage. Like Trudeau, he would consider it the inevitable cost of war. And like Trudeau, he would plan on getting away with it.

The next hitman.

SOURCES AND ACKNOWLEDGMENTS

For more than three decades, the authors of this book have been investigating the Hells Angels, organized crime, and law enforcement. Julian cowrote two books on the biker gangs with William Marsden: *The Road to Hell* and *Angels of Death*, which provided background for their historical roots recounted here. He cowrote and directed the documentary *Kings of Coke* and drew on his interviews for the story of the West End Gang in this book. Lisa Fitterman was the court and justice reporter for many years for the *Montreal Gazette*, covering several biker trials and getting to know defense lawyers and prosecutors who gave assistance to this book.

We could not have written *Hitman* without the detailed and dedicated work of our fellow journalists on the crime beat, starting with Paul Cherry, the current crime reporter for the *Montreal Gazette*, along with his colleagues at that paper who covered the beat over the years: Eddie Collister, Peggy Curran, William Marsden, and Rod MacDonell. At *La Presse*, Daniel Renaud continues to break stories, while André Cédilot dominated the field for years. Eric Thibault, at the *Journal de Montréal*, follows in the footsteps of Michel Auger, the king of Quebec crime reporters, who survived an assassination attempt by the Hells Angels. In Toronto, the *Globe and Mail*'s Tu Thanh Ha has kept a steady eye on the Montreal crime scene.

And of course there was the venerable, if not always tasteful, coverage by *Allo Police*. Special thanks to Karine Perron, who has painstakingly kept and maintained the archives and photos from that tabloid.

For books on the Hells Angels, readers can consult the excellent *The Biker Trials: Bringing Down the Hells Angels* by Paul Cherry; *Le parloir—Manigances et déchéance de Maurice "Mom" Boucher* by *Journal de Montréal* reporters Eric Thibault and Félix Séguin; and Jerry Langton's *Showdown: How the Outlaws, Hells Angels and Cops Fought for Control of the Streets.*

The best book on Montreal's unique Irish outlaws is D'Arcy O'Connor's *Montreal's Irish Mafia: The True Story of the Infamous West End Gang.*

For the Mafia in Canada, the definitive works are *Mafia Inc.: The Long, Bloody Reign of Canada's Sicilian Clan* by André Cédilot and André Noel; *Business or Blood: Mafia Boss Vito Rizzuto's Last War* by Peter Edwards and Antonio Nicaso; and *The Sixth Family: The Collapse of the New York Mafia and the Rise of Vito Rizzuto* by Lee Lamothe and Adrian Humphreys.

An overview of Canadian organized crime can be gleaned from *The Encyclopedia of Canadian Organized Crime: From Captain Kidd to Mom Boucher* by Peter Edwards and Michel Auger and from Steven Schneider's *Iced: The Story of Organized Crime in Canada.*

Book publishing in Canada can be cutthroat and perilous in its own way. As always, we could never have survived without the help of our literary agents, John Pearce and Hilary McMahon at Westwood Creative Artists. At HarperCollins, we had the superb backing of editor-in-chief Jennifer Lambert and senior editorial director Brad Wilson, and the hard work of copyeditor Sue Sumeraj. Special thanks to Jim Gifford, now at Simon & Schuster, for first approaching us to do this book.

Although we have been covering crime and the justice system

for decades, this is our first joint project together. We could not have done it without the support of our family and friends, who encouraged us and tolerated our long absences.

And to our readers over the years, thank you for your valued support and encouragement.

Keep in touch, stay safe.

Julian Sher
www.juliansher.com

Lisa Fitterman
www.lisafitterman.com

Montreal, April 2025

NOTES

PROLOGUE: DEATH COMES CALLING

1 **"What's he doing?":** This and all subsequent quotes from Darlene Weichold come from interviews with the authors.

CHAPTER 1: THE YOUNG POPEYE

10 **"Motorcycles are just like baseball bats":** Mark Wilson, "Cycle Gangs and Police—A New Climate," *Montreal Star*, November 24, 1969.

11 **"Back then, in '68 and most of '69":** This and all subsequent quotes from John Dalzell come from an interview with the authors.

12 **"I want to show my mother that I am good":** This and subsequent quotes from Yves Trudeau come from newspaper accounts of his testimony at the coroner's inquest, multiple trials, and his own bail hearings.

12 **"C-I-L has served industry with explosives for 140 years":** C-I-L website, www.cilexplosives.com.

13 **"finich 'cause I eats my spinach":** Catchphrase of cartoon character Popeye the Sailor, created by E.C. Segar in 1929.

13 **"These are people who are attracted to this family":** This and all subsequent quotes from Dr. Louis Morissette come from an interview with the authors.

14 **"make whoop-whoop whoopie night and day":** "Montreal Ranks All-Time Top 5 Songs about Montreal," *Montreal Gazette*, October 27, 2012.

CHAPTER 2: THE FIRST KILL

30 **"'Apache' the 'Best' Killer in Canada":** "'Apache' le 'meilleur' tuer au Canada," front page headline, *Allo Police*, March 16, 1986.

CHAPTER 3: HITMAN FOR THE HELLS

32 **"Whadda ya got?":** *The Wild One*, Columbia Pictures, December 1953.

32 **"He's not a big guy":** Interview with Julian Sher for *Angels of Death: Inside the Bikers' Empire of Crime*, cowritten with William Marsden (Toronto: Knopf Canada, 2006), 37.

33 **"In the '60s, we got a lot of publicity":** *Organized Crime in America: Hearings Before the Committee on the Judiciary, United States Senate, Ninety-eighth Congress*, January 1983, U.S. Government Printing Office, 549.

33 **"The seventies were a gangster era for us":** Ralph "Sonny" Barger with Keith and Kent Zimmerman, *Hell's Angel: The Life and Times of Sonny Barger and the Hell's Angels Motorcycle Club* (New York: Harper Perennial, 2009), 177–88.

CHAPTER 4: THE NOISY BARBARIANS

41 **"To kill was a necessity":** Richard Desmarais, "Testimony in Joliette: My Sister Was the Only Female Member of the Popeyes," *Allo Police*, June 22, 1986.

41 **"Bikers: Hordes of Noisy Barbarians":** Michel Auger, "Bikers: Hordes of Noisy Barbarians," *La Presse*, April 5, 1979.

41 **"They are willing to use violence":** Auger, "Bikers."

46 **"But she loved this boy":** Jennifer Hunter, "Neighbours stunned by horrible deaths," *Montreal Gazette*, May 29, 1980.

CHAPTER 5: THE IRISH CONNECTION

50 **"They grew up poor":** This and all subsequent quotes from D'Arcy O'Connor come from an interview with Julian Sher for *Kings of Coke*, Crave TV, 2022.

50 **"The West End Gang is great":** This and all subsequent quotes from Dan Burke come from an interview with Julian Sher for *Kings of Coke*, Crave TV, 2022.

51 **"What made Dunie a good crime boss?":** This and all subsequent quotes from Melvin Mingo come from an interview with Julian Sher for *Kings of Coke*, Crave TV, 2022.

52 **"I always put my .44 Magnum under the bed":** This and all subsequent quotes from André Savard come from an interview with Julian Sher for *Kings of Coke*, Crave TV, 2022.

53 **"It makes sense that Dunie":** This and all subsequent quotes from Ken Sweeney (a pseudonym) come from an interview with Julian Sher.

55 **"Near the park, there is a school":** Eddie Collister, "Police Fear Gang War after Westmount Blast," *Montreal Gazette*, October 28, 1981.

55 **"The man just fell out":** Scene from *Kings of Coke*, Crave TV, 2022.

55 **"I opened the car door":** D'Arcy O'Connor, *Montreal's Irish Mafia: The True Story of the Infamous West End Gang* (Toronto: HarperCollins, 2014), 140.

55 **"I knew it was a bomb right away":** Collister, "Police Fear Gang War."

55 **"He died in my arms":** Collister, "Police Fear Gang War."

56 **"It was probably a settling of accounts":** Eddie Collister, "Hospital Releases Car Bomb Victim," *Montreal Gazette*, October 29, 1981.

56 **"Police Fear Gang War after Westmount Blast":** Collister, "Police Fear Gang War."

56 **"Things could really go pop":** Collister, "Hospital Releases Car Bomb Victim."

56 **"You were taken from us without a goodbye":** Obituaries, *Montreal Gazette*, October 27, 1982.

59 **According to André Cédilot:** André Cédilot, "Règlement de comptes relié à la drogue?," *La Presse*, July 16, 1983.

CHAPTER 6: A CONTRACT FOR REVENGE

62 **"I shot a dead man":** O'Connor, *Montreal's Irish Mafia*, 149.

63 **According to a later court filing:** United States v. Ross, October 11, 1994, https://casetext.com/case/us-v-ross-108.

63 **"The king is dead":** Scene from *Kings of Coke*, Crave TV, 2022.

64 **"When I first met Allan Ross":** This and all subsequent quotes from Jeffrey Boro come from an interview with Julian Sher for *Kings of Coke*, Crave TV, 2022.

64 "You could stop Allan Ross on the street": Interview with Julian Sher for *Kings of Coke*, Crave TV, 2022.

64 "He tried to get away with everything": Interview with Julian Sher for *Kings of Coke*, Crave TV, 2022.

65 "The West End Gang was an extraordinary surprise": Interview with Julian Sher for *Kings of Coke*, Crave TV, 2022.

CHAPTER 7: THE BOMBING

68 "It was necessary to find a way": Peggy Curran, "I Killed 4 with Bomb in Gift TV Set: Ex-Angel," *Montreal Gazette*, August 28, 1985.

69 "What starts off as a squadron": "A Timeline of the Hells Angels," *New York Times*, February 13, 2013.

71 "I've never seen anything like it": David Johnston, "Drug Dealers' War Suspected," *Montreal Gazette*, November 26, 1984.

71 "The door to our apartment was shattered": Johnston, "Drug Dealers' War Suspected."

72 "Suddenly there was a violent explosion": Johnston, "Drug Dealers' War Suspected."

72 "I thought my ears were gone": Johnston, "Drug Dealers' War Suspected."

72 "We were blown out of bed": Johnston, "Drug Dealers' War Suspected."

73 "Drug Dealers' War Suspected": Johnston, "Drug Dealers' War Suspected."

74 "seated in a circle facing the device": Forensic report by investigator Paul Riendeau, November 1984, Bibliothèque et Archives Nationales du Québec.

74 "They're off the scene as of today": "Bomb Likely Killed Its Makers: Police," *Montreal Gazette*, November 27, 1984.

74 "Bomb Likely Killed Its Makers: Police": Headline, *Montreal Gazette*, November 27, 1984.

74 "The Bomb Exploded in Their Hands": André Cédilot, "La bombe leur aurait explosé dans les mains," *La Presse*, November 27, 1984.

74 "work accident": "Un accident du travail," *Allo Police*, December 2, 1984.

75 "The Mad Bomber was a freelance hitman": Interview with Julian Sher for *Kings of Coke*, Crave TV, 2022.

75 **"Dunie was my best friend":** Interview with Julian Sher for *Kings of Coke*, Crave TV, 2022.

CHAPTER 8: THE MASSACRE

78 **"Everybody bowed down to him":** Interview with Julian Sher for *The Road to Hell: How the Biker Gangs Are Conquering Canada*, cowritten with William Marsden (Toronto: Knopf Canada, 2003).

81 **"In joining the Hells Angels":** This and all subsequent quotes from Réjean Lessard come from his bail hearing, reported by Paul Cherry, "Ex-Hells Angels Boss: 'I Wouldn't Hurt a Fly," *Montreal Gazette*, February 4, 2006.

82 **"I can't wait until this is over":** La Presse Canadienne, "Procès de quatre Hell's: Témoignage incriminant du délateur Coulombe," *La voix de l'Est*, October 7, 1986.

83 **"There was nothing to sign for":** Peggy Curran, "Hell's Angels Plotted to Kill Laval Bikers, Trial Told," *Montreal Gazette*, October 7, 1986.

84 **"I was in my car, keeping watch":** This and subsequent quotes from Coulombe's testimony are from La Presse Canadienne, "Procès de quatre Hell's."

87 **"I saw the reason on March 24":** Peggy Curran, "I Was Held at Gunpoint During Killings: Biker," *Montreal Gazette*, November 4, 1986.

CHAPTER 9: A TIMELY REFUGE

93 **"This was where the action was":** This and all subsequent quotes from Mario Dumont come from an interview with the authors.

CHAPTER 10: THE HITMAN BECOMES A TARGET

99 **"talked too much":** Peggy Curran, "Biker Killed in St. Basil 2 Weeks after 5 Others Died," *Montreal Gazette*, August 21, 1985.

100 **"Forget the cash":** Pierre-A. Champoux, "Les Hell's Angels ont été trahis! 'Apache' Trudeau dévoile tous leurs secrets," *Allo Police*, September 8, 1985.

101 **"Police say they were acting on a tip":** Sarah Scott and Eddie Collister, "Judge Orders Release of 5 Hell's Angels," *Montreal Gazette*, April 13, 1985.

102 **"It was nothing but a publicity stunt":** Scott and Collister, "Judge Orders Release."

102 **"I'll believe it when I see the bodies":** Scott and Collister, "Judge Orders Release."

103 **"In Montreal Sessions Court":** Scott and Collister, "Judge Orders Release."

103 **"The charges and seizures are only secondary":** Scott and Collister, "Judge Orders Release."

CHAPTER 11: A FATEFUL DECISION

107 **"This was nothing but a big police fishing expedition":** Susan Semenak, "Hell's Angels Sue Quebec for $358,300," *Montreal Gazette*, April 20, 1985.

109 **"paradise for drug dealers":** David Johnston, "Overcrowded Bordeaux Jail Is Paradise for Drug Dealers," *Montreal Gazette*, March 31, 1984.

112 **"I have killed for them":** Jerry Langton, Cold War: How Organized Crime Works in Canada and Why It's About to Get More Violent. (Toronto: HarperCollins, 2015), 109.

112 **"I was as good as dead already":** Peggy Curran, "Angels' Leaders Had 12 Bikers Executed: Witness," *Montreal Gazette*, August 29, 1985.

CHAPTER 12: OUT OF THE SHADOWS

118 **"My role, as minister of justice":** Presse Canadienne, "Hell's Angels: L'enquête répart à zéro," *Le Devoir*, July 30, 1985.

119 **"a stickler, a man who squeezes between the commas":** Michael Farber, "Jangling Chains Identify Inquest," *Montreal Gazette*, September 12, 1985.

122 **"behind the trigger":** Curran, "Biker Killed in St. Basil."

125 **"Some are missing, and some have been found":** Pierre-A. Champoux, "Les Hell's Angels ont été trahis!," *Allo Police*, September 8, 1985.

126 **"Everyone, really, except for Brutus Geoffrion":** Champoux, "Les Hell's Angels."

126 **"We wrap it in a sleeping bag":** Champoux, "Les Hell's Angels."

126 **"No rape, no burn, no shoot":** Peggy Curran, "Gangs Killing Off Wild Ones Who No Longer Fit In," *Montreal Gazette*, September 14, 1985.

127 **"We knew who shot him":** Champoux, "Les Hell's Angels."

127 **"Charlie Hachey owed $145,000":** Champoux, "Les Hell's Angels."

127 **"You're going to see how the HA have become so powerful":** Champoux, "Les Hell's Angels."

127 **"I calculated everything":** Alain Saint-Ours, "Au procès de Claude Brousseau," *Allo Police*, June 22, 1986.

128 **"That night, Paul April learned":** Champoux, "Les Hell's Angels."

128 **"You are my Hells' brothers":** Champoux, "Les Hell's Angels."

129 **"Like cats and dogs":** Peggy Curran, "Bomb in TV Killed 4: Ex-Angel," *Montreal Gazette*, August 28, 1985.

129 **"In Laval, these were guys":** Champoux, "Les Hell's Angels."

129 **"It's for this that I lost my chapter":** Champoux, "Les Hell's Angels."

130 **"Yes, I read his book":** Champoux, "Les Hell's Angels."

130 **"My sister is dealing with this":** Champoux, "Les Hell's Angels."

130 **"That last time, I didn't like it at all":** Champoux, "Les Hell's Angels."

CHAPTER 13: THE TRAP

137 **"I will provide a doctor's note to support this":** Rollande Parent (PC), "Un chef des Hell's écope de six mois," *La Tribune*, September 25, 1985.

138 **"profound amnesia":** Parent, "Un chef des Hell's."

138 **"I'm not here to investigate":** Parent, "Un chef des Hell's."

138 **"I don't remember":** Peggy Curran, "Court Frees Hell's Angel Linked to Biker Slayings," *Montreal Gazette*, September 26, 1985.

CHAPTER 14: THE CONTROVERSIAL DEAL

142 **"Who Will Get Michel Blass":** Michel Auger, "Who Will Get Michel Blass—The SQ or a West End Gang Killer?," *Journal de Montréal*, September 1985.

144 **"We can see for ourselves":** René Laurent, "Underworld Killer Has Deal to Spend Only Seven Years in Prison," *Montreal Gazette*, February 27, 1986.

146 **academic researchers later found four photocopied pages:** Mathilde Turcotte, *Quand policiers et délinquants négocient: Analyse de la relation contrôleur-source humaine*, Université de Montréal, January 2008, https://papyrus.bib.umontreal.ca/xmlui/bitstream/handle/1866/6534/Turcotte_Mathilde_2008_these.pdf.

147 **"We didn't have much to go on":** René Laurent, "Ex-Hell's Angel Pleads Guilty in 43 Slayings," *Montreal Gazette*, March 1, 1986.

148 **"You buy what is convenient for you to get":** William Marsden, "True Confessions of Murderer Who Killed 43 Times," *Montreal Gazette*, March 18, 1986.

148 **"These witnesses are like puppets for the police":** Marsden, "True Confessions."

149 **"Consider Yves (Apache) Trudeau":** Editorial, "Shrugging Off Slaughter?," *Montreal Gazette*, March 21, 1986.

149 **"fact of life":** "Marx May Limit Deals for Criminal Informers," *Montreal Gazette*, March 12, 1986.

CHAPTER 15: "HE WAS LYING"

152 **"Tell me, Mr. Trudeau":** This and all subsequent quotes from Daniel Rock come from an interview with the authors, supplemented by court files and final arguments he provided.

154 **"Let's give Dionne another chance":** Alain Saint-Ours, "Apache confirme: Il a été payé entre $5,000 et $200,000 pour ses 43 meurtres," *Allo Police*, June 22, 1986.

155 **"He has pulled a fast one":** Saint-Ours, "Apache confirme."

155 **"I had friends there who owed me":** Saint-Ours, "Apache confirme."

155 **"Okay, I did what you asked":** Saint-Ours, "Apache confirme."

155 **"You practically did it in my own backyard":** Saint-Ours, "Apache confirme."

155 **"To kill was never a pleasure":** Saint-Ours, "Apache confirme."

160 **"I stated the truth, but forgot some details":** Saint-Ours, "Apache confirme."

161 **"First Defeat!":** Headline, *Allo Police*, June 29, 1986.

162 **"The career of the informant":** Richard Desmarais, "Erreur grave," *Allo Police*, June 29, 1986.

CHAPTER 16: A RARE VICTORY

164 **"We missed him by a hair":** Eloise Morin, "Hell's Angels Boss Sought for Murders," *Montreal Gazette*, February 26, 1986.

165 **"Beer cost nothing":** Peggy Curran, "Hell's Angels Plotted to Kill Laval Bikers, Trial Told," *Montreal Gazette*, October 7, 1986.

167 **"I'm not an informer":** Curran, "Hell's Angels Plotted."

167 **"dressed to the nines":** Christian Richard, "Le Nez y a assisté! Il a tout vu! Dans le repaire de Lennoxville," *Allo Police*, November 15, 1986.

168 **"Raise your hands":** Germain Tardif, "Gilles 'la Nez' Lachance raconte ce qu'il a vu lors de la tuerie de Lennoxville," *La Presse*, November 4, 1986.

168 **"No bloody guns in the clubhouse!":** Tardif, "Gilles 'la Nez' Lachance."

169 **"I saw what happened on March 24":** Tardif, "Gilles 'la Nez' Lachance."

170 **"His lawyer argues that the man's wife isn't dead":** Peggy Curran, "Judge at Hell's Angels Trial to Instruct Jury on Monday," *Montreal Gazette*, November 15, 1986.

170 **"I was bought":** Peggy Curran, "Angel Murder Trial. 1 Freed, 3 Found Guilty," *Montreal Gazette*, December 4, 1986.

CHAPTER 17: "ZERO CREDIBILITY"

172 **"fears that criminals might get the message":** Editorial, "Shudder and Bear It," *Montreal Gazette*, August 2, 1986.

174 **"I didn't sleep much":** This and all subsequent quotes from Christiane Filteau come from an interview with the authors.

CHAPTER 18: "MERCENARIES OF PERJURY"

177 **"These men are mercenaries of perjury":** Christian Richard, "Apache Trudeau et Mike Blass perdent un autre procès!," *Allo Police*, May 23, 1987.

177 **"These two killers have found a new power":** Richard, "Apache Trudeau."

177 **"Apache Trudeau and Mike Blass Lose Another One!":** Richard, "Apache Trudeau."

180 **"I did not hesitate":** Christian Richard, "Lucky et Conan acquittés," *Allo Police*, January 31, 1988.

181 **"Dear scoundrels and trash":** Robert LaHaye, "Aux délateurs!," *Allo Police*, June 21, 1987.

CHAPTER 19: SAFE BEHIND BARS

187 **"Savoie calls out of the blue":** This and subsequent quotes from Dave McGee come from an interview with Julian Sher for *Kings of Coke*, Crave TV, 2022.

189 **"You don't understand":** Interview with Julian Sher for this book.

189 **"Your new TV and VCR is on its way":** O'Connor, *Montreal's Irish Mafia*, 166.

CHAPTER 20: A BLOODY LEGACY

194 **"I'll tell you honestly":** This and all subsequent quotes from André Bouchard come from an interview with Julian Sher for *The Road to Hell*.

196 **"They'd steal your information":** Sher and Marsden, *The Road to Hell*, 68.

196 **The commission's final 1,700-page report:** Commission d'enquête chargée de faire enquête sur la Sûreté du Québec, 1998, https://www.bibliotheque.assnat.qc.ca/guides/fr/les-commissions-d-enquete-au-quebec-depuis-1867/7712-commission-poitras-1998.

199 **"All the company you kept":** Lisa Fitterman, "Star Witness a Chronic Liar, 'Mom' Trial Told," *Montreal Gazette*, November 20, 1998.

200 **"the incarnation of justice in Quebec":** Lisa Fitterman, "The Avenger," *Walrus*, May 2013.

200 **"How could we not appeal?":** Fitterman, "Avenger."

CHAPTER 21: WHAT WENT WRONG

207 **"I didn't have no choice for thinking":** CBC, "Hitman," *Fifth Estate*, 1982, https://www.cbc.ca/player/play/video/1.2841895.

CHAPTER 22: A FINAL CRIME

209 **When prosecutor Sonia Paquet looked at the file:** The description of events and dialogue in this chapter come from an interview with Sonia Paquet by the authors.

212 **"Apache's Going to Have to Sing a New Tune in Court":** James Mennie, "Apache's Going to Have to Sing a New Tune in Court," *Montreal Gazette*, March 20, 2004.

212 **"Hells Angels Hitman up on Sex Charges":** Headline, *Montreal Gazette*, March 22, 2004.

212 **"king of hitmen":** André Cédilot, "Le roi de tuer à gages encore épinglé," *La Presse*, March 19, 2004.

212 **"Yes, he has benefited from our protection":** Mennie, "Apache's Going to Have to Sing a New Tune."

214 **"Your Honor, I'll have to be kept in isolation":** Christiane Desjardins, "Quatre ans de prison de plus pour 'Apache' Trudeau," *La Presse*, July 15, 2004.

215 **"It must be noted that during your life":** Excerpt from sentence rendered by Quebec Court Judge Michel Dionne, file 700–01–050973–042, July 14, 2004.

215 **"Definitely there is embedded":** Excerpt from file 700-01-050973 -042.

CHAPTER 23: THE DEATH SENTENCE

220 **"Then, at the end of the hearing":** Interview with Paul Cherry by the authors.

221 **"What do you think about death?":** Paul Cherry, "He Killed at Least 43, Now Ex-Biker Faces Death," *Montreal Gazette*, July 16, 2008.

222 **"It wasn't looked upon well by the others":** Cherry, "He Killed at Least 43."

222 **"no sign suggesting a potential for aggressiveness":** Cherry, "He Killed at Least 43."

CHAPTER 24: THE FALLEN ANGELS

227 **"My identity was the [Hells Angels]":** Paul Cherry, "Hells Angels Killed Their Own in Lennoxville Purge," *Montreal Gazette*, March 24, 2015.

227 **"I sincerely regret participating":** Cherry, "Hells Angels Killed."

228 **"I am not the same man":** Cherry, "Hells Angels Killed."

228 **"a model of compliance":** Cherry, "Hells Angels Killed."

228 **Mayrand would never betray:** Cherry, "Hells Angels Killed."

229 **"Your fidelity to the Hells Angels":** Cherry, "Hells Angels Killed."

229 **"Carroll is alleged to have been involved":** Interpol website, https://www.interpol.int/en/How-we-work/Notices/Red-Notices/View-Red-Notices#1994-41113.

230 **"I don't use violence to solve my problems":** Elias Abboud, "Hells Angels Assassin-Turned-Informant Granted Escorted Outing from Prison," *CBC News*, October 17, 2018, https://www.cbc.ca/news/canada/montreal/hells-angels-stephane-gagne-1.4865333.

EPILOGUE

233 **He was pushed into "forced retirement":** Eric Thibault and Félix Séguin, "Crime organisé: retraite forcée pour l'ex-chef des Hells Angels, Salvatore Cazzetta," *Journal de Montreal*, November 22, 2022.

234 **Woolley . . . had been forging alliances:** Daniel Renaud, "Crime organisé: une alliance décapitée," *La Presse*, November 20, 2015.

INDEX